CHAO$
AND
COMPROMI$E

CHAO$
AND
COMPROMI$E

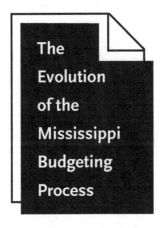

The
Evolution
of the
Mississippi
Budgeting
Process

Brian Pugh

University Press of Mississippi / Jackson

The University Press of Mississippi is the scholarly publishing agency of
the Mississippi Institutions of Higher Learning: Alcorn State University,
Delta State University, Jackson State University, Mississippi State University,
Mississippi University for Women, Mississippi Valley State University,
University of Mississippi, and University of Southern Mississippi.

www.upress.state.ms.us

The University Press of Mississippi is a member
of the Association of University Presses.

First printing 2020

∞

Library of Congress Cataloging-in-Publication Data

Names: Pugh, Brian A., author.
Title: Chaos and compromise: the evolution of the Mississippi budgeting
process / Brian A. Pugh.
Other titles: $i Title appears on item as: $a Chao$ and compromi$e
Description: Jackson: University Press of Mississippi, 2020. | Includes
bibliographical references and index.
Identifiers: LCCN 2020016828 (print) | LCCN 2020016829 (ebook) | ISBN
9781496830197 (hardback) | ISBN 9781496830241 (trade paperback) | ISBN
9781496830203 (epub) | ISBN 9781496830210 (epub) | ISBN 9781496830227
(pdf) | ISBN 9781496830234 (pdf)
Subjects: LCSH: Allain, William Alexander, 1928–2013. | Mabus, Ray, 1948– |
Fordice, Daniel Kirkwood, 1934–2004. | Musgrove, David Ronald, 1956– |
Barbour, Haley, 1947– | Bryant, Phil (Dewey Phillip), 1954– |
Budget—Mississippi. | Mississippi—Appropriations and expenditures. |
Mississippi—Economic policy.
Classification: LCC HJ2053.M7 P74 2020 (print) | LCC HJ2053.M7 (ebook) |
DDC 352.4/809762—dc23
LC record available at https://lccn.loc.gov/2020016828
LC ebook record available at https://lccn.loc.gov/2020016829

British Library Cataloging-in-Publication Data available

Contents

Foreword

Budgeting. What thoughts or feelings do you have when you hear that word? For many, it conjures thoughts of a lot of mind-numbing numbers that don't make sense, addition and subtraction, revenue estimates and projected expenditures, deficits and surpluses—topics that could be interesting or intriguing only to economists, corporate financial officers, or government budget officers. For everyone else, which is most of us, budgeting is not enticing at all but instead is a boring, tedious, or dreaded subject, one that we only reluctantly think about when we are attempting to make ends meet, by trying to keep our household expenses in line with our income and savings.

But Brian Pugh's first book, *Chaos and Compromise: The Evolution of the Mississippi Budgeting Process*, is perhaps surprisingly not a dull discussion of numbers or a technical analysis that only a budget officer or financial expert could love. How was he able to take a seemingly mundane topic like government budgeting and not only keep it from being dry or boring but also create a readable narrative that is not difficult to understand and is even interesting?

To answer that, let's begin with his impressive credentials: Brian is uniquely qualified by both his education and his breadth of practical experience to craft a detailed, authoritative story of Mississippi budgeting, because he is both an academician and a practitioner in various aspects of the field, with extensive budgeting experience in both the legislative and executive branches of Mississippi state government. So his perspective on budgeting is that of both a scholar and a practitioner, and that combination of perspectives enables him to provide an insightful and balanced view of budgeting from both disciplines.

Brian's academic credentials include master's and PhD degrees in public policy and administration, with an emphasis on public budgeting and finance. He has been intimately involved with budgeting from the beginning of his career, first working as a practitioner as a budget analyst with the Legislative Budget Office, then as the director of finance for the governor, and finally as the deputy state fiscal officer and deputy executive director of the Department

of Finance and Administration (DFA). While working in the latter two positions, he also taught classes as an adjunct professor at Jackson State University,
and he is currently an adjunct professor at Mississippi State University. His
knowledge and experience in government budgeting were gained through
the hands-on, down-in-the-numbers developing of budgets in two different
branches of government, and then by overseeing all state budgeting actions as
a high-ranking budget administrator in the executive branch while at the DFA.

Chaos and Compromise tells the story of the state budget process in Mississippi from the beginning of statehood up to the present day, providing a
comprehensive overview and in-depth analysis of budgeting in Mississippi and
how the process has changed over time. It shows and explains how the balance
of power over the budget between the legislative and executive branches evolved
during that time, primarily through legislation and court decisions, and some
key executive actions. It also looks at the political history of the state from the
early twentieth century forward, viewed through the lens of the state's budget
process, with a spotlight on a number of the key people who were involved in
those decisions and actions. So, while following the budgeting narrative, the
reader will also learn about a number of interesting aspects of state government and history, and the relationships and interplay for power between the
governors and the legislature. There has previously been a lack of in-depth
literature about Mississippi budgeting, and this book addresses that void by
providing the most extensive account of the budget process in Mississippi that
I have seen; and it is filled with much detailed information about a variety of
people and events, some that are better known and others more obscure.

The book is heavily documented, using and citing official government documents and other public records from the executive and legislative branches, campaign documents, letters, newspaper reports, and legislative general laws—any
form of communication or record that the public has access to, so that readers
who want to see an original source can find it and read it for themselves. In
addition, it includes comments from interviews with several key participants
in the process, in order to help document newspaper articles and provide
more detailed information about a topic, both where other documentation was
available and where there was no written record. Throughout the book Brian
just lays out and reports the facts of the events as he has uncovered them, not
attempting to persuade the reader that any procedure, process, or change is
better than another, and maintaining a fully objective viewpoint until briefly
at the end, where he provides some commentary.

Brian has written this book for the serious scholar and academician as
well as for the general reader who has an interest in Mississippi government,
politics, or history and how it currently works and how it worked in the past.

It includes sufficient details and documentation for the academic reader, while also being enlightening and even entertaining for the general reader, by providing numerous tidbits of interesting information. All of the technical or arcane terminology that is used in budgeting and the legislative process is thoroughly defined, explained and put in context so that even those who are not budget experts can readily understand it. The book was not written primarily for budget practitioners, who by the nature of their work will necessarily be focused on the present-day process and don't have the need for going back into the history of budgeting. But because it provides that detailed historical information, the book can be used as a resource or reference to help those persons better understand the current process in which they practice by knowing its historical context.

Chaos and Compromise extensively focuses on the administrations of the six most recent governors, beginning with Bill Allain in 1984. It examines each of those governor's budget goals, priorities, successes, and failures, and their relationships and battles over budgeting with the legislature, and the significant actions and events that transformed or affected state budgeting during that time. All of the landmark Mississippi Supreme Court decisions regarding constitutional separation of powers in which the governors and the legislature battled for control over the budget process are covered in depth, as well as the major legislation enacted along the way that changed state budgeting. The legislature almost totally dominated the budget process during the mid-twentieth century, with the governors not being able to have much impact with the limited power they had, until Bill Allain won his separation of powers lawsuit against the legislature, filed when he was attorney general and decided by the Mississippi Supreme Court right before he took office as governor in 1984. That case, *Alexander v. State of Mississippi by and through Allain*, and the resulting legislation enacted in response to the decision, the Mississippi Administrative Reorganization Act of 1984, changed the budget process in Mississippi forever, in significant ways that still reverberate today.

I was working for the legislature during all six of those governors' time in office, and I participated in, experienced, or witnessed much of what is covered in the book. So the details of most of those events and actions should have been fully familiar to me, but I found that was not the case, as the book provided me with a number of revelations and surprises. Through his examination of official documents, conducting interviews, and use of other sources, Brian uncovered many interesting, behind-the-scenes aspects of those events that I never knew about before, so his book has broadened my knowledge and understanding of those times of which I was a part.

I think that anyone who has more than a little interest in Mississippi budgeting, politics, or history will be informed, enlightened, and probably even entertained by *Chaos and Compromise*, and academicians will be pleased to have for the first time a comprehensive and fully documented explanation of the budget process and its history.

—Ronny Frith

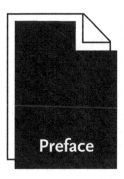

Preface

Public budgets reflect elected leaders' priorities, and the study of public budgeting is a way to understand those priorities. One cannot fully comprehend Mississippi's budget-making process without first understanding Mississippi's storied political past. Mississippi policy makers today share the same reluctance of giving the executive branch too much power as did the state's early constitutional framers, especially regarding the taxpayers' money. This book examines public budgeting in Mississippi and the single largest impact on the state's present-day budget-making process, the Mississippi Administrative Reorganization Act of 1984, and other contributing factors that followed. The reorganization act cannot be properly addressed without first understanding why the act was passed in the first place. The reorganization act was not passed by the legislature voluntarily, but as a result of the court's decision in *Alexander v. State of Mississippi by and through Allain* (1983), which proved to be the most important separation of powers case in modern history of the state.

This book shows how the *Alexander* case not only shaped Mississippi's budget-making process back in the early 1980s, but still shapes it to this day. The *Alexander* case made clear that budget control is an executive function, which proved important nearly three and one-half decades later in another separation of powers case that specifically addressed Mississippi's budget, *Representative Bryant W. Clark and Senator John Horhn v. Governor Phil Bryant et al.* (2018). In addition to covering important legislation and litigation that contributed to the budget-making process, this book also covers governors' contributions to the process and the roles that they played after budget reform.

Chapters 1 through 10 all offer objective contributions to the Mississippi budget-making process, and a majority of the material used for those chapters are well-documented public records. The public records were supplemented by a few interviews of key public officials who were involved in the budget-making process. The conclusion is the only time that subjectivity is included in the book, which is deliberate. Following the conclusion in Appendix I is the *Affidavit of Brian A. Pugh*, which was used in the *Clark v. Bryant* case to explain Mississippi's budget-making process to the Chancery Court of Hinds County, Mississippi.

This book is an interpretative narrative that attempts to explain the evolution of Mississippi's budget-making process in a precise, readable format that can be understood by Mississippi taxpayers, all of whom should have a vested interest in the end result of that process. Public budgeting at the state level determines how much funding will be available for state spending on programs that citizens care about, and there is no better way of knowing where governors' and legislators' priorities are regarding those programs than to look at their budgets.

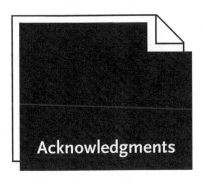

Acknowledgments

Two of the exciting aspects of writing this book have been getting the chance to explore Mississippi's budget-making process as an academic field of study, and the opportunity to work with budget practitioners responsible for putting budget theory into practice. No academician has contributed more to the research of Mississippi budgeting than Mississippi State University's Professor Emeritus Dr. Ed Clynch. Dr. Clynch's research has been an inspiration to me, and I am happy to pick up where he left off. I'd also like to recognize the following budget practitioners: former State Fiscal Officer and Executive Director of the Mississippi Department of Finance & Administration (DFA) Cecil Brown, current State Fiscal Officer and Executive Director of the DFA Laura Jackson, Deputy Director of the Legislative Budget Office (LBO) Howard Brown, and House Budget Officer Lee Anne Robinson. I learned a great deal from all of these individuals, and they all contributed in some capacity to this book and my budget career more than they know. I had the pleasure of working with all of them personally in my role as a legislative budget analyst at the LBO and as Deputy State Fiscal Officer and Deputy Executive Director at the DFA.

I am grateful to attorneys Krissy Nobile and Justin Matheny, with the Attorney General's Office, for their indirect contribution to Mississippi's budget process. I had the pleasure of working with Nobile and Matheny in the court case *Representative Bryant W. Clark and Senator John Horhn v. Governor Phil Bryant et al.*, to explain the difference between budget making and budget control. I was fortunate enough to witness them successfully argue *Clark v. Bryant* before the Mississippi Supreme Court. I am also grateful to Gov. Phil Bryant, who placed his trust in me to advise him on all budget matters and for making me his director of finance; knowing that the governor counted on me encouraged me to work extremely hard every day. While I believe that history will look favorably on many fiscal accomplishments proposed by Bryant that successfully made it through the legislative process, I am most proud of legislation that fell short, such as the Mississippi Working Families Tax Credit. The unsuccessful earned income tax credit would have allowed low-to-moderate-income families the opportunity to take advantage of a nonrefundable tax credit.

I would also like to acknowledge Ronny Frith for all of his support and help with the manuscript. Ronny has served as a Legislative Attorney for the Mississippi House of Representatives for over forty-two years, and his institutional knowledge of the legislative process is second to none. Ronny worked with me for the entire duration of this project, and he devoted countless hours to reading the manuscript for clarity and accuracy. He provided editing recommendations and offered lots of constructive criticism, which made the manuscript better. Nevertheless, I am solely responsible for any errors or erroneous interpretations.

Last but certainly not least, I would like to thank my wife, Dominique, and my daughters, Robin and Mae. My family aided in the effort by making my life enjoyable during the process. They sacrificed countless hours of family time and tolerated long stretches of Daddy's writing time so that the manuscript could be completed.

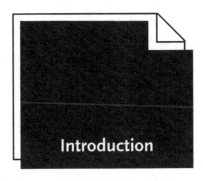

Introduction

By the time Mississippi was admitted to the Union as a state in 1817, it had examples of nineteen other states to imitate, each of which had its governmental structure divided into three separate branches—legislative, judicial, and executive. States gained admission to the Union over a span of three centuries, and the level of power given to the separate branches of government was far from uniform among the states. Some state constitutions placed a strong emphasis on the "trias politica" or simply "separation of powers,"[1] while others were vague and placed little emphasis on the political doctrine. By the time that Mississippi adopted its constitution that is still used today, the Mississippi Constitution of 1890, the doctrine of separation of powers was no longer a political theory, but a policy put into practice. Mississippi Supreme Court Chief Justice Neville Patterson explained in 1984:

> By 1890 separation of powers was no longer a mere political theory from the untested works of Locke and Montesquieu. There was available years of experience by the federal sovereign whose constitution implied but did not express separation of powers. Additionally, there was the example of other states of the union, each of which had divided its powers of government into three branches.[2]

The Mississippi Constitution of 1890 strongly emphasized the separation of powers among the three individual branches of government. Mississippians enjoyed seventy-three years of statehood with a clear understanding of the government's separation of powers. Prior to the current constitution, each of the previous constitutions—those of 1817, 1832, and 1868—unequivocally required the three distinctive branches to be vested in separate and disparate departments of government.[3] The separation of powers served the state well, giving each of the three branches the ability to check the powers of the other branches. Although Mississippi's 1890 constitution aspired to strengthen the constitutional mandate for separation of powers, loose interpretations of the document allowed the legislature to encroach on executive powers, which eventually led to lawsuits being filed by legislators and the attorney general's office in 1982.

A disproportionately large amount of power is vested in the Mississippi Legislature under the current state constitution, which includes the authority to appropriate all funds in the state treasury. The question that eventually led to litigation was never whether the Mississippi governor should be involved in the appropriation process, because that responsibility was clearly given to the legislature and is not unique to Mississippi. Legislatures in all fifty states have the authority to appropriate funds and approve the budget process. However, authority to oversee the implementation or control of the budget is what varies from state to state and is sometimes called into question. Encroachment by the legislature on the "budget control" component of the budget execution phase is what led to (among other things) some Mississippi officials questioning whether legislators should be so heavily involved in this phase. In the early 1980s, a total of thirty-six legislators[4] served on the Commission of Budget and Accounting and eight other executive boards and commissions. Budget control infringement by the legislature was a major reason why the constitutionality of legislators serving on those boards and commissions was challenged.[5]

The executive branch of government does not have the ability to appropriate funds and is dependent on the legislature to fund its agenda items. The simplest way for governors to advance their fiscal agenda and get things paid for is to work in collaboration with the legislature, but working together is challenging. Governors inform the legislature of what they want by submitting a budget proposal, and that budget proposal or executive budget recommendation (EBR) can serve as a vehicle to advance the governor's policy agenda.

The effective utilization of executive budgets was by far the most positive effort made to strengthen the power of governors in the twentieth century. Executive budgets were not only a way for governors to express policy priorities; they were also used to reflect agency needs. Additionally, budget reviews and resource allocations could be used by governors to control and direct executive agencies.[6] This method of executive persuasion to control agencies is not unique to states alone and can also be used at the national level by the president of the United States. Some states provide more executive power to their governor over the budget than that given to the president, while other states grant considerably less budget authority. Mississippi's power granted to its governor was, and still is, significantly less than other states', especially before 1984.

It is the governor's job as chief executive to persuade legislators to approve his or her executive budget proposal with little or no modifications.[7] Article 5 of the Mississippi Constitution begins by declaring that "the chief executive power of this state shall be vested in a Governor," but prior to 1984, state agency directors had little allegiance to the governor and much loyalty to the legislature, because agencies were at the mercy of the Commission of Budget and Accounting, which was dominated by legislators. Governors were also aware of the legislature's power pertaining to the budget and understood the importance of compromise.

Successful governors found out early on the importance of cooperating with the legislature. Furthermore, governors who knew the importance of compromise prior to winning office were even more likely to have success with the legislature. In April 1962 Mississippi State Representative William Winter, who was later elected governor, in 1980, addressed an audience at Centre College in Danville, Kentucky, stating, "It is especially in legislative activity that the problem of accommodation by way of compromise comes up most frequently. . . . I cannot recall a single instance in which any piece of legislation that might be termed controversial was ever passed without some modification in the nature of compromise."[8] Winter understood that the same level of compromise necessary to work with other legislators could also be used by executives when dealing with the legislature.

When Winter decided to run for governor in 1975, his second attempt at the office, he listed his positive relationship with the legislature as an advantage he had over his opponent. While campaigning at an event sponsored by the Greater Meridian Chamber of Commerce, Winter explained that he had the know-how to cooperate with all 174 members of the legislature, more so than his opponent. Winter explained, "Legislators will work with me. I know. I have worked with them."[9] After Winter was elected governor in 1980, he used his longstanding acquaintance with legislative members to have his preferred candidate, Jim Cofer, selected as staff director of the legislatively dominated Commission of Budget and Accounting, which was the agency responsible for recommending the state budget and promoting economy and efficiency in the management of the state's finances.

The Mississippi Legislature's unilateral control over appropriations made compromise a necessity for any chief executives wishing to advance their agenda. Governors could not get their agenda items paid for without first convincing the legislative body that their executive proposals were worthy of taxpayers' hard-earned money. Even talented governors with years of legislative experience found it challenging to get legislators to support their EBR in its entirety, and usually learned early on that a legislative/executive collaboration was by far the easiest formula for getting priorities paid for in the state of Mississippi.

This book explores significant actions taken by the legislative, judicial, and executive branches of government that affected the Mississippi budgeting

process. Significant budgeting legislation is covered, including: the passage of
S.B. 356, which gave the governor the authority to prepare and submit a budget
recommendation in 1918; the passage of the Administrative Reorganization
Act of 1984; the passage of the Budget Reform Act of 1992; and the passage
of the Financial and Operational Responses That Invigorate Future Years
(FORTIFY) Act during the First Extraordinary Session of 2017. The intent of
the first couple of chapters is to provide a historical perspective of the Mississippi budget process and to give the reader an overall understanding of how
legislation, litigation, and executive orders (to a lesser extent) all contributed
to the present-day budget-making process. The establishment of the Budget
Commission in 1932 and the Commission of Budget and Accounting in 1955,
two commissions that played very important roles in the budget-making process, is also discussed. Interventions by the courts, which eventually led to a bill
creating a legislative budget-making process, while simultaneously establishing
legislative and executive roles in the process, is discussed. Additionally, the
major reorganizations that affected the budget-making process are discussed,
along with a brief description of the roles played by the legislative and executive branches of government and their respective staffs.

   In addition to discussing important budgeting laws, this book takes a more
detailed look at six of Mississippi's modern-day governors—Bill Allain, Ray
Mabus, Kirk Fordice, Ronnie Musgrove, Haley Barbour, and Phil Bryant—to see
the methods used for getting the legislature to include them in the budgeting
process. Some governors wanted to be heavily involved in the budget-making
process, while others had more of a laissez-faire approach.

   Two of the six governors, Musgrove and Bryant, served as members of the
legislature. It is hard to say with certainty whether or not the two governors
with legislative experience had an advantage in persuading the legislature to
support their agenda items or to include them in the budget process. However,
it is safe to assume that the relationships built and experience gained by them
while serving as members of the body certainly helped them understand the
dynamics of the legislative process.

   Bill Allain did not serve in the legislature; however, he did have experience
working with the legislature as state attorney general, although the relationship
was far from ideal. Allain was the attorney general that brought the suit that
resulted in the eventual demise of the Commission of Budget and Accounting.
In 1982 the Hinds County Circuit Court heard the case and declared that the
practice of legislators serving on executive boards was an unconstitutional
violation of separation of powers. The state supreme court upheld the lower
court's decision a year later. Ironically, the supreme court's decision was rendered
on November 28, 1983, only a few weeks after Bill Allain was elected governor.

After the Commission of Budget and Accounting was dismantled by the courts, the legislature attempted to preserve as much of its power as possible by passing S.B. 3050, which established a legislative budget process. The bill created the Joint Legislative Budget Committee (JLBC), a ten-member joint house and senate committee (later expanded to fourteen, in 1999), under the leadership of the speaker of the house and lieutenant governor, which was responsible for recommending a legislative budget. Musgrove and Bryant gained tremendous budgeting experience serving on the JLBC, both as lieutenant governor (Musgrove in 1996–2000 and Bryant in 2008–2012).

Mabus also did not serve in the legislature, but he too had experience working with legislators; he worked for the governor's office during the Winter Administration (1980–1984). It is safe to say that Mabus, similar to Allain, had a rocky relationship with some members of the legislature prior to being elected governor. Mabus was one of the youthful staffers that Senate Finance Committee chairman Ellis Bodron derogatorily labeled the "Boys of Spring" during the Winter Administration, which became a badge of honor to the members.[10] Neither Fordice nor Barbour had real political ties to the legislative leadership because both houses had Democratic majorities at the time of their elections. Fordice was the first Republican governor in the state of Mississippi since Reconstruction,[11] and Barbour was the second. Not only did Fordice and Barbour lack a connection to the legislature, neither had ever served as an elected government official prior to winning their respective gubernatorial elections.

The governors discussed in this book had very diverse backgrounds, and they also used different strategies for dealing with the legislature. Some were clearly more successful than others. Some of the governors elected to work directly with the legislative body to get support for their fiscal agenda items, while others decided to go straight to the citizens of Mississippi. This book is not meant to determine which governor had the best method for getting agenda items paid for; instead, the intent is to examine any contributions made to change or improve Mississippi's budget-making process. Furthermore, this book shows how the budget-making process has evolved over time to become what it is today.

CHAO$
AND
COMPROMI$E

Chapter 1

The Origin and Evolution of Mississippi's Budget Process and Control over It

One cannot discuss Mississippi's budget process without first understanding the control of Mississippi government's power structure, which has changed significantly over time. Mississippi's first constitutional convention convened in the town of Washington in Adams County to finalize a draft constitution and voted, after deliberating and amending the proposed document, to adopt Mississippi's first constitution.[1] The convention delegates signed the constitution on August 15, 1817;[2] it was a simple and brief document consisting of a mere eighteen pages.[3] The Mississippi Constitution of 1817 established a weak executive and a strong legislative branch of government, and it provided for an independent judiciary, the latter being similar to that of the US Constitution. Mississippi's early constitutional framers were reluctant to give the executive branch too much power, because they were still suspicious toward a powerful executive. Political scientist Tip H. Allen Jr. explained why the young state was hesitant to give the executive branch too much power, stating "Mississippians still remembered their nation's bitter conflicts with the British king and colonial governors, as well as their own recent feuds with territorial governors."[4]

The feud came with Mississippi's very first territorial governor, Winthrop Sargent (May 7, 1798–May 25, 1801), who was appointed by President John Adams and later dismissed by President Thomas Jefferson. Governor Sargent was a Harvard-educated aristocrat, as well as a Massachusetts Puritan and devout Federalist, who clearly did not connect with Mississippians. Governor Sargent acknowledged in a private letter to Secretary of State John Marshall that he was not "over anxious of popularity [and] I shall never be so far Degraded, as to become the Machine of the Multitude."[5]

The first Mississippi Constitution gave the legislature a tremendous amount of power, including the ability to appoint all major state officials except for the popularly elected governor and lieutenant governor and the gubernatorially appointed judges. However, some of the legislature's power was taken away just fifteen years later when a constitutional convention convened in Jackson in September 1832 to draft a new state constitution. The Mississippi Constitution of 1832 was passed after six weeks of work, and similar to the Constitution of 1817, the new constitution was a short document of only eighteen pages.

The Mississippi Constitution of 1832 was a product of the democratic theme in America, known as Jacksonian democracy, which stressed greater participation by the people in the political process. Historian J. F. H. Claiborne described the Mississippi Constitution as "imperfect indeed, but the freest in the world."[6] Legislators no longer selected most of the constitutional officials, because those positions were now elected by the people, and the people also gained the ability to elect all judges. Electing all judges by popular vote was quite innovative at the time, making Mississippi the first state to do so, and by 1961 all states had followed Mississippi's example.[7] The Constitution of 1832 was clearly a gain for the people regarding the judicial branch, but the executive branch remained weak under the new constitution.

Mississippi's next constitution, the Mississippi Constitution of 1868, was unconventional in two major ways compared to the first two, because it was born of military defeat in the Civil War, and because eighteen of the ninety-seven delegates elected were black. Mississippi was under the supervision of Gen. Edward Ord after the conclusion of the war, and he called for a convention that would write a new constitution that would meet Congress's requirements for the state's restoration into the Union. The Mississippi Constitution of 1868 was framed after delegates assembled in Jackson and drafted the twenty-four-page document. It provided the executive branch with more power, compared to the 1817 and 1832 constitutions, giving the governor the authority to appoint judges with the consent of the senate—thus eliminating the elective judiciary of the 1832 constitution. Furthermore, the governor's term was extended to four years, instead of the two-year terms granted in the previous two constitutions, with no limitation on succession. In other provisions, the legislature was directed to meet annually, and the state's first poll tax was introduced, which was intended to support education and not to prevent people from voting.[8]

The Mississippi Constitution of 1890 reversed the trajectory taken by the 1868 constitution and reverted back to the tradition of a weak governor, and further diminished the strength of the office by making the governor ineligible for immediate reelection. One benefit gained by the governor in the new constitution was the partial veto over appropriation measures. The 1890 constitution also mandated biennial legislative sessions instead of the annual legislative sessions called for in the previous constitution. One constitutional barrier affecting the legislature's ability to increase public spending was the requirement that all bills raising revenue receive a three-fifths vote in the Mississippi Senate and House of Representatives.[9]

The constitutional convention finished its work on the 1890 constitution by late October, and the final document was formally adopted on November 1, 1890. The Mississippi Constitution of 1890 is still the state's basic law, because a constitutional convention has not convened since 1890. The constitution does not mention a constitutional convention, but the assumption is that the legislature has the authority to call one. One major criticism of the 1890 constitution is that the executive branch suffers from a lack of power and executive functions because the constitution provides for the independent popular election of heads of key executive departments.

In Mississippi the governor does not have the number of will and pleasure appointments that provide governors in other states with backdoor leverage over budget proposals. Government officials that are appointed by executive officials in most states, such as state insurance commissioners and transportation commissioners, are elected in Mississippi, further diluting executive influence. Although the legislature lacks the constitutional or statutory powers to govern or select the professional department heads elected by the people, they still control the agencies' appropriations and may sometimes try to use that as leverage for controlling some agency decisions.

Legislative Dominance over the Budget

The Mississippi Legislature dominated the budget process for just over one hundred years following the end of Reconstruction in 1877, with the exception of a few decades in the early-to-mid-twentieth century. The legislature did not control the budget process by giving itself blatant authority; instead, it controlled the budget process by weakening the influence of the executive branch of government. Mississippi governors lack the constitutional and statutory budgetary powers of chief executives in many other states. The Mississippi Legislature has allowed the governor to be a part of the budget preparation and proposal phase since the early 1900s but has rarely paid attention to the executive budget recommendation (EBR).

The legislature established the Commission of Budget and Accounting in 1955 to replace the Budget Commission, an executive commission created in

1932, which gave themselves control over the budget-making process. The old Budget Commission had no legislators serving on it, while the new five-member Commission of Budget and Accounting was made up of four legislators and the governor. Today's budget process consists of two budget recommendations sent to the full legislative body, one being sent by the governor and the other by the Joint Legislative Budget Committee (JLBC), which the legislature established in 1984. Historically, the latter budget recommendation has been used as the starting point for deliberation on appropriations when the legislative session begins. The JLBC membership currently consists of fourteen individuals, and they are all legislators except for the lieutenant governor, an executive branch official who presides over the senate. The JLBC and its staff are discussed at length in chapter 3.

Executive Involvement

The legislature gave the executive branch of government the authority to submit a budget recommendation in 1918 when it approved S.B. 356 on March 27 of the legislative session.[10] The senate bill empowered and directed the governor to prepare and submit to the legislature a budget for handling the state's affairs for the biennial period (today the legislature meets annually, and an annual budget is submitted). State agencies that were supported in whole or in part by state funds were required to submit to the governor's office a detailed estimate of expenditures necessary for the biennial period, along with an explanation of the changes compared to the previous year's appropriation. The governor was given the authority to revise the estimates submitted by the agencies and offer his own recommendation to the legislature.

S.B. 356 also gave the governor the responsibility for properly summarizing the revised expenditures and making sure that they did not exceed revenue. The governor also had to provide detailed revenue sources for all of the recommended expenditures. Further requirements by the law mandated that the governor make a part of the budget an official statement by the auditor of public accounts. The auditor of public accounts was then directed to furnish an official budget document consisting of the state income from all sources and expenses, as well as disbursements, for all purposes as shown by the books in the auditor's office for each of the two preceding years. Finally, a detailed statement of the bonded and other indebtedness of the state had to be submitted, along with the revenue and expenditure statement, to show a true picture of the state's financial condition. The governor's budget had to be mailed to each member of the legislature ten days prior to the convening of the legislative session; the governor then had to present the budget on the first day of the session. For thirty-seven years after the passage of S.B. 356—1918 through 1955—the Mississippi budget was prepared by the executive branch and submitted to the legislative branch for consideration.[11]

Gov. Theodore G. Bilbo was in office when S.B. 356 passed, and he was the first governor to submit an executive budget under that act. Bilbo was a very controversial governor, but he found ways to get the legislature to support his fiscal agenda. Bilbo believed that the rich should pay more and the poor should pay less. In his inaugural address to the legislature, Bilbo explained that the remedy for the state's poor financial situation was "a complete revision of our whole fiscal system under which . . . the tax burden is not only not equal and uniform, as provided in the Constitution, but falls heaviest on those least able to bear it, and in its imposition is grossly unjust, unequal and inequitable."[12] He inherited a large budget deficit when he entered office and was successful in recommending several tax measures to correct the situation.

Jackson Daily News editor Fred Sullens, a huge opponent of Bilbo, begrudgingly admitted that "we must give the devil his due and frankly admit that Theodore's administration has been one of substantial achievements."[13] Positive words from Bilbo's editorial antagonist Sullens was no small matter. It was quite apparent that Sullens was no fan of Bilbo, describing him as "a pimp and frequenter of lewd houses." Bilbo's response to Sullens showed that the resentment was mutual when he retorted that Sullens "is a degenerate by birth, a carpetbagger by inheritance, a liar by instinct, an assassin of character by practice, and a coward by nature!"[14] Bilbo proved to be both a filthy-mouthed orator as well as a governor who could balance a budget, at least during his first term (1916–1920). Bilbo was elected to a second term (1928–1932) and had little budget success, leaving office with a huge budget deficit.

Bilbo accomplished his fiscal agenda during his first term while having a less-than-stellar relationship with many members of the legislature. Prior to becoming governor in 1916, a youthful Senator Bilbo was accused by fellow senators of taking bribes and was nearly expelled from the Mississippi Senate. The hearing to expel Bilbo was held on April 14, 1910, and the senate fell one vote short of the two-thirds majority required to dismiss him, with the final vote count being 28 to 15. The senate asked Bilbo to resign after it failed to remove him, but he refused. After Bilbo's refusal to resign, a resolution was adopted, by a vote count of 25 to 1, condemning his acceptance of a bribe and calling him "unfit to sit with honest, upright men."[15]

During his first term, Bilbo was successful in getting the legislature to support his fiscal agenda to raise taxes on the rich, but the legislature did not fund his whole budget request. With Bilbo, as with other governors, the final budget approved by the legislature in most cases was significantly different from what the governors recommended. Legislatures in other states rarely ever approve executive budgets in their entirety without some modifications.

Martin S. Conner was inaugurated as governor of Mississippi on January 19, 1932, during the worst depression in American history. Governor Conner was fully aware that he could not dig Mississippi out of the financial crisis alone and knew that it would take a collaborative effort with the legislature. He acknowledged in his inaugural address the grim reality of the disruption in the state economy that he and the members of the legislature had to confront:

> We assume our duties when men are shaken with doubt and with fear, and many are wondering if our very civilization is about to crumble. The problems presented to us by this unprecedented, worldwide condition demand for their solution sane minds, clear vision, and courageous hearts. . . . In our deliberations here we must speak frankly and act justly.[16]

Conner became familiar with the state's revenue problems when he served as speaker of the house and had to work with Lt. Gov. Lee Russell, who was thought to have "run the Senate for Bilbo."[17] Then-Speaker Conner and Russell did not get along well. "Despite their personal animosity, Conner and Russell served on a special committee between the 1916 and the 1918 legislative sessions with Alfred Stone, Bilbo's appointee to the new tax commission. Bringing national experts to Jackson, they sought ways to end Mississippi's chronic shortage of tax revenue."[18] Although Conner prided himself on his commitment to fiscal responsibility, he understood that drastic measures had to be made to overcome the state's financial crisis.

Governor Conner inherited a bankrupt treasury and a $13 million deficit from Bilbo's second term. The "Bilbo administration had bequeathed to its successors a near-empty treasury with a balance of only $1,326."[19] Conner proposed a 3 percent sales tax to the legislature to eliminate the deficit.[20] Conner did not hide his thoughts of what would happen should the legislature fail to pass a tax increase. He explained:

> If you will enact a three percent tax upon sales, together with other revenue measures . . . I am prepared to accept full responsibility for the result. . . . If you fail to adopt this program or neglect to make provisions for other suitable and fair means, and as a result, the state's obligations are not met, its credit not restored . . . I warn you now, in all kindness of spirit, and give notice to the people of Mississippi, that I decline to share the responsibility which will be yours."[21]

Connor knew that he would have to get support from key legislative leaders in order to get the sales tax passed. He solicited help from four of the most influential legislators—Speaker of the House Thomas L. Bailey, Rep. Walter Sillers, Rep. Laurence Kennedy, and Rep. Joseph George, who were known as the "Big Four"—to essentially guarantee that the act would pass. Conner's relationship with members of the Big Four went back to his days as a legislator. "Sillers joined Conner and Bailey to form a clique to run the House of Representatives" before eventually bequeathing "the speakership to Bailey when he resigned to run for governor."[22] Conner's relationship with the Big Four proved advantageous in getting the tax increase passed.

The Emergency Revenue Act of 1932 was the "most spectacular fight during [the 1932 legislative] session," and it became law with the passage of H.B. 328.[23] "By a change of one vote the Emergency Revenue Act was passed and signed into law by Governor Conner on April 26, 1932. It provided for a 2 percent retail sales tax."[24] With the enactment of the sales tax, Mississippi became one of the first states in the nation to pass a sales tax. The tax increase eventually fixed the revenue problem, and when Conner left office in 1936, the state had a $3 million surplus.[25] Alfred Holt Stone, chairman of the State Tax Commission, was responsible for the administration of the sales tax, and he stated that "[t]he first six months of operation in Mississippi has resulted in the collection of revenues to the amount of $1,173,721. . . . We have gone far enough, however, to justify the statement that the administration of the law has been satisfactory."[26] Conner contributed a great deal to the efforts of returning Mississippi to solvency during the Great Depression, but the state "could not have approached even partial success without the aid of the federal government."[27]

Budget Commission

The financial crisis caused by the Great Depression, along with a critical report on Mississippi government issued by the Brookings Institution, led to legislation being passed to address the fiscal problems.[28] The legislative reaction to the financial crisis and critical report resulted in the passage of H.B. 205 on May 5, 1932, which created the Budget Commission that was charged with promoting economy and efficiency in the management of the state's finances.[29] The legislation designated the governor as ex-officio director of the budget, and the chairman of the State Tax Commission as the assistant director. The assistant director was given the duty of preparing and submitting to the governor a balanced state budget, consisting of all expenditures and revenue, for consideration every other year. The necessary clerical assistance needed to prepare the budget was provided by employees of the governor and the State Tax Commission's office without extra compensation. The attorney general was required to provide any necessary legal advice or services that the Budget Commission might need.

Governor Conner was the first director of the Budget Commission, and Alfred Holt Stone was the first assistant director, since he chaired the State Tax Commission. Although the governor was responsible for appointing the chairman of the State Tax Commission, once he made his appointment, the chairman would serve six years in that position, outlasting the governor's four-year term.[30] The State Tax Commission, like other state agencies, was heavily influenced by the legislature, because it was dependent on the legislature for its appropriation. Knowing that the governor could not dismiss him after he was appointed, Stone was probably more likely to be loyal to the legislature, because governors would come and go, while legislative leaders, who were involved in the budget process, were there for a much longer period of time. Furthermore, the governor did not decide how much funding the State Tax Commission would receive, because funding levels for agencies were determined by the legislature.

The structural makeup of the Budget Commission was clearly established to be an executive agency. However, agencies sometimes got confused when trying to determine who made some of the budget decisions that were recommended to the legislature, because some agencies believed that legislators had indirect involvement with and influence over the Budget Commission. This claim was debatable, but confusion with regard to the status of the commission was undeniably evident. An article published in the *Jackson Clarion-Ledger* in June 1953 alluded to confusion concerning the Budget Commission when it explained that the commission "is considered something of an arm of the executive department on the one hand and of the legislature on the other."[31]

H.B. 205 required the assistant director to submit a balanced state budget, and he was given the authority to demand any information or records from state entities that were necessary for preparing the state budget. The legislature gave the assistant director supervision over every state agency and/or department that was supported in whole or in part by the state. This was done to secure uniformity and accuracy of accounts and efficient conduct of its financial affairs, according to the legislation.

The state budget was prepared by the assistant director and staff under the governor's instructions. Governors operating under H.B. 205 could have elected to be more involved in the budgeting process, because they had the option to accept or reject the prepared budget recommendation, but in most cases, they simply endorsed the assistant director's plan.[32] The assistant director's influence basically ended at the conclusion of the budget preparation and proposal phase, because the legislature did not have to seek assistance from the Budget Commission after it made its recommendation to the legislature.

One power given to the Budget Commission that went beyond the budget preparation and proposal phase was the ability to allow state agencies to exceed their appropriation during emergencies. The legislature could deal with emergencies if it was in session, but this authority allowed the Budget Commission to address emergencies occurring at any time. During such emergencies, the governor had to set out his full reasons for approving excess spending, and the commission had to limit the time and prescribe the conditions in which the emergencies applied.

In 1952 the legislature passed S.B. 613, which amended the statute pertaining to the Budget Commission.[33] The duties of the Budget Commission did not change; it was still charged with promoting economy and efficiency in the management of the state's finances. The purpose of amending the statute was to clarify and prescribe the methods of employing and fixing salaries of the personnel of the commission. The legislation gave significant power to the executive branch by giving the governor the authority to appoint an executive secretary who would be responsible for carrying out the provisions of all laws pertaining to the Budget Commission and running the Budget Commission office. The governor was not only given the authority to appoint the secretary; he was also in charge of setting the secretary's salary.

Prior to the passage of S.B. 613, the staff of the State Tax Commission was responsible for most of the administrative work needed to formulate a state budget. But the amended statute now allowed the new executive secretary to employ his own staff, who were subject to dismissal by the secretary with the governor's approval. Altering the method of hiring the staff assured allegiance to the governor and took away all the power that was previously held by the chairman of the State Tax Commission while serving as assistant director of the Budget Commission.

Mississippi Commission of Budget and Accounting

The executive-centered Budget Commission was abolished in 1955 when the legislature passed H.B. 177 to create the Mississippi Commission of Budget and Accounting, which totally changed the budget-making process by transforming it into a legislatively dominated process.[34] The newly created commission made it clear that the legislature thought that budget decisions were best decided on by members of the legislature, because 80 percent of the new members of the commission were legislators.

The Commission of Budget and Accounting consisted of the governor serving as ex-officio chairman and four legislators. Gov. Hugh White served as the first chairman of the commission, and the remaining members of the commission were the following legislators: J. O. (Click) Clark, president pro tempore of the senate; Sen. Earl Evans Jr., chairman of the Senate Finance

Committee; Rep. H. Tyler Holmes, chairman of the House Appropriations Committee; and Rep. Hilton Waits, chairman of the House Ways and Means Committee. The commission was later expanded to eleven members, and the additional six members were all legislators, except for the lieutenant governor, who presides over the senate.

Having members of the executive and legislative branches of government serving on the same commission that controlled both the budget preparation and proposal phase and other budgeting functions was very uncommon, in other states as well as in Mississippi. Prior to the creation of the new commission, Mississippi was similar to other states and allowed the executive branch to submit a budget recommendation to the legislature, and then the legislature accepted some of the recommendations while also rejecting some of them. It seemed odd that the legislature would want to be involved in recommending a budget to itself, and this new method was clearly outside the norm of other states. Charles Hills of the *Jackson Clarion-Ledger* explained that the legislative "act as adopted by both houses . . . has created a far-reaching system of checking state operational costs and estimating of new budgets."[35]

One could easily interpret the creation of the Commission of Budget and Accounting as legislative overreach, but Gov. Hugh White did not seem to see it that way. When asked by newsmen about his opinion of the bill and if he would sign it, White explained that he had not yet read the act and had to study the bill before deciding to sign it or not. Although he admitted to not reading the bill, he indicated that he was fairly certain that he would sign it and create the new commission. White concluded to the newsmen that he had not yet made his decision, but "[I] understand, however, that the act is a good one."[36]

Similar to the Budget Commission, the Commission of Budget and Accounting controlled spending authority and management of all state agencies, departments, and institutions. The new commission, like the previous one, was required to submit to the legislature an overall balanced budget of the entire expenditures and revenue of the state for each biennium. The commission had to submit the budget prior to the first day of December before the legislature convened for the legislative session. Although some of its authority was the same as the Budget Commission's, the Commission of Budget and Accounting was given many more duties.

The Commission of Budget and Accounting's business and day-to-day operations were administered by an executive secretary who was appointed by the commission and served at the will and pleasure of the commission. The legislation also gave the secretary the authority to appoint a staff. The secretary was required to consult with the Finance Committee of the senate and the Ways and Means and Appropriations Committees of the house of representatives whenever the committees needed assistance during the legislative session. The staff responsible for administrative support that was needed to create the budget recommendation answered directly to the secretary.

The commission selected W. R. Carbrey of Columbia, Mississippi, as the first executive secretary; prior to being appointed, Carbrey served as executive secretary of the Budget Commission.[37] Soon after his appointment, Carbrey fell ill, and Frank W. Ellis Jr. and Joe B. Keith had to "perform immediate initial preparation for the setting up of the new budget."[38] While Carbrey was ill, Ellis served as acting secretary. Carbrey eventually resigned the position in 1956, and the commission named Ellis the executive secretary.

Ellis was quite candid about the Commission of Budget and Accounting's influence on the legislature. Agencies were rarely ever thrilled about the commission's recommendations and were accustomed to appealing to the legislature to get their way. Ellis explained that most agency heads end up going to the legislature "either to say how glad [they are] or how mad [they are]" and went on to add that "history shows that the legislature usually accepts the recommendations of the [. . .] commission."[39] The reason that the legislature generally took the advice of the commission was due to the makeup of the commission. Most of the legislators serving on the commission were experienced legislative leaders and usually more knowledgeable on budgeting matters, which is why their legislative peers were more likely to take their recommendation. Additionally, the full legislative body dealt with many issues throughout the legislative session and simply had no time to review all of the agency requests, therefore making them quite dependent on their legislative colleagues who were members of the commission. Gov. James Plemon "J. P." Coleman, chairman of the commission, explained in 1957 how he did not see any prospects for salary increases for state employees and went on to mention that some agencies may get their budgets cut. It was not at all uncommon for governors to make premature, broad statements pertaining to budget increases or decreases, similar to the statement made by Coleman, knowing that the final decision would be left up the legislature.

The commission's first biennial report clearly showed that the legislature listened to the Commission of Budget and Accounting more than it had to the Budget Commission. The EBR submitted by the Budget Commission for the 1954–1956 biennial period was a recommended amount of $137,251,000, and the final amount approved by the legislature was $168,030,877, a difference of $30,779,877, or a whopping 22.43 percent. The Commission of Budget and Accounting submitted its first recommendation for the 1956–1958 biennial period for $183,003,897, and the final amount approved by the legislature was $186,125,587, a difference of only $3,121,690, or a mere 1.7 percent.[40]

The commission had its critics, especially when it came to revenue estimating. Three years after the creation of the commission, State Auditor Boyd Golding thought that the commission did a very poor job of anticipating incoming revenue. Golding explained that the auditor's office handles all of the "incoming money" and "outgoing money" and is in a "better position" to determine the financial picture of the state. Furthermore, Golding stated that the commission and its predecessor, for the past decade, had "consistently missed" its revenue estimates, and he predicted that the general fund would be depleted by July 1, 1958, although the state would actually have a surplus of "around $28-million."[41]

Today, a professional revenue estimating committee consisting of the state economist, who is employed at the University Research Center, and the Department of Revenue (previously known as the State Tax Commission) predicts revenue estimates for the fiscal year and makes a recommendation to the legislature and governor to be jointly adopted.[42] The revenue estimate is then used as a starting point for the legislative budget recommendation (LBR) and the EBR. Although Mississippi law gives revenue estimating authority to the University Research Center and the Department of Revenue only, three other agencies assist in this process, including the Legislative Budget Office (LBO), the Office of the State Treasurer, and the Department of Finance and Administration (DFA). It is ironic that the agencies that informally assist with revenue estimating today do not include the Office of the State Auditor, which was quite critical of the revenue estimating process in 1958.[43]

Legislative Encroachment on Executive Functions

Mississippi's budget-making process consists of three formal phases: budget preparation and proposal, legislative budget approval, and budget execution. The specific component of the budget execution phase that is the focal point in this book is budget control. Budget proposal and control are both responsibilities of the executive branch in most states, and the legislatures are responsible for the approval phase. The terms *budget proposal* and *budget recommendation* are used interchangeably throughout the book. With the creation of the Commission of Budget and Accounting, Mississippi became unique, because the legislative branch of government was now involved in all three phases of the budget-making process. There is also an informal fourth phase, the review/reporting phase, which is not discussed, because it is not mandatory for all Mississippi agencies.[44]

First, the commission was in charge of the budget preparation and proposal phase, because agencies had to submit their budget requests to the commission, and the commission then submitted a budget recommendation to the full legislative body. Secondly, Mississippi statutes and judicial decisions gave the legislature the sole responsibility of adopting budgets and appropriating funds, which is still the case today. The legislative approval phase is best explained as a time when it is the executive branch's job to "step back and leave it in the hands of the legislature."[45] Finally, the budget control component of the budget execution phase, which was by far the most controversial in Mississippi, had extensive legislative involvement because legislators were serving as board members of key executive branch agencies and participated in the control and administration of agency programs. Additionally, the commission itself, which was also dominated by legislators, exercised budget control functions over executive agencies. The executive agencies that were dominated by legislative members were in violation of the state constitution's separation of powers. Because of legislative influence over the budget process, agency directors who were selected by boards and commissions (and nonlegislative members of those boards) were more likely to take "their cues from . . . legislative board members."[46]

Chapter 2

Legislative Power Weakened

It was clear that the Commission of Budget and Accounting held a substantial amount of power over the budget-making process, because it was heavily involved with the preparation and control of the budget. Although the executive branch was annoyed with the legislative domination over the process, it recognized the rights granted by law for the legislature to be a part of the preparation and approval phases. However, legislative involvement in the budget control component of the budget execution phase was beginning to draw negative attention, because most spending decisions were made at this phase, allowing the legislature to function "as a de facto quasi-parliamentary system with state agencies responsible to the legislature."[1] In the early 1980s, a total of thirty-six legislators were serving on the Commission of Budget and Accounting and eight executive boards and commissions that were directly responsible for implementing government services to citizens of Mississippi. The constitutionality of legislators serving on executive boards and commissions was eventually challenged when Attorney General Bill Allain filed suit on April 7, 1982, to have the legislators removed from those boards.

Hinds County Circuit Court

Judge Charles Barber of the Circuit Court of the First Judicial District of Hinds County heard the "separation of powers" case for three days in November 1982, with testimony from Attorney General Allain and Ed Brunini, the Jackson attorney representing the legislators. Oddly enough, the legislators never denied the fact that the constitution clearly separates the powers of government among the three branches of government. Brunini explained to Judge Barber that there is "no such thing as the schoolboy notion of a complete separation of powers," because each case has to be viewed "in its own situation." Allain responded that the legislators are "not even denying that these are executive boards. They just keep talking about this blending, this melding of responsibilities. Their idea of cooperation is that there should be a member of the legislature sitting right up there with you [pointing to Judge Barber]....When do you start this blending....Where are you going to stop?" implying that the legislature will next start interfering with judicial functions.[2] On February 3, 1983, Judge Barber declared the controverted statutes unconstitutional to the extent they authorized legislators to sit on the executive boards. Furthermore, Judge Barber's order removed the legislators from the executive boards and commissions, with the exception of Rep. Charles Young (who served on the Board of Corrections before he became a legislator), and ousted them from the legislature (legislators never actually vacated their legislative seats).[3] The court's final judgment was to become effective on January 1, 1984.

Supreme Court

The thirty-six legislators appealed the verdict to the Mississippi Supreme Court, and they were taken by surprise when all nine justices joined in a unanimous opinion on November 23, 1983, that upheld the lower court's decision. The case, *Alexander v. State of Mississippi by and through Allain* (1983), was concerned with the rights and prerogatives of the executive and legislative branches of state government. The separation of powers lawsuit was taken to the supreme court for an interpretation of Article I, Sections 1 and 2 of the Mississippi Constitution of 1890. The two debatable sections in need of clarification were:

Section 1. The powers of government of the state of Mississippi shall be divided into three distinct departments, and each of them confided to a separate magistracy, to-wit: those which are legislative to one, those which are judicial to another, and those which are executive to another.

Section 2. No one person or collection of persons, being one or belonging to one of these departments, shall exercise any power properly belonging to either of the others...

The supreme court's sentiment for upholding the lower court's verdict was not surprising based on Chief Justice Neville Patterson's simple opening paragraph of his opinion describing the situation. Chief Justice Patterson explained that "[i]n broad terms the issue presented is whether Article I, Sections 1 and 2 should be interpreted faithfully . . . or whether it should be interpreted loosely so that efficiency in government through permissive overlapping of departmental functions becomes paramount to the written word."[4]

The supreme court declared that a loose interpretation of the Mississippi Constitution, for the sake of efficiency, is clearly a violation of the law and gave the legislature seven months, until July 1, 1984, to remove its members from the boards and commissions in the executive branch. The supreme court's separation of powers decision gave the executive branch authority over budget control, while the legislature continued to control the budget proposal and legislative approval phases in the budget process. Although the separation of powers lawsuit made it clear that the governor was responsible for budget control, the legislature still would be able to influence and control agencies indirectly in this phase, because they could always retaliate against disobedient agencies by providing less funding in the next fiscal year.

The Final Budget Proposal by the Commission of Budget and Accounting

The Commission of Budget and Accounting submitted its final budget proposal to the legislature for the 1984 session in the fall of 1983. This particular budget proposal was not only unique in the fact that it was the last one ever to be submitted by the soon-to-be obsolete commission but also peculiar because the commission elected to present two budgets for the legislature's consideration. The law at that time required the commission to prepare a balanced budget in which the general fund expenditures could not exceed the estimated revenues.[5] Because of the down economy, the commission was forced to reduce budgets by over $240 million from legislative appropriations since FY 1981 in order to comply with the law requiring a balanced budget. The commission explained, "These funding reductions, taken to maintain a balanced budget, have seriously eroded the state's ability to provide basic essential services that the citizens of Mississippi need and deserve."[6] The commission decided that it wanted to recommend the appropriation of more funds than the anticipated revenue would cover, so it submitted a balanced budget and an alternate, unbalanced budget. A statute that has since been repealed allowed the commission, at the time, to propose an alternative budget that was approximately $68 million higher than the anticipated revenue estimate.[7] The commission felt that it fulfilled its statutory obligation by adopting the balanced budget, in which the general fund expenditures and revenues both totaled $1,360,000,000. However, the alternate budget totaling $1,428,089,389 was the commission's preferred budget.

The alternate budget proposal was used in a way to recommend additional funding that could come only from the legislature and not the commission. It was a consensus among the committee members that the estimated revenue that would be collected during the next fiscal year would not adequately support the essential functions of state government. The commission felt that the alternate budget was necessary because it believed that the functions of state government would be severely harmed under the commission's statutorily required budget of $1.36 billion. The alternate budget did not include any new programs, and it was intended to provide the same level of services as provided in FY 1984.[8]

Mississippi Administrative Reorganization Act of 1984

The supreme court's decision in the *Alexander* case temporarily set the legislature back some in the budget-making process. The court's order to remove the legislature from the budget-control component of the budget execution phase instantly increased the executive branch's power in the budget process. The legislature responded to the supreme court's decision by passing S.B. 3050 during the 1984 legislative session, a 350-page bill that removed all legislators from all executive branch boards and commissions, while simultaneously consolidating a number of agencies under the governor's office.[9] That act, which was known as the Mississippi Administrative Reorganization Act of 1984, abolished the Commission of Budget and Accounting and created the Joint Legislative Budget Committee (JLBC) to make recommendations regarding budget making to the entire legislative body and the state Fiscal Management Board (FMB) to carry out budget control. The JLBC and the FMB were both responsible for the budget preparation and proposal phase. The creation of the FMB, which was composed of the governor and two other members appointed by the governor with the advice and consent of the senate, enhanced the power of the governor in the budget process. The governor was made chairman of the board, and no board action could be valid without the governor's approval along with one other member's,[10] which basically gave the governor veto power over FMB actions. The governor was also given the authority to hire an FMB director and six analysts, which strengthened his control over FMB actions. In addition to implementing the budget through budget control, the FMB was also given the responsibility of producing an executive budget recommendation (EBR).[11]

The FMB was given jurisdiction over the functions of state government that were previously under the Commission of Budget and Accounting, placing them under a Bureau of Budget and Fiscal Management and a Bureau of Administration. The Bureau of Budget and Fiscal Management consisted of the following divisions: budget, fiscal management, and bond advisory. The divisions that made up the Bureau of Administration included purchasing, insurance, and administrative. The reorganization act also centralized and placed a number of governmental units within the Office of the Governor that were not previously there.[12]

The legislature preserved as much power as possible by establishing a legislative budget-making process and creating the JLBC to administer the process. The JLBC consisted of the lieutenant governor and the same legislative members that made up the constitutionally infirm Commission of Budget and Accounting, and excluded the governor. The JLBC consisted of eleven members when first established and was increased to fourteen members in 1999. The initial JLBC members, postreorganization, consisted of the following: Brad Dye, lieutenant governor; Thomas L. Brooks, president pro tempore of the senate; Sen. Bob Montgomery, chairman of the Senate Finance Committee; Sen. Glenn Deweese, chairman of the Senate Appropriations Committee; Sen. Robert L. Crook; C. B. (Buddie) Newman, speaker of the house of representatives; Rep. F. Edwin Perry, chairman of the House Appropriations Committee; Rep. H. L. Meredith, chairman of the House Ways and Means Committee; Rep. Ted J. Millette; and Rep. James C. Simpson. The JLBC was now responsible for producing a legislative budget proposal that was completely independent of the executive budget produced by the FMB.

The JLBC was given a professional staff, called the Legislative Budget Office (LBO), consisting of a director and seven analysts. Bobby Greenlee was selected by the JLBC to serve as the director of the LBO, and many of the budget analysts on his new staff previously served as analysts for the Commission of Budget and Accounting. Other budget analysts who had previously worked for the Commission of Budget and Accounting went to work for the FMB after the commission was dissolved. While Jim Cofer served as the director of the Commission of Budget and Accounting, Greenlee had served as one of the deputy directors. The duties of the LBO included providing fiscal support necessary to enable the JLBC and the legislature to adopt a balanced state budget. For LBO staff to assist the JLBC in adopting a state budget, it was necessary for LBO analysts to work closely with state agencies, in order to better understand their budget needs. Prior to making a staff recommendation to the JLBC, Greenlee explained that his staff "worked with the 175 state agencies presenting budget proposals and came up with recommendations."[13] The JLBC then reviewed the staff recommendation, made changes, and then made their own recommendation based on information compiled and analyzed by their staff. The JLBC proposal was known as the LBR, and the LBR was one of the two budget proposals presented to the full legislative body. The other budget proposal was the EBR, recommended by the FMB, which is discussed in the next chapter.

The two budget recommendations proposed for the 1985 legislative session constituted the first time that competing recommendations had ever been made in Mississippi's history.[14] Although the legislature increased the executive involvement in the budget process substantially in S.B. 3050, legislative leaders were intentional in drafting the bill in a way to preserve the legislature's dominance over the budget preparation and proposal phase. Gov. Bill Allain was the first governor postreorganization to present a budget proposal, and his passive approach to his recommendation was likely because he thought that the "legislature would disregard his budget."[15] Allain was correct in his assumption that legislators would place little emphasis on his executive budget and that they would pay more attention to the budget prepared by the JLBC.[16]

Prior to the passage of the reorganization act, the Commission of Budget and Accounting, which consisted of legislative leaders and the governor, adopted an annual general fund revenue estimate that was used as a starting point for the budget recommendation, and the commission also adopted the final revenue estimate (known as the "sine die estimate") that was used to build the next fiscal year's budget during the legislative session. A year after the reorganization act was passed, the legislature passed a law specifying that the legislature's sine die estimate was the official state estimate.[17] Although the law gave sole authority to the legislative branch—more specifically the LBO—for adopting the sine die estimate, the state fiscal officer, under the guidance of the governor, was given the responsibility of reducing budgets if revenue estimates failed to meet projections.[18]

The legislature would not have abolished the powerful Commission of Budget and Accounting if it had not been forced to do so by the courts. Legislation has been passed in the years following the 1984 supreme court decision that tweaked the budget-making process, but none of the legislation was on the scale of the Mississippi Administrative Reorganization Act of 1984. The legislative branch enjoyed many years of budget domination before the constitutionality of legislators serving on executive boards and commissions was challenged, and although some budget powers were lost, the legislature was the one charged with coming up with a solution to the problem. The legislature passed S.B. 3050, which satisfied the court's separation of powers issue while simultaneously preserving as much legislative power as legally allowed. Although the legislative branch fared well postreorganization, many legislators were not happy that they were forced to reorganize the budget process in the first place. The reorganization act remains the most drastic change to the budget-making process to this day, and while it was a small setback for the legislative branch, the legislature has continued to find ways to keep the upper hand over the process.

Chapter 3

The Budget Process, Postreorganization, under Allain

There was not an individual affected more by the Mississippi Administrative Reorganization Act of 1984 (S.B. 3050, passed during the 1984 legislative session) than Bill Allain. Allain was the attorney general who brought the suit against the legislators who were serving on executive boards and commissions, which resulted in the demise of the Commission of Budget and Accounting. Allain was ironically elected governor a few weeks before the Mississippi Supreme Court rendered its decision that upheld the Hinds County Circuit Court's earlier decision declaring the practice of legislators serving on executive boards and commissions as an unconstitutional violation of separation of powers. The supreme court's decision on November 28, 1983, made Allain the first governor to serve under the reorganization act.

It was a bit puzzling that Governor Allain did not take more of an initiative toward establishing spending priorities, since he was the one responsible for the abolishment of the Commission of Budget and Accounting. The staff of the Fiscal Management Board (FMB) was said to have made proposals to Allain for funding ongoing programs and spending plans for fund balances, based on public statements that he made, and Allain was thought to have accepted his staff's recommendation with little comment. The FMB staff would develop a plan and present it to Allain, explaining, "Governor, we believe these are your priorities," according to an Allain staffer.[1] Regardless of whether Allain was passive in the development of his budget proposals, he was quite successful in getting the legislature to approve key priority items on his fiscal agenda throughout his four-year term.

On November 15, 1984, Allain proposed an optimistic inaugural executive budget to the legislature. He recommended $1,491,185,205 in general funds for his FY 1986 budget recommendation,[2] which was nearly 7 percent higher in general funds than the previous fiscal year's budget. Allain's recommended general fund increase was somewhat surprising because of the tough economic times that the state had been undergoing. Times were so bad that the Commission of Budget and Accounting had been forced to reduce general fund spending levels by 5 percent in August of 1983.[3] Allain was fully aware of the economic challenges and explained to the legislature, "The State of Mississippi is amidst austere economic times. Mississippi has tremendous needs—and these needs far exceed our state's available resources."[4] Included in Allain's first budget recommendation was a 5 percent salary increase for state employees. He explained in his budget proposal that state employees are the most important resource that the state has and that the state's fiscal constraints have prevented them from being adequately compensated. "The financial picture for state government continues to be bleak; however, provisions must be made for salary increases," explained Allain.[5] It was likely of little concern to Allain that the Joint Legislative Budget Committee (JLBC) did not follow his lead and recommend state employee pay raises in the committee's legislative budget recommendation (LBR); what mattered to him was that he expressed to state employees and the general public what his priorities were in his executive budget recommendation (EBR).

The argument can easily be made that Allain did not get the general fund increases that he requested in his first budget recommendation because of the sluggish economy. Budget appropriations had been cut from FY 1981 through FY 1986 by over $287,400,000.[6] Because of his awareness of the budget woes, Allain presented a solution to the problem in his FY 1987 budget proposal that would transfer $380,153,403 from special funds to the general fund. This simple conversion of special funds to general funds would have made the total FY 1987 revenue estimate $1,940,153,403.

The actual FY 1986 revenue estimate was 28 percent lower than the amount that Allain thought could be generated by including the converted special funds. Knowing that such a drastic change to the budget had no chance of getting legislative approval without a proper explanation, Allain explained that the "amount represents operating funds other than federal, local or self-generated funds and those funds held in trust for someone else. It is long past time for the Legislature to make provisions for combining all funds so that there will be better management and control of them."[7] Unfortunately for Allain, the legislature did not see it his way, totally ignored his proposal, and continued appropriating general and special funds the same way as in the past. Allain did not request that the legislature convert special funds into general funds in his FY 1987 budget proposal, but he still thought that it was a good idea and needed. Allain explained in his proposal:

> The Executive Budget Recommendation follows the traditional definition of "general" and "special" funds, and is presented in that format for your convenience and to facilitate comparison with prior years and with the Legislative Budget Office's recommendation. However, I still feel strongly that all state money should be placed into a single fund so that all agencies, regardless of the source of their funds, are treated equally and without preference.[8]

Allain's first two budget proposals to the legislature for FY 1986 and FY 1987 were not well received, but that does not mean that he did not eventually succeed in getting some of the items from his fiscal agenda passed. Allain's third budget proposal was less optimistic than his first two proposals, and he seemed far less enthused by the document. Allain submitted a balanced budget for FY 1988 within the confines of the consensus general fund revenue estimate established by the FMB and the JLBC, which basically level funded most agencies. Allain's administration got off to a good start and was initially influential in the budget process; however, toward the end of his term, his administration seemed to lose momentum regarding the budget. Allain was so disengaged in the budget process in the latter part of his administration that he, "as a lame duck, did not release a budget" for FY 1989.[9]

Allain's Fiscal Accomplishments

Fiscal accomplishments in which Governor Allain found success throughout his term in office included: (1) influencing the content of S.B. 3050, which created the FMB, by threatening the legislature with a veto of the bill, (2) getting the legislature to statutorily create a centralized administrative office that he previously set up by executive order, and (3) successfully getting the legislature to transfer special funds from the Mississippi Highway Department to the general fund. The first accomplishment was achieved when Allain was successful in getting the legislature to take his desires into consideration by agreeing to set up the FMB and allowing him to make the two appointments to the three-member board, with him serving as chairman of the board.[10] Allain was very interested in having the new FMB members approach the management of state government like a business, and he thought that he could achieve that goal by appointing two business-minded individuals to the board. Allain explained in an interview when discussing his new appointees that the two individuals selected should succeed in "making government operate as much like a business as it can."[11] The next accomplishment was achieved when Allain issued Executive Order No. 526 that created the Office of Administrative Services and later got legislation passed to statutorily create the new office. The final accomplishment of Allain was his recommendation to redirect earmarked highway department funds away from the highway department to help assist with the hardship caused by the financial crisis of 1986.[12] The legislature responded by directing the agency to transfer $10 million of highway department funds to the Bureau of Building, Grounds and Real Property Management during the 1986 session by passing S.B. 2654. The legislature also directed the agency to transfer $12 million of highway department funds to the general fund during the 1987 session by passing S.B. 3039, to ease the burden on the budget.

Establishment of the Fiscal Management Board

In addition to creating the JLBC to carry out the budget preparation and proposal phase for the legislative branch of government, the reorganization act created the FMB to carry out the budget preparation and proposal phase and budget control component of the budget execution phase for the executive branch. The first meeting of FMB was held on July 2, 1984, which was intended to be an "organizational meeting" featuring a review of policies, procedures, and a few budgetary matters, along with the election of a vice-chairman.[13] Governor Allain appointed John Callon and Mike Sturdivant to serve as board members. The latter was ironically a Democratic primary opponent of Allain's in the 1983 governor's race, finishing third behind Evelyn Gandy and Allain. As governor, Allain served as chairman of the FMB, and he had lots of control over the board because he was responsible for appointing both members, and no board action could be valid without the governor's approval along with one other member's approval.

The first action taken during the inaugural meeting of the FMB was chief justice of the Mississippi Supreme Court, the Honorable Neville Patterson, administering the oath of office to John Callon and Mike Sturdivant in order for them to serve on the board. Sturdivant was then elected vice-chairman of the FMB upon a motion by Callon. Allain succeeded in appointing two experienced and successful businessmen to the board: Callon operated an oil and gas company, Callon Petroleum Co., in Natchez for a number of years, and Sturdivant was a millionaire businessman who had farming interest in the Delta and also operated a company that ran hotels in four southeastern states.[14]

The second line of business at the board meeting was to appoint a state fiscal officer. Sturdivant offered a motion to appoint Jim Cofer as state fiscal officer, Callon seconded the motion, and the board's ratification of Cofer made him the first state fiscal officer. Before his appointment as state fiscal officer, Cofer had served as the director of the Commission of Budget and Accounting, so he was not at all new to Mississippi budgeting. Shortly after being approved as state fiscal officer, Cofer presented the FMB with a progress report on the reorganization and transition since the passage of the reorganization act. Additionally, the board voted to implement the recommendation of FMB staff concerning implementation of the FY 1986 Executive Budget, which was to move away from line item budgets and toward a modified zero-based budget for FY 1986.[15]

Centralized Administrative Support

One of the first actions taken by Governor Allain following the passage of the reorganization act was to issue an executive order creating a new administrative office to provide centralized administrative support for the governmental units placed within the Office of the Governor by the act. Issued on June 4, 1984, Executive Order No. 526 established an Office of Administrative Services within the Office of the Governor to provide that support. The mission of the new office was "[t]o perform personnel and business support functions for designated governmental agencies, divisions, and offices operating programs under the authority of the Governor."[16] Other than relying on the legislature for a budget appropriation, the Office of Administrative Services was completely independent of the legislature.

The Office of Administrative Services was created to "provide and perform [. . .] administrative functions" for specific governmental agencies, such as "centralized fiscal management support functions," among many other administrative duties.[17] The governmental agencies supported by the office consisted of the following: the Division of Medicaid, the Mississippi Emergency Management Agency (MEMA), the Governor's Office of General Services, the Bureau of Budget and Fiscal Management, and the Governor's Budget Office. The latter two agencies were directly involved in making the budget. The centralized fiscal management support functions were to be performed by the Division of Business Services of the Office of Administrative Services, and this division's responsibilities included interpreting state legislation pertaining to fiscal affairs; analyzing fiscal policies and procedures in order to recommend needed changes; reviewing appropriate historical budgetary data in order to prepare or assist in preparing budget requests for supported governmental agencies; and attending legislative budget hearings to answer questions pertaining to budget requests.

Allain issued Executive Order No. 542 on November 2, 1984, which rescinded Executive Order No. 526 but continued the operation and function of the Office of Administrative Services. Executive Order No. 542 was in furtherance of the reorganization act, which mandated that the administrative functions of several agencies under the purview of the governor be centrally managed to bring about more efficiency, less cost, easier control, and an avoidance of duplication. Two major additions to Executive Order No. 542 were the creation of a centralized administrative pool of employees for administrative and management purposes and the use of a cost allocation plan.[18] The sponsoring agencies included in the centralized administrative pool were the Division of Medicaid, the Governor's Office of General Services, the Fiscal Management Office, and MEMA. Directors of those agencies were able to assign designated personnel, without loss of employee rights and benefits, to the central administrative pool under the governor's direction.

Statutory Establishment of the Office of Administrative Services and Funding for It

Governor Allain included a sum of $408,965 in his FY 1986 EBR for the Office of Administrative Services, but the JLBC recommended nothing for the newly created office in its budget proposal. When the full legislative body convened for the 1985 legislative session, the legislature passed S.B. 2510, which established the Office of Administrative Services statutorily, effective on July 1, 1985.[19] The legislature also passed S.B. 2991, which appropriated $381,874 for the FY 1986 expenses of the new office and authorized twelve full-time positions.[20] The entire amount appropriated was in general funds, and three-quarters of the funding went toward salaries. More specifically, the legislature appropriated $292,842 for salaries, $1,000 for travel, $79,032 for contractual services, and $9,000 for commodities. Although Allain did not get his full appropriation request for the Office of Administrative Services, the mere shortage of $27,091 was not enough to disrupt any major operational plans for the new agency.

S.B. 2510 was authored by Sen. Robert Crook and Sen. Glen Deweese, both members of the JLBC, and it amended a number of existing statutes pertaining to multiple fiscal matters in addition to statutorily creating the Office of Administrative Services. Section 35 of the bill created the Office of Administrative Services within the Governor's Office of Federal-State Programs, but the bill specifically stated that the "Office of Administrative Services shall be a separate and distinct office from the Division of Administration of the Governor's Office of Federal-State Programs."[21] The bill basically set the office up the way that Governor Allain had it in his executive orders.

Staffing the Office of Administrative Services

Soon after the issuance of Executive Order No. 526, the governor selected Edwin R. Ling to be the first executive director of the Office of Administrative Services, beginning June 18, 1984. Prior to accepting the position, Ling was a counsel for the National Aeronautics and Space Administration (NASA). Ling was obtained through the "loan" of a federal executive to the state for a one-year period, beginning June 18, 1984, with potential for an extension by NASA's National Space Technology Laboratories, under Title IV of the Intergovernmental Personnel Act of 1970.[22]

The Office of Administrative Services' initial staff came from the following sponsoring agencies: the Division of Medicaid, MEMA, the Fiscal Management Office, and the Governor's Office of General Services. The Division of Medicaid provided four employees, MEMA provided two, the Fiscal Management Office provided one, and the Office of General Services provided three. NASA agreed to pay Ed Ling's salary of $67,950, so there was no initial cost to the state. Excluding the position for the director, because it was paid for by the federal government, the final number of positions approved by the State Personnel Board (SPB) on September 13, 1984 was twelve, for a total cost of $213,848.64.

Ling experienced some difficulties early on with the new agency but remained optimistic that things would get better. Chief among these difficulties, which Ling confessed to Allain in a letter approximately a year after Executive Order No. 526 was signed, was the development of a team of disciplined professionals devoted to providing quality services in a timely manner, and the presence of institutional bias that sometime impeded progress. Ling reported that "[t]he year has been one of twists and turns—a rather bumpy course, in addition, if not downright rocky. It has not been without its satisfaction and success, though."[23] As pessimistic as Ling's letter sounded concerning the difficulties, his overall outlook was very positive on the agency's progress. Ling concluded the letter explaining that "[t]he future is bright. This Office has made its way past the initial shoals and is approaching deeper, smoother water ahead."[24]

Critical Legislative Report

Things took a turn for the worse for the Office of Administrative Services when a critical staff report was released by the Joint Legislative Committee on Performance Evaluation and Expenditure Review (PEER). The JLBC, not surprisingly, had requested that PEER conduct a review of the Office of Administrative Services to assess the degree of duplication with client agencies and determine the necessity for continued funding. Rep. Hillman Frazier,

PEER Committee chairman, authorized the PEER staff to conduct the review. The PEER staff report concluded that the office had not provided satisfactory centralized fiscal management and personnel services; additionally, the report went on to explain how the desired economic and managerial benefits were not produced either. Ling was not at all happy with the PEER staff report and assured Governor Allain that the report "does not accurately reflect the performance and activities of this Office—or of the undersigned."[25]

Controversial Highway Department and Funding for It

Governor Allain and the legislature started out on positive terms when it came to funding for the Mississippi Highway Department in his first year as governor. Allain was successful in getting funds transferred from the highway department to the Bureau of Building, Grounds and Real Property Management and to the general fund in his first two years as governor, although he had to work much harder to accomplish his goals in the second year. The disagreement between the legislature and the governor's office eventually led to Allain vetoing the FY 1987 appropriation bill for the highway department on April 9, 1986, and having to call a special session to fund the agency.

Allain's FY 1986 budget proposal for the Mississippi Highway Department was very favorable to the agency, and Allain actually recommended more funding for the agency than it had requested. The highway department requested $204,441,882 in federal funds and $202,303,199 in special funds, for a total request of $406,745,081; the agency did not request any general funds. Allain recommended for the agency $240,070,140 in federal funds, $213,118,011 in special funds, and $20,000,000 in general funds—a total funding recommendation of $473,188,151, which was 16 percent higher than requested. In addition to the general fund recommendation, Allain also expected for the agency to have access to $10,000,000 in interest earnings, which was not reflected in his EBR, for a total of $30,000,000 needed to match federal funds to initiate new construction projects in FY 1986.[26] The legislature ended up appropriating $468,002,977 to the highway department, which was not far from Allain's recommendation. The legislature did not authorize the expenditure of the $10,000,000 in interest earning during FY 1986 as requested by Allain. However, during the 1986 session, the legislature directed the agency to transfer $10,000,000 in special funds to the Bureau of Building, Grounds and Real Property Management for FY 1987. So the governor and legislature appeared to be somewhat on the same page in FY 1986 when it came to highway funding.

Funding for the highway department the next year took a turn for the worse between Allain and the legislature. In Allain's FY 1987 EBR, he proposed transferring $380,153,403 of special funds to the general fund, of which $229,271,701 would come from the highway department. Instead of funding the highway department with federal and special funds as in the past, Allain proposed funding the agency with more general funds than special funds. He recommended the following funding for the highway department: $167,815,561 in general funds; $245,199,814 in federal funds, and $41,038,599 in special funds—a total funding recommendation of $454,053,974, which was $13,949,003 below the FY 1986 level. The legislature did not take Allain's advice to transfer the special funds into the general fund, and they also funded the highway department using the same funding sources as in previous years.

Allain was not at all pleased with the legislature for disregarding his recommendations pertaining to the highway department, so he decided to veto H.B. 1367, the agency's appropriation bill, which appropriated $436,453,974 to the department. Although the amount appropriated by the legislature was less than what was recommended in the EBR, Allain was actually unhappy that the agency was cut by a smaller percentage than other agencies. He explained in his veto message that:

> the Highway Department, with its $436 million budget, has been cut less than 4 percent, and has, in fact, been allowed to increase its salary category. The Highway Department, apparently, will not have to face the massive layoffs that other State agencies will face. In addition, while these other State services sustained budget reductions during fiscal year 1986, when we had to cut the budget by $72 million, the Highway Department lost only about $632 thousand.[27]

Allain understood that a developed transportation system was a great need for Mississippi; however, he did not think that transportation was more important than "needs for higher education, economic development, health care, law enforcement or mental health." Those services had been cut by 12 to 15 percent compared to the highway department's less than 5 percent cut. Additionally, Allain argued that any savings cut from the highway department's budget "could materially assist the delivery of other essential services of State government."[28]

Allain was forced to call a special legislative session after he vetoed the appropriation bill for the highway department. During the First Extraordinary Session of 1986, the legislature passed S.B. 2001, which funded the highway department at $424,453,974, some $12,000,000 less than the amount appropriated in the vetoed bill.[29] Allain wanted the unallocated $12 million to go into the general fund for FY 1987,[30] but the legislature instead transferred the funds to the general fund for FY 1988. Allain did not get all of the money he wanted for the programs that would have been funded from reducing the highway department budget. But getting the legislature to redirect earmarked highway funds to the general fund to help assist during the sluggish economy showed the legislature that he would not sit by idly and allow them to exclude him completely from budget decisions.

Strictly Executive Budget Functions

In addition to having the sole authority to veto legislation and call special legislative sessions, both of which Governor Allain exercised when dealing with the budget of the highway department, Mississippi's chief executive also has the ability to direct the state fiscal officer to reduce allocations of general funds and certain special funds to state agencies' operating budgets if revenue collections are underperforming.[31] The executive branch is statutorily required to keep revenue in line with expenditures. In order to do that, the governor can direct the state fiscal officer to make agency operating budget cuts in varying amounts, but no budget reductions for individual agencies may exceed 5 percent over the course of the fiscal year without all agency budgets being cut by at least 5 percent. Furthermore, the governor can exempt individual agencies from budget cuts as long as the reductions to any other agencies do not exceed 5 percent. For example, if the State Board of Health is cut by 5 percent in the first round of budget reductions and the Division of Medicaid is exempted, the State Board of Health cannot be cut any more until the Division of Medicaid and all other agencies have been cut by 5 percent. After the budgets for all agencies have been cut by 5 percent, then any additional budget reductions must be by a uniform percentage and across the board to all agencies.

Tough economic times forced Allain to order budget cuts totaling $47 million in November 1985. Most agencies were cut by 4.32 percent in the first round of budget reductions. A second round of budget reductions was made in January 1986 that took the agency cuts up to the 5 percent cap; however, Allain decided to exempt several programs in elementary and secondary public education. If a third round of budget reductions had taken place during the fiscal year, state law would have required the inclusion of elementary and secondary education in those cuts. Adjusting agency expenditures downward when revenue collections fail to equal the projection is considered a budget control measure and, as such, is strictly an executive function. Under the supreme court's decision in the *Alexander* case, the legislature is totally excluded from budget control.

Chapter 4

Temporarily Enhanced Executive Influence over Budget Decisions under Mabus

Ray Mabus served as state auditor from 1984 to 1988 prior to serving as governor and was quite familiar with Mississippi's budget-making process, but his budget knowledge did not come from being state auditor. The Office of the State Auditor did not and still does not have a direct involvement in the budget-making process, but it does have an indirect involvement similar to other agencies. The indirect involvement comes when the state auditor, like all agency heads, submits a budget request to the legislature for an appropriation. The state auditor was not and still is not a member of the unofficial revenue estimating committee. However, Mabus found a way to insert himself into fiscal affairs while serving as state auditor. On July 1, 1985, the auditor's office under Mabus adapted the state's accounting system to allow for financial reporting based on generally accepted accounting principles (GAAP). Furthermore, his office published a single audited comprehensive annual financial report (CAFR) for the state for FY 1986, which was the first of its kind in Mississippi. This single financial report replaced separate reports that were usually issued for each of the 133 state agencies at that time.

Mabus explained that there were numerous benefits to a single report: "Legislators, other public officials, and private citizens will have timely access to key financial data about Mississippi in one document; the major requirements of bond rating companies and investors will be satisfied; and accounting for and reporting of state funds will be greatly improved," he explained.[1] Mabus's idea to produce a single CAFR was so well received that the legislature passed a law requiring a single financial report, instead of the separate agency reports produced in the past. However, the legislature took the responsibility of publishing the state CAFR away from the Office of the State Auditor and gave it to the Fiscal Management Board (FMB). State Fiscal Officer Thomas Campbell explained in the FY 1987 CAFR, "This is the second CAFR produced by the State and represents our continued commitment to financial reporting excellence."[2]

Although Mabus was essentially uninvolved in the budget-making process in his role as state auditor, he was far from a novice in that area. Mabus was very instrumental, while serving as legislative liaison during the William Winter Administration, in getting the Mississippi Education Reform Act of 1982 passed and funded. Education reform was very expensive and required a new funding formula. Early in the battle for education reform, Mabus predicted a financial challenge. "Anytime you change the way you're going to distribute money you're going to get a fight," he explained.[3] Mabus would continue believing that education needed additional funding after being elected governor years later.

Governor Mabus, similar to his predecessor Allain, was successful in the early stages of his administration and was initially influential in the budget process. Mabus's positive relationship and cooperation with the legislature led to early funding for his fiscal agenda items. When asked about the legislature's working relationship with the new governor, Lt. Gov. Brad Dye stated, "I have found him exceedingly easy to work with. He seems to have a real grasp of the needs of the state."[4] Speaker of the House Tim Ford echoed similar comments made by the lieutenant governor. "We didn't always agree on how we wanted to get something done, but I think we addressed his programs," explained Ford. The legislative leadership was aware of the newly elected governor's popularity with the public and was quite accommodating to his fiscal agenda at first.[5] However, toward the end of Mabus's four-year term, his administration appeared to lose momentum regarding the budget, especially when revenue started to decline.

Mabus came to office with the intentions of drastically changing government, especially in the area of education. His agenda included raising elementary and secondary teachers' salaries and reorganizing the executive branch of Mississippi's state government. Additionally, Mabus proposed the issuance of bonds to fund a capital improvement plan, which was not guaranteed when dealing with legislative leadership that was accustomed to taking a more conservative approach and paying cash for long-term state capital needs.

Mabus was aware of the fact that his fiscal agenda could not be accomplished without additional revenue, but he opposed increasing either of the two largest state revenue generators, which were (and are to this day) sales and individual income taxes. A participant in the budget process explained that

"Mabus was always looking for schemes to generate new money without a general tax increase."[6] Mabus was open to increasing minor sources of revenue, and he also proposed several failed revenue-raising ideas, including a lottery to support educational spending. But the legislature did not adopt his revenue ideas. Toward the end of his administration, Mabus had lost nearly all of the momentum gained in his first two years. Revenue-generating schemes and the governor's refusal to raise taxes were hardly the only reasons for Mabus's lack of success in the final two years of his term. The case can be made that the primary cause of the governor's failure to further advance his fiscal agenda was the absence of natural revenue growth in the economy.

Mabus' Fiscal Accomplishments

Governor Mabus achieved multiple goals on his fiscal agenda at the beginning of his administration. The first accomplishment occurred when the governor vetoed S.B. 2214, which would have weakened executive discretion over budget cuts by mandating that the FMB, chaired by the governor, uniformly reduce budgets when revenue did not meet expectations. The second accomplishment was when Mabus was successful in getting the legislature to increase elementary and secondary teachers' salaries after an updated general fund revenue estimate at the beginning of the 1988 legislative session suggested that additional revenue was available. The third accomplishment occurred when Mabus succeeded in getting the legislature to support a couple of his reorganization ideas that were recommended by the Executive Branch Reorganization Study Commission, such as establishing the Department of Finance and Administration (DFA) and abolishing the state charity hospitals along with the Eleemosynary Board. The reorganization committee claimed that nearly $6.4 million would be saved by abolishing the state charity hospitals and the Eleemosynary Board, and Mabus proposed and succeeded in getting those funds diverted into the state Medicaid program. The final accomplishment was getting the legislature to issue general obligation bonds to fund capital improvement projects, which freed up general funds to be spent on other government services. The governor's bond package died during the 1989 regular legislative session because the house and senate members could not reconcile their differences, which forced Mabus to promptly call a special session to address the issue. H.B. 3 was eventually passed during the special session with bonding authority for $78.1 million for capital improvement projects during FY 1990. S.B. 3192 was passed during the next regular legislative session, providing a total of $69.5 million in general obligation bonding authority.

Legislature's Crafty Attempt to Weaken Executive Budget Authority

Governor Mabus was fortunate to have entered the governor's office with a good understanding of the budget-making process. The knowledge that he gained while working on Governor Winter's staff truly paid off and proved to be quite valuable. Part of the reason for the early success of the Mabus Administration was the governor's willingness to work with the legislature. Senate Appropriations Committee chairman Jack Gordon explained at the conclusion of the 1989 legislative session that the governor's relationship with the legislature was good. "[Mabus] practiced a lot of restraint, and I think that's part of his success," Gordon said. "He's been able to be very compromising on some things."[7] One thing that Mabus was unwilling to compromise on was S.B. 2214, which would have practically removed all flexibility of the FMB in making budget reductions if signed into law.

The legislative branch dominated the budgeting process for most of Mississippi's history and had all intentions of keeping it that way. The executive branch gained a little power in the budget-making process in the mid-1980s because of judicial intervention, not by legislative choice. The Mississippi Administrative Reorganization Act of 1984 abolished the legislatively dominated Commission of Budget and Accounting and created in its place the FMB and the Joint Legislative Budget Committee (JLBC).[8] It would be difficult to dispute that the legislation favored the JLBC over the FMB. The legislature intentionally preserved as much power over the budget process as legally allowed. However, one clear advantage given to the executive branch was the ability to cut budgets when revenue did not meet expectations. This power had to be given to the executive branch because the legislature no longer could legally exercise budget control functions. S.B. 2214 was originally introduced to make several technical changes to statutes under the jurisdiction of the FMB, but during the legislative process, amendments were added to the bill that drastically changed its purpose. Legislators downplayed the significance of the bill, claiming that it simply leveled the playing field for agencies when cuts had to be made. S.B. 2214 passed the senate and was amended in the house and then was sent to a conference committee to work out the differences.

Four of the six conferees for S.B. 2214 were members of the JLBC. Sen. Jack Gordon was one of those conferees, and he was fully aware of what the bill would do if passed. The conference committee report was adopted by both houses, and the final bill was sent to the governor for his signature. Mabus vetoed the bill, showing the legislature that he would not allow it to impede executive powers without a fight. As passed, S.B. 2214 would have forced the FMB to impose reductions uniformly on all agencies, which would have basically required across-the-board cuts. Mabus explained in his veto message:

This change runs counter to my entire philosophy about state budgeting: priority programs should be established and adequately funded. Requiring uniform percentage budget reductions on all agencies prevents any attempt to set priorities. In addition, it ignores the ability of agencies to withstand budget cuts. It may be easier for some agencies to take a greater percentage budget cut than others. . . . The changes in Senate Bill No. 2214 preclude any of this flexibility and priority budgeting. Across the board cuts do not promote quality in state programs and removes the ability of the [FMB] to make cuts where they can be absorbed in the most fair and equitable manner.[9]

Legislators were aware of the governor's popularity, so they decided that overriding the governor's veto was a matter not worth fighting for. Although Mabus was not intentionally trying to upset the legislature by vetoing that bill, it would have been hard for him to explain to the general public that the teacher pay raises that he campaigned for could be taken away if revenue did not meet expectations. In addition to vetoing S.B. 2214, Mabus also vetoed a large salary increase for county supervisors. A pay increase for supervisors would not have been included in the governor's budget recommendation, because county supervisors are paid with local funds and not state funds. Having the veto stand came as a surprise to some legislators, because vetoing the legislation would not have resulted in a savings to the state budget. When asked by the press about the governor's veto of the proposed salary increase for county supervisors, Gordon stated, "Years ago, I think it would have been overridden."[10]

Veto power for a governor is an important tool, and it is always considered a victory when vetoes are not overridden. Some vetoes are symbolic and insignificant, while others are substantial and have a huge effect on government. Mabus's veto to preserve executive budget authority, associated with budget control, was arguably the most significant achievement for the executive branch in the budget-making process since the creation of the FMB in 1984.

Funding for Education

As a candidate for governor in 1987, Ray Mabus promised that he would raise elementary and secondary teachers' salaries to the average of the salaries in the southeastern states. More specifically, he promised to raise teachers' salaries by about $3,700 per teacher on the first day of the 1988 legislative session. In the second month of the 1988 legislative session, Governor Mabus released his official education plan, titled "An Investment in Mississippi's Future: Priority Funding for Education," and explained that the result of the election "signified a reaffirmation of the intense support of the citizens of Mississippi for substantial reform and improvements in the educational system of Mississippi."[11] Aware that the promise he made during his campaign to get a teacher pay raise on the first day of the session did not occur, Mabus altered his plan slightly once he realized that more time was needed. A primary component of his official education plan for the future of Mississippi was to "raise teacher salaries to the 'Southeastern' average in the first year."[12] The target average pay raise in the plan called for an increase of $3,712. That figure was compiled using 1987–1988 data from the State Department of Education, which used the amount of the present differential between the Southeastern average and the Mississippi average. Twelve southeastern states[13] were compared, with Virginia paying the most at $28,020 and Mississippi paying the least at $20,750. Calculating the teachers' salaries in all twelve states, the average salary came out to be $24,462. Mabus's education plan also called for funding increases for universities and the community and junior college system, but this was not the primary focus of his education plan.

The teacher pay raise bill (H.B. 601) that was eventually passed by the legislature and signed by Mabus[14] was approximately $3,802 per teacher, on average, which was higher than the amount specified in Mabus's plan. The pay raises were to be funded over two years and were originally estimated to have a cost of $65.5 million in FY 1989 and $117 million in FY 1990.[15] However, the legislature ended up funding a bulk of the pay raises in the first year instead of the second. H.B. 601 also created the Education Reserve Fund[16] to provide additional education funding for the Minimum Education Program, institutions of higher learning (IHL), and the State Board of Community and Junior Colleges. The Mabus Administration received the most praise for getting pay raises for teachers, and his first legislative session was viewed by many to be one of the most successful sessions of any governor in modern times.

A large number of legislators thought that Governor Mabus was off to a great start, but that sentiment was not shared by all. One lawmaker suggested that the initial success of Mabus's first legislative session could only be considered relative. When asked about the accomplishment of Mabus's first legislative session, Sen. Hob Bryan asked, "Do you say he's successful for passing an extremely good pay raise? Or do you say he's a failure because it's not the southeastern average on the first day? I think that's analogous to many other situations."[17] Although candidate Mabus was too optimistic when configuring a timeline for accomplishing the pay raises, the increases passed by the legislature ended up being the highlight of the 1988 legislative session. Another reason that the teacher pay raise was so significant is that Mabus did not recommend the increase in an executive budget recommendation (EBR), because he was not yet elected governor—instead, he made the proposal on the campaign trail directly to the citizens of Mississippi.

Mabus's first EBR was submitted for FY 1990, and the total funding level proposed was significantly higher than in the previous fiscal year. Mabus recommended a total of $1,907,270,448 in general funds for FY 1990, which represented a net increase of $101,443,955, or 5.6%, over FY 1989. The bulk of the recommended increase was for public education's Minimum Education Program. The governor's budget proposal recommended a total of $790,326,125 for the Minimum Education Program, which was $48,662,699 over the FY 1989 level.[18] Teachers' salaries were funded through the Minimum Education Program at that time. Of the increased amount recommended, $42,899,743 in general funds was to annualize the teacher pay raises awarded in FY 1989.

The full legislature did not need much convincing from the governor's office to provide funding to annualize the teacher pay raise awarded in FY 1989 during the 1989 legislative session, because the JLBC had proposed additional funding for the pay increase in its fall budget proposal. The JLBC's FY 1990 budget recommendation for the Minimum Education Program was not far off from the governor's recommendation. The FY 1990 budget proposal adopted by the JLBC for the Minimum Education Program was $786,801,558, a difference of less than half of 1 percent compared to the Mabus proposal. The legislature recommended an increase to the program of $47.5 million for salary increases and increments.[19] Although Governor Mabus received a majority of the credit for the teacher pay raise, many legislators were quick to point out that it was a collaborative effort by the governor's office and the legislature.

Mabus was successful in his first two years at getting additional education funding for his fiscal agenda items, but he did not have much success in his last two years. In his FY 1991 budget proposal, Mabus recommended that the first statewide lottery be dedicated constitutionally to Mississippi's B.E.S.T. (Better Education for Success Tomorrow) program. He anticipated that the net proceeds from the first statewide lottery would be around $55 million in the first year, which was included in his budget proposal.[20] Mabus was aware that Mississippi's 1890 Constitution prohibited gambling, but he thought that the legislature should allow voters to decide whether they wanted a statewide lottery to fund B.E.S.T. In order to get that issue on the ballot, two-thirds support in both the house and senate was needed. However, the lottery would cover only a portion of the cost needed to fully fund B.E.S.T., because the total cost of the governor's plan was $500 million over three years. The lottery was supposed to raise about $180 million during that same period, and the rest of the funds needed were supposed to come from growth in the state's economy. In 1989 Mabus estimated the economy to grow at 5.5 percent in each of the next three years.[21]

Legislative leaders were not comfortable with Mabus's plan to finance the $500 million B.E.ST program. However, legislators appeared to want him to succeed overall. House Speaker Tim Ford said that he was "exploring the option of adding a 6 percent bracket to the state's personal and corporate income tax to raise $55 million for education reform," but Mabus refused the idea of raising taxes. In response to the idea of raising taxes, Mabus stated, "I don't think we need a tax increase. I don't think it's a good idea and I'm the one on the spot."[22]

Legislators urged the governor to come up with an alternative funding plan during a meeting of a House Select Committee charged with studying education reform, but Mabus refused to do so. "I don't have a Plan B. What I do have is a conviction that we've got to help the children. I think what we've come up with is a reasonable financing plan and I want to see that through," explained Mabus.[23] Former House Education Committee chairman, and long-time education advocate, Rep. Robert Clark believed that education was too important for Mabus to not have a contingency plan in place, and he also believed that the governor's plan was in trouble. "It looks like our method of funding this all-important package is on very shaky ground . . . and it looks like [the governor] or the Legislature ought to start looking for Plan B," said Clark.[24] Mabus continued to object to numerous requests by legislators to come up with alternatives to a lottery to fund the program.

There is sufficient evidence to show that the legislature wanted the B.E.S.T. program to succeed. During the 1990 regular legislative session, the house passed H.B. 1523, and the senate passed S.B. 2507, which enacted Mississippi's B.E.S.T. program into law.[25] However, both bills had the following language at the end of the bill:

This act shall take effect and be in force from and after July 1, 1990, provided that the Legislature by concurrent resolution adopted by the House and Senate in session prior to July 1, 1990, declares that sufficient funds are dedicated and made available for the implementation of this act.[26]

Enjoying a small victory after both bills passed, Mabus was forced to call a special legislative session to get funding for his B.E.S.T. program. Mabus called the legislature back into session on June 18, 1990, and many items were placed on the calendar, but those receiving the most attention pertained to a lottery and B.E.S.T. Although legislation was passed to provide for extensive regulation, licensing, and taxation of legalized gambling that had been authorized during the 1990 regular legislative session,[27] the legislature did not pass a lottery or put any other funding mechanism in place to fund B.E.S.T. Not only were legislators pessimistic about the amount of revenue that Mabus claimed a lottery could generate, they were equally pessimistic about economic growth needed to fund B.E.S.T. over time. So, even though the B.E.S.T. program had been enacted into law, it never took effect or was implemented, because the condition at the end of each bill was not met.

Instead of the economy growing by 5.5 percent in 1990 through 1992, such as Mabus predicted, revenue collections actually took a turn for the worse and fell short of expectations. The State of Mississippi had revenue shortfalls for FY 1990, FY 1991, and FY 1992, and budget cuts were needed to cover the shortfalls for the latter two fiscal years.[28] It was much easier for the legislature to support Mabus's fiscal agenda when the economy was strong, but it proved to be quite challenging to obtain legislative support when the economy was not performing well, because his fiscal agenda items required revenue that was not available.

The economy never rebounded during the Mabus Administration, but that did not stop him from continuing, with no success, to request funding for B.E.S.T. in his last two EBRs. The FY 1992 EBR proposed by Mabus was by far the most unrealistic. The jointly adopted general fund revenue estimate by Mabus and the JLBC totaled $1,987,697,000; however, Mabus's budget included additional revenue totaling $149,240,656. The governor's budget proposal included a revenue statement showing how the additional revenue would be generated, and the largest revenue generator shown was an estimated $65 million from video card machines. At this point, many members of the legislature had already stopped taking Mabus's revenue-generating ideas seriously. The inevitable outcome was that the legislature never appropriated funds or passed a lottery or other revenue generating mechanism to fund B.E.S.T.

Reorganization Commission

The 1980s turned out to be the decade of reorganization for Mississippi government. The Mississippi Administrative Reorganization Act of 1984 was the most comprehensive government reform act in modern times in Mississippi, and it changed the organizational structure of the state's government significantly. However, that reform act was not the choice of the legislature but was forced on the legislature by judicial action. Newly elected Governor Mabus began the discussion of additional government reform soon after taking office. The government reform proposed to the legislature by Mabus was different from the reform a few years earlier, because it was optional and not mandated by a court order.

In response to Mabus's desire to reform government, the legislature passed S.B. 2260 during the 1988 legislative session, which authorized the governor to appoint a twenty-five-member Executive Branch Reorganization Study Commission.[29] The commission was directed by the legislation to "conduct a comprehensive study of the organizational structure of the executive branch of state government" and "issue a report making specific recommendations to the legislature for the reorganization of the executive branch of government." The bill became effective on March 11, 1988, and it required the commission to present a final report and recommendation to the governor and legislature by October 1, 1988. The final report was to be accompanied by proposed legislation that included the commission's recommendations.

Government Reform

Mabus wanted to streamline state government by reducing the 135 or more state agencies, boards, and commissions to no more than 15. After carefully examining the recommendations made by the study commission, Mabus proposed a new reorganization plan in October 1988 to consolidate the executive branch of state government by cutting down the number of boards, commissions, and agencies and consolidating them into eleven executive departments. The governor's proposal to restructure the executive branch of state government would have altered and/or created the following major departments: Department of Finance and Administration, Department of Revenue, Department of Economic and Community Development, Department of Public Safety, Department of Human Services, Department of Health, Department of Mental Health, Department of Corrections, Department of Cultural Affairs, Department of Wildlife Conservation, Forestry and Parks, and Department of Environmental Quality. Mabus estimated that the reorganization would have an estimated savings of $31.9 million.

The gist of the Mabus reorganization plan, based in part on the commission's study, was to reduce the size of the executive branch of government, which he though would "dramatically improve the delivery of services and save the state money by cutting down on waste and duplication." He believed that the plan would make government more accountable and responsive to the citizens of Mississippi, because the elected governor would be appointing the executive department heads instead of the numerous unelected boards and commissions. "If agencies don't perform, you'll know who to blame. At present, that is too often not the case," Mabus explained.[30]

Mabus decided not to call a special session to deal with reorganization in October, because legislators and committee leaders indicated to him that they would consider the reorganization bill very early in the regular 1989 legislative session. Mabus took the leadership at their word and patiently waited for the next legislative session to deal with reorganization; he believed that the reorganization discussion was only the beginning. Mabus explained that his reorganization plan was "a first step, not the last" and would save the state lots of money. Mabus cited two examples of how his plan would allow the state to do more with less. First he explained that the Department of Economic Development would expand services at $300,000 below the $8.9 million agency budget for FY 1989 with fifteen fewer people. Second he said that his plan would save around $7 million by closing the state charity hospitals and the Eleemosynary Board, and the funds would be put in Medicaid's budget. The Mabus Administration explained that the additional funds spent on Medicaid would generate an additional $28 million in federal funds to care for Mississippians. "Our resources are too precious, and our needs too great for us not to reorganize the executive branch," explained Mabus.[31]

Mabus was not successful in getting the legislature to buy into his executive reorganization plan in its entirety, which he claimed would make government more efficient while simultaneously saving the state lots of money. Mabus was critical of the decision to not fully implement his reorganization plan, believing that neither the senate's nor the house of representatives' plan went far enough, but he believed that the effort made by the latter was far superior to the former. On January 24, 1989, Mabus praised the house on its vote that night for smaller, more effective state government, explaining that "I applaud the House. Even though the bill doesn't go as far as Mississippi needs, it is a good start, and it clearly is better than the Senate version."[32] The legislature ultimately passed H.B. 659, which slightly reorganized government, and Mabus signed the bill into law.[33]

Although the act to restructure the executive branch of state government that the legislature passed fell far short of Mabus's expectations, the governor still felt the need to take credit for the good that came out of the watered-down bill. Mabus later pointed out that a PEER report recognized that "reorganization is clearly working" and that "an annual recurring savings of at least $928,744" was one of the outcomes of government reorganization.[34] The reorganization bill altered the makeup of a few agencies while also creating some of the new agencies recommended by Mabus; however, the legislature elected to keep a great majority of the boards and commissions exactly the way they were, and the number of agencies, boards, and commissions of the state still exceeded one hundred.

Fiscal Management Board Abolished and Department of Finance and Administration Created

One of the major accomplishments of H.B. 659 was the creation of the DFA. The act transferred to the DFA the powers and duties previously held by the FMB, including the responsibility of submitting the governor's EBR as well as all budget control measures. Prior to the passage of H.B. 659, the governor essentially controlled the FMB because he statutorily chaired the three-member board, and his vote was required along with one other member's in order for a measure to pass. Furthermore, the other two FMB members were appointed by the governor. The governor's influence was not diminished at all with the creation of the DFA, because the executive director of the new agency served at the pleasure of the governor.

When Mabus first started the discussion about executive reorganization, it was no secret that the legislature was reluctant to make all of the changes that would be recommended by him. Moreover, some legislators were quite direct in letting the public know that Mabus's reorganization plan, as proposed, would more than likely never come to fruition. When asked about the chances of Mabus's executive reorganization proposal passing intact, Lt. Gov. Brad Dye replied, "I don't think that will happen." House Speaker Tim Ford had similar sentiments concerning reorganization, stating, "I do not anticipate a massive reorganization, but I feel there will be some reorganization depending on the effectiveness of the individual state agencies." However, one particular agency that legislators felt would come into fruition from the beginning was the DFA. House Appropriations Committee chairman Charlie Capps explained, while being questioned about reorganization, that the legislature would "likely pass legislation to coordinate the collection, expenditure and oversight of state money, now handled piecemeal by several agencies, into a new Department of Finance."[35] The legislature was aware that the powers being given to the newly created DFA already lay in the purview of the executive branch, and the legislative branch would not be giving up any legislative authority. Mabus was unsuccessful in getting a majority of his executive reorganization ideas in the final bill, but the legislature pretty much created the DFA like the governor wanted.

H.B. 659 organized the DFA into the following divisions: (a) Division of Budget and Policy Development; (b) Division of General Services; (c) Division of Financial Management; and (d) Division of Support Services. The responsibilities given to the DFA were numerous and went well beyond budget and finance. It was given the responsibility for administering programs related to general services, public procurement, insurance, bond advisory duties, federal-state programs, and the state's aircraft operation. Although all of these were important, the primary responsibility was fiscal matters, because the act mandated that the executive director would also be the state fiscal officer.

The new act officially made the DFA the executive agency responsible for the budget preparation and proposal phase (that is, the EBR) and budget control. DFA responsibilities specifically listed in H.B. 659 that were directly or indirectly related to the budget-making process included the following duties and powers:

to provide administrative guidance to the various departments and agencies of state government; to facilitate the expedient delivery of services and programs for the benefit of the citizens of the state; to analyze and develop efficient management practices and assist departments and agencies in implementing effective and efficient work management systems; to conduct management review of state agencies and departments and recommend a management plan to state departments and agencies when corrective action is required; to allocate the federal-state program funds to the departments responsible for the delivery of the programs and services for which the appropriation was made; to collect and maintain the necessary data on which to base budget and policy development issues; to develop and analyze (fiscal) policy recommendations to the governor; to develop and manage the executive budget process; to prepare the executive branch budget recommendations; to review and monitor the expenditures of the executive agencies and departments of government; and to manage the state's fiscal affairs.

Successfully getting the DFA created was a huge accomplishment for Mabus. The DFA was created to help manage and support the basic functions of state government, along with managing the state's fiscal affairs. Its broad scope loosely resembled a combination of the General Services Administration (GSA) and the Office of Management and Budget (OMB) on the federal level. A majority of the responsibilities given to the DFA with the passage of H.B. 659 in 1989 still remain with it today. After it proved that centralized administration was a benefit to the State of Mississippi, the legislature, often without executive requests, further enhanced the agency's duties and powers throughout the years.

Bond Funding for Capital Improvement Projects

None of the phases in Mississippi's budget-making process include bonding. Neither the executive nor the legislative budget proposals typically recommend the issuance of bonds in their respective budget documents. Additionally, bonds do not go through the Appropriations Committees in either house. The legislature authorizes bonding primarily through the Finance Committee in the senate and Ways and Means Committee in the house. The topic of bonding was significant in budget making during the Mabus Administration, because he claimed that general funds could be saved by financing capital improvements, rather than appropriating funds for the improvements.

Mabus recommended a Comprehensive Five-Year Capital Improvement Plan in his FY 1990 EBR, which was the first proposal of its kind. The plan was for FY 1991 through FY 1994. Mabus was aware of the legislature's reluctance to finance capital projects because of the added debt service payments that would follow as a result of issuing the bonds, but he felt that the state's infrastructure needs were approaching critical levels and needed to be addressed. In a letter to the legislature, Mabus stated:

> Many of you are rightfully concerned about the issuance of additional State general obligation debt. The federal experience with deficit financing has proven that fiscal conservatism and control of the issuance of debt must be maintained to ensure the financial integrity of future generations of Mississippians. On the other hand, the failure to responsibly address the state's capital needs can also haunt future generations as state mental institutions, university buildings, junior colleges, parks and office facilities crumble and decay. In many instances, renovation needs have reached the critical stage. We must maintain our infrastructure. The long-term cost of crumbling facilities and constant repair will far exceed the cost of today's renovations and replacement.[36]

Mabus's FY 1990 budget proposal showed in great detail that his capital improvement plan would indeed require more general obligation debt being issued, but he insisted that "much of the cost of that debt service would be recovered" through various measures, such as decreased rents, more federal funds generated as a result of the capital improvements, and increased self-generated special funds, such as state parks admission fees. "In fact, many of the projects are self-funding," Mabus said.[37] Mabus went on to explain that the state could construct new buildings or acquire privately owned buildings that are currently being leased by agencies and use the funds that would have gone toward lease payment to pay off the debt.

The legislature was receptive to the capital improvements bond idea proposed by Mabus, and both the house and senate attempted to pass bond bills out of their respective chambers during the 1989 regular legislative session. Unfortunately, legislators could not reconcile the differences between the senate and house versions, which eventually caused the bills to die. After the legislature failed to pass a bond bill, Mabus called a special legislative session that resulted in the legislature passing a compromise bond bill.[38] The legislature passed H.B. 3 during the 1989 special legislative session, which provided Mississippi with a capital improvement program and the bonding authority for the following projects: $73.1 million for specifically approved projects; $2 million for discretionary roofing and waterproofing projects; and $3 million for discretionary asbestos-abatement projects.[39]

The total bonding authority provided from the passage of H.B. 3 was $78.1 million, and the projected twenty-year debt service on the total authority was projected to be approximately $148 million. Mabus claimed that the projected accumulated savings—from diverting rent to debt service, anticipated federal funding as a result of capital improvements, and savings on operating costs—would total just over $86 million, for a projected net cost to the State of Mississippi of $62 million on a $78 million capital investment.[40] Although the anticipated savings to the general fund was speculative, proponents of Mabus considered the compromise bond bill passed during the 1989 special session to be a huge success and truly believed that it would save the state money.

Mabus was also successful in securing bonding authority during the 1990 regular legislative session, when the legislature passed S.B. 3192, which provided for a total general obligation bonding authority of $69,485,000.[41] Among the other projects that were funded, S.B. 3192 provided bond funds for what the Mabus Administration referred to as the 1991 Governor's Capital Improvement Program (CIP). Mabus explained that the key to the CIP was what was called the "flow-of-funds." The projected gross debt service on the total bonding authority in the bill was anticipated to be $132,369,949. Mabus claimed that an aggregate estimated general fund savings of $100,739,184 would be realized, for a net estimated impact on the general fund of $31,630,765. "This scenario indicates a net impact to the General Fund over the life of the debt of about $29.4 million. Of course, once the bonds are paid, these savings will continue to benefit the General Fund year after year. I project this scenario will 'pay back' the General Fund in less than 26 years," explained Mabus.[42]

As with the fate of his fiscal agenda pertaining to education spending, Mabus also lost momentum in his influence over bonding in the latter part of his administration. Mabus's comprehensive five-year plan for the CIP proposed in his FY 1990 budget was well received and got a positive reception from the legislature. Additionally, Mabus also fared well in getting more bonds issued for FY 1991. But as the economy started to decline, the legislature's appetite for issuing bonds began to weaken. Realizing that revenue was scarce, Mabus shifted his focus to his number one priority, which was getting more education funding. Mabus became so focused on getting funding for B.E.S.T. that he seemed to forget about his plan for the CIP altogether. The stressed economy, coupled with the governor's new priority of funding B.E.S.T., overshadowed the governor's plan for the CIP, to the point that his FY 1992 EBR did not even mention the CIP.

Poor Economic Conditions and Government Operations

During the latter part of the Mabus Administration, the economy took a turn for the worse, and the only way to pay for Mabus's B.E.S.T. program was for the state to generate more revenue. Mabus's proposed lottery never came into fruition, but that did not stop him from continuing to propose the adoption of one. Although he was convinced that a lottery would generate a significant amount of revenue, it was never intended to be the primary mechanism for financing B.E.S.T. While addressing the House Select Committee charged with studying education reform in 1989, Mabus estimated that natural growth in the state's economy would finance approximately two-thirds of the cost of B.E.S.T. However, the committee heard reports from staff represented by the Legislative Budget Office (LBO) and the Joint Legislative Committee on Performance Evaluation and Expenditure Review (PEER) that challenged the validity of Mabus's revenue projections. Both agencies believed that the governor's revenue projections were too optimistic.[43]

Mabus attempted to discredit the LBO and PEER staffers' opinions regarding revenue projections by stating that they were "[t]he same folks [that] told us we'd be $100 million in the hole" after teachers' salaries were raised to the southeastern average.[44] The LBO and PEER ended up being right about revenue and Mabus wrong. The US officially went into recession in July 1990, and it lasted through March 1991.[45] The year following the recession, the economy struggled to regain ground that was lost during the economic slowdown.[46]

Former state fiscal officer Cecil Brown explained that the recession really hurt the second half of the Mabus Administration. "As state fiscal officer, I was constantly on the phone with the State Tax Commission checking on revenue collections while also communicating with the Treasurer's Office checking on cash. I then had to decide which bills the state was going to pay and not pay," explained Brown.[47] At the direction of Governor Mabus, he was forced to reduce agency budgets to better deal with the struggling economy. The fiscal agenda quickly went from figuring out how to pay for new programs to finding a way to adequately continue the operation of state government.

The DFA allowed some agencies to use current year funds to pay for the previous year's expenditures, which was prohibited by law. Executive director of PEER John Turcotte wrote a letter to Brown on January 7, 1991, expressing a concern with year-end spending practices.[48] Brown was no longer serving as state fiscal officer, because he had accepted a position as Mabus's chief of staff, but he was still very involved in the process. In a response letter to Turcotte, he explained that he was also concerned with the practice but believed that the legislature was okay with him allowing it. Brown said that both Appropriations Committee chairmen knew of the practice and approved of the state meeting its financial obligations. He explained:

On August 29, 1988, I talked on the telephone with Jack Gordon and Charlie Capps regarding the payment of [. . .] expenses incurred prior to June 30, 1988, from FY 89 appropriations. I described the problem to both chairmen and they agreed that the requisitions should be honored, the bills should be paid, and we would collectively work out recommendations to the Legislature for corrective action. Regretfully, to date no action has been taken.[49]

In addition to the letter, Brown appeared before the PEER Committee on January 22, 1991, to discuss the year-end spending practices. He provided three primary reasons for the DFA's approval of deficit spending by agencies: (1) the practice seemed to have the blessing of the legislature, (2) the DFA believed that the disallowance of the practice might "shut down" state government, and (3) the DFA concluded that the statutes were not clear with regard to the legality of such spending practices.

The PEER Committee was not satisfied with Brown's explanation and responded with a report titled "Deficit Spending in Mississippi State Government." The committee took exception to the position of the DFA regarding deficit spending, and it explained that state statutes clearly provide that deficit spending is illegal, and agencies, particularly the DFA, must rely on legislative mandates (state statutes) rather than legislative discussions to determine legal compliance requirements. Furthermore, the report recommended that agencies adhere to spending limits established through the appropriations process.[50]

The economy continued to deteriorate during the Mabus Administration, and the state had revenue shortfalls from FY 1990 through FY 1992. Budgets were cut in FY 1991 and FY 1992 by approximately $90 million and $74 million, respectively.[51] The PEER Committee conducted a follow-up review of deficit spending and concluded that "state agencies, as a whole, did not incur substantial obligations at the end of fiscal year 1991 to be paid from fiscal year 1992 appropriations."[52] The legislature forced the executive branch to follow the law and stop allowing deficit spending, regardless of the effect. Mabus never secured funding for his prized B.E.S.T. program, and he ended up losing his reelection bid to political newcomer Kirk Fordice.

Chapter 5

The Legislature's Intervention with Budget Reform

The legislature did not blame Gov. Ray Mabus for the budget woes that occurred in the late 1980s; legislative members were aware that the distressed economy was one of the primary causes of the revenue shortage that led to budget problems. However, the legislature did grow frustrated with Mabus's unrealistic revenue figures used in his executive budget recommendations (EBR) and reacted by passing H.B. 796 during the 1991 legislative session, which essentially strengthened existing law pertaining to submitting a balanced budget.[1] Mabus's budget recommendations were very confusing to the public, because the total amount of revenue used in his budget recommendations was significantly higher than that proposed by the legislature in its legislative budget recommendations (LBR). This was because Mabus would include proposed sources of revenue that did not yet exist. H.B. 796 prohibited this practice by requiring the governor to use in his budget recommendation only those revenues available under existing laws and not include any proposed revenues that would become available only after the enactment of new legislation.

After passing H.B. 796, the legislature continued its efforts to strengthen the budget process by passing H.B. 505, known as the Budget Reform Act of 1992, during the next legislative session.[2] With the exception of the passage of the Mississippi Administrative Reorganization Act of 1984, which created the Joint Legislative Budget Committee (JLBC) and the Legislative Budget Office (LBO), no other legislation in recent history affected the budget-making process more than the Budget Reform Act of 1992. In a continual effort to further advance Mississippi's budgeting process, the legislature also passed the Mississippi Performance Budget and Strategic Planning Act of 1994, which never really gained momentum and ended up being of no real consequence to the budgeting process.[3]

Budget Reform Act of 1992

The Budget Reform Act of 1992 was approved by the governor on May 7, 1992, enacting some of the most far-reaching and beneficial changes to Mississippi's budgeting process in recent memory.[4] The bill was authored by Rep. Charlie Capps, chairman of the House Appropriations Committee and member of the JLBC. The senate passed a companion bill, S.B. 2706, which was authored by five senators, including two who served on the JLBC.[5] Those two were Sen. Dick Hall, chairman of the Senate Appropriations Committee, and Sen. Paul Richard Lambert, chairman of the Senate Finance Committee. After the Senate Appropriations Committee had passed H.B. 505, the House Appropriations Committee did not take up S.B. 2706.

Central features of H.B. 505 dealt with restructuring the reserve fund and setting limitations on total annual appropriations from the general fund. Additionally, the bill mandated that an in-depth review and analysis of the state budget process, in comparison to that in other states, be conducted by the JLBC with the assistance of the LBO, University Research Center, State Tax Commission, and any other agencies necessary. The bill did not require adoption of a completely new budget process, such as was proposed in previous sessions, but instead required the JLBC to make recommendations for additional improvements that could work in collaboration with the reforming provisions of H.B. 505 and further improve Mississippi's budget process.[6]

Reserve Funds

One of the primary reasons that the budget reform act was passed was due to the lack of reserves in place during the late 1980s and early 1990s. A proper reserve could have helped alleviate the fiscal stress caused by the down economy during those years. Mississippi's revenue collections fell short of projections, similar to many other states, because the nation went into a recession in July 1990. Mississippi's budget was cut in FY 1991 and FY 1992 by approximately $90 million and $74 million, respectively. The cuts were painful and disruptive to the state, because there was essentially no contingency plan in place in the event that revenue fell short of projections. "There were no reserve account balances and there were no cushions in the budgets in the form of unappropriated balances. In its efforts to address all the mandates, demands, and commitments, the [l]egislature, for ten years, had been appropriating virtually all available funds."[7]

The Working Cash-Stabilization Reserve Fund, which was created in H.B. 505, was and still is known as the "rainy day fund." The purpose of the rainy day fund was to "set aside [. . .] projected revenue as an unappropriated contingency against a revenue shortfall."[8] Section 2 (1) of H.B. 505 created the rainy day fund and explained how it was to work:

> There is created in the State Treasury a special fund, separate and apart from any other fund, to be designated the Working Cash-Stabilization Reserve Fund, into which shall be deposited one hundred percent (100%) of that portion of the unencumbered General Fund cash balance that exceeds Six Million Dollars ($6,000,000.00) at the close of the fiscal year ending June 30, 1992, and one hundred percent (100%) of the unencumbered General Fund cash balance at the close of each succeeding fiscal year until such time as the balance in the fund reaches Forty Million Dollars ($40,000,000.00). After the balance in the fund reaches Forty Million Dollars ($40,000,000.00), fifty percent (50%) of the unencumbered General Fund cash balance at the close of each fiscal year, not to exceed seven and one-half percent (7-1/2%) of the General Fund appropriations for such fiscal year, shall be deposited into the fund.[9]

Section 2 went on to explain that the remainder of the year-end unencumbered cash after funds are transferred to the rainy day fund would remain in the general fund, until the balance of the rainy day fund reached 7.5 percent of appropriated general funds for the fiscal year. When that threshold had been met, 50 percent of the unencumbered cash balance would be transferred into the Education Reserve Fund.[10] After the formula-driven transfers to the rainy day fund and Education Reserve Fund were satisfied, the legislature would then be able to use the unencumbered cash in the general fund for cash flow needs for the next year, deficit appropriations, or regular appropriations.

In addition to creating the rainy day fund, H.B. 505 abolished the General Fund Stabilization Reserve and General Fund Reserve, which were two funds created by the legislature when it passed H.B. 627 in 1982.[11] The General Fund Stabilization Reserve and General Fund Reserve were created for the sole purpose of preserving the fiscal integrity of the State of Mississippi, but they proved to be inadequate to accomplish that purpose. The former was a proper stabilization reserve, while the latter was discretionary. Adequate stabilization reserve funds are accompanied by rules that encourage states to save when times are good in order to stabilize budgets when times are bad.[12]

The General Fund Stabilization Reserve and General Fund Reserve were inadequate because funds were available only if there was a surplus remaining in the state's general fund at the end of the fiscal year. So if the legislature overappropriated or revenues did not exceed expectations, no funding was available to be distributed into the two funds. Another problem with H.B. 627 was the formula for the distribution of the funds when there was a surplus. If there was a surplus at the end of the fiscal year, only one-fourth of the funds went to the General Fund Stabilization Reserve, and it could be used only for covering any unforeseen deficits in revenue. The remaining three-fourths went into the General Fund Reserve, which could be used at the discretion of the legislature. H.B. 627 would have been much stronger if only the General Fund Stabilization Reserve had been created and 100 percent of surplus funds were to go into it.

The newly created Working Cash-Stabilization Reserve Fund was far superior to the two reserve funds that it replaced, because it was accompanied by a requirement that only 98 percent of estimated general fund revenue could be appropriated by the legislature. With the 2 percent set-aside requirement in place, the state no longer had to exceed revenue estimates in order for funds to go into the reserve fund; instead, the revenue only had to meet expectations. Furthermore, if the revenue fell short of expectations, the 2 percent set-aside would serve as a cushion. The act also provided for immediate fund transfers and fund consolidations that resulted in a rainy day fund beginning balance of $46.9 million to begin FY 1993.[13] Although the 2 percent set-aside requirement contributed greatly to the success of the rainy day fund, this was not the first time that spending less than 100 percent of the anticipated revenue was proposed.

Appropriation Limitations

In 1986 Rep. Charlie Williams requested a study of the state's reserve funds, which included measures by which appropriations would be limited to less than 100 percent of available funds.[14] Representative Williams's recommendation in 1986 to limit appropriations to less than 100 percent of available revenue would have likely had a better chance of passing if he had been a member of the JLBC. Unfortunately, he was not a member of the committee, and the legislature continued to appropriate most of the anticipated revenue, and on some occasions all of it. When the budget reform act was enacted in 1992, Representative Williams was much more influential in fiscal matters, serving as the chairman of the powerful House Ways and Means Committee and as a member of the JLBC. There were other JLBC members who believed that the state should not spend all of its revenue, so Representative Williams was not the only member pushing for the 98 percent limitation that was eventually adopted in 1992. The specific provision of H.B. 505 that addressed the 2 percent set-aside was Section 11, which read as follows:

> Beginning with the appropriations for Fiscal Year 1994, the total sum appropriated by the Legislature from the General Fund for any fiscal year shall not exceed ninety-eight percent (98%) of the General Fund revenue estimate for that fiscal year developed by the Tax Commission and the University Research Center and adopted by the Joint Legislative Budget Committee, plus any unencumbered balances in general funds that will be available and on hand at the close of the then current fiscal year.

The legislature's appropriation limitation coupled with the existence of an effectively structured rainy day fund placed Mississippi ahead of most states in budget management and in the appropriation process.[15] However, having laws that mandated setting aside revenue proved to be less effective over the years, because the legislature began suspending the requirements whenever it pleased, allowing it to appropriate 100 percent of revenue.

Legislative Study of the Budgeting Process

The budget reform act required JLBC to undertake a comprehensive study of state budgeting, which required the assistance and cooperation of multiple other states and national organizations. The purpose of the study was to produce findings and recommendations from a comprehensive review of the state budget system compared to the other forty-nine states. The bill's provision for the study had the following requirements:

> The Joint Legislative Budget Committee shall study and review the state budgeting system and make comparisons with and evaluations of other budgeting systems in use in other states. The study shall review financial and economic conditions and the associated performance of the budget systems. In reviewing the state budget system, the study shall include an analysis of budget preparation, data gathering and evaluation, development of budget recommendations, revenue forecasting, reporting of revenue collections, appropriation tracking and reporting and tax expenditure reporting.[16]

The legislative staff's methodology used for the study involved the following: (1) thoroughly examining Mississippi's budget system; (2) written questionnaires to executive budget offices in the other forty-nine states; (3) telephone interviews with legislative and executive budget and fiscal officers in other states; (4) specialized surveys of southeastern states regarding revenue estimating practices and tax expenditure reporting; (5) interviews and discussion with university researchers on state budgeting and with officials of national associations such as the National Conference of State Legislatures, the National Association of State Budget Officers, the Council of State Governments, and the Federation of Tax Administrators; and (6) research of the literature on state budgeting systems, formats, and other related matters. The materials obtained by the legislative staff were thought to be the only known collection in existence of budget books from every single state, at the time of the study.[17]

The study found that Mississippi did face significant problems with fiscal stress caused by poor economic conditions and expenditure growth exceeding revenue growth. However, Mississippi's budget process could not be directly faulted for either of those two problems. "The budget process has no control over economic conditions and, likewise, the budget process cannot control the fact that expenditure growth exceeds revenue growth"[18] The legislature explained that budget reform would help to alleviate the cited problems but not get rid of them altogether.[19]

The study also found that Mississippi's existing budgeting system, after budget reform, was effective because it already consisted of priority setting, program analysis, and performance measurement, which are three of the most important elements of a budget system.[20] Yet the study found that the elements in its current format did not exist in a vacuum. In order for the elements to be more effective, the study concluded that the system should be enhanced and its operation and effectiveness improved by integrating the three elements more. Individually advancing each element through integration produces a budgeting system with greater impact[21] This so-called greater impact was referred to in the study as the Measured Performance-Priority, Program Accountability Concept (M-PAC).

The study concluded that the Budget Reform Act of 1992 had initiated very important changes in the state's financial operations and that the basic framework of the existing system should be retained; however, the study found that the system should be improved by the adoption of numerous recommendations found in the report. Some of the recommendations introduced new procedures, while others involved pushing to accelerate the full implementation of changes previously initiated. The specific recommendations included: (1) revising and changing existing programs to enhance the M-PAC; (2) priority ranking of programs; (3) continuing performance evaluations of successful state systems that link goal setting and priority budgeting, and then formally establishing them in the budget process; and (4) monitoring more closely the implementation of the Statewide Automated Accounting System (SAAS), which provides the accounting tools for program budgeting and performance evaluation. Speaker of the House Tim Ford expressed his satisfaction of the study's recommendations, explaining that some of the recommendations had already been incorporated into the budget process and that other changes would be reflected in the appropriation process during the 1993 legislative session.[22]

The budget reform act changed the budget-making process greatly, and it created a rainy day fund that was much more effective than the previous two reserve funds that were abolished by the act. Furthermore, the act called for a 2 percent set-aside requirement that when combined with the rainy day fund put Mississippi in a position to better handle the state finances when the economy performed poorly. The budget reform act also required the JLBC to undertake a comprehensive study of state budgeting that further enhanced the budgeting changes made by the passage of H.B. 505. Many of the successful budget modifications passed in the budget reform act are still used today, and some of the reform measures are believed to be among the most effective changes ever made to the budget process in Mississippi.[23]

Mississippi Performance Budget and Strategic Planning Act of 1994

One of the specific requirements of the JLBC's comprehensive study mandated by the budget reform act was to "review financial and economic conditions and the associated performance of the budget systems."[24] The study devoted an entire chapter to performance titled "Planning-Priorities, Performance and Accountability." As a result of the study, the legislature passed S.B. 2995, which created the Mississippi Performance Budget and Strategic Planning Act of 1994.[25] The processes and procedures established by the act were derived in large measure from recommendations contained within the study.

S.B. 2995 required agencies to include in their budget requests a definition of the mission, a description of the duties and responsibilities, financial data relative to the various programs operated by the agency, and performance measures associated with each program of the agency. Furthermore, the bill required agencies to include a five-year strategic plan in an addendum format. The new performance measures and strategic planning requirements were set to be reflected in agencies' budget requests beginning in FY 1996. The legislation mandated that the agencies' performance measures be developed by cooperative efforts of the LBO, the Department of Finance and Administration (DFA), and the agency itself, and required the LBO and the DFA to jointly approve the performance measures prior to being included in the agencies' budget requests.

The performance measures and strategic planning concept adopted by Mississippi closely resembled those of Texas, which was one of the states reviewed in the comprehensive study. At the time of the study, Texas had recently adopted a new strategic planning process, which was set to be submitted in September of 1992 to cover the six-year period of 1992–1998. The Texas law mandated that all state agencies prepare strategic plans, and it required the plans to be submitted prior to the submission of the agencies' budget requests. Texas identified four elements of the process: planning, budgeting, implementation, and evaluation. The plan had two stages: the first involved defining the agency mission, goals, and philosophy; and the second set out outcome measures and output measures. The primary focus of the plan was to put an emphasis on results and not efforts. It is ironic that Mississippi decided to model its new plan after Texas, because the Texas plan was just being launched and did not have a proven track record.

Mississippi's performance budget and strategic planning act did not accomplish the goals that it set out to do. Sure, agencies were required, and still are today, to submit performance measures and a strategic plan when submitting their budget requests; however, the legislature rarely ever used the information to determine how much funds would be appropriated to agencies. Furthermore, some agencies recognized that neither the performance measures nor the strategic plans were getting much attention from the legislature and begin to put little effort into what was submitted.

Chapter 6

Executive–Legislative Conflict under Fordice

Gov. Kirk Fordice had never held a public office before being elected governor, and he was generally unfamiliar with the details of Mississippi's budget-making process. However, he signed the legislature's Budget Reform Act of 1992 (H.B. 505, passed during the 1992 legislative session)[1] into law during his first year in office, not because he thought that it was great, but because he thought that anything was better than the existing budget process. At the beginning of the legislative session in which the act was passed, Fordice said during his State of the State address, "In all good conscience, we must set aside the old smoke and mirrors method of budgeting and immediately reform our fiscal policy."[2] One component of the budget reform act that Fordice was pleased with was a set-aside of 2 percent of projected revenue as an unappropriated contingency against revenue shortfalls. Even though Fordice stated during his address that he would like to see the legislature set 3 percent aside,[3] he was okay settling for 2 percent. Fordice believed that a set-aside for emergency expenditures was beneficial for any organization, regardless of whether it was public or private.

Although Fordice was unfamiliar with public budgets, he was no stranger to private-sector budgets. Prior to being elected governor, Fordice served as the chief executive officer of Fordice Construction Company in Vicksburg, Mississippi.[4] He learned early on in his administration that public budgeting was not the same as private-sector budgeting, and that it was no easy task serving as Mississippi's chief executive officer. Fordice found out that managing the state's nearly $6 billion total budget[5] came with many restrictions, and that he did not have complete control over the budget, as he might have wished. Additionally, Fordice's budget approach ran counter to the perspectives of most of the legislators, and they responded by making his job extremely difficult.

Governor Fordice and the legislature had a strained relationship from the start because of a stark contrast in their respective political thinking, especially fiscal philosophy. The philosophical differences were magnified because Fordice was the first Republican governor in over a century, while the legislature was dominated by Democrats.[6] The governor wanted to "cap the growth of recurring General Fund expenditures" and limit borrowing for capital projects, in order to decrease debt service payments.[7] Additionally, Fordice felt that it was unnecessary to expand government services and believed that a significant tax cut was needed instead.[8] In his final executive budget recommendation (EBR) to the legislature for FY 2000, Fordice stated, "The highest priority of my fiscal agenda has always been the delivery of a significant tax cut to hardworking Mississippi taxpayers."[9]

Most legislators did not share Fordice's fiscal agenda views because they thought that state government was underfunded and needed to grow, and they believed that a significant tax cut was out of the question. Between FY 1992 and FY 2000, during Fordice's two terms as governor, general fund revenue collections increased by just over $1.4 billion, or 71 percent.[10] Fordice thought that the fiscal dividend produced by the expanding economy should have been used to reduce taxes, while the legislature thought that it should have been used to expand government services. Throughout the Fordice Administration, the fiscal philosophy of the latter ended up winning out because of the Democratic supermajority held in both chambers.

Although the legislature rejected most of Fordice's fiscal agenda items, they did accomplish a few things working together. Fordice explained in his final budget recommendation that in retrospect, he and the legislature "jointly worked toward and achieved a good number of fiscal accomplishments during the past seven years including the 98% rule, Working Cash-Stabilization Fund, capital gains exemption, elimination of the marriage penalty, bridge rehabilitation, Master Teacher pay plan, and additional funding for law enforcement."[11] But for the most part, Fordice was unsuccessful in convincing the legislature to adopt his top priorities, which included significant tax reductions, limiting expenditure growth, and a limitation on general obligation bonded indebtedness. Although Fordice's taxing and spending philosophy ran counter to the legislature's philosophy, the general public seemed to approve of Governor Fordice overall, because he was overwhelmingly elected to a second term, becoming the first governor to succeed himself in more than one hundred years.[12]

Fordice's Fiscal Accomplishments

Fordice's fiscal accomplishments consisted of the following: (1) persuading the legislature to abolish the state income tax on capital gains from sales of shares or assets of Mississippi companies, (2) getting the legislature to eliminate the "marriage penalty" in the state income tax code, and (3) encouraging the legislature to adhere to the 2 percent set-aside requirement in order to increase the state's savings. The other collaborative accomplishments mentioned in Fordice's FY 2000 EBR were significant as well, but the argument can be made that the legislature would have provided additional funding for bridge rehabilitation, teacher pay increases, and law enforcement increases whether Fordice requested those items or not, so those items are not discussed.

Fordice received a big win during the last year of his first term when he persuaded the legislature to abolish the income tax on capital gains from sales of shares or assets of Mississippi companies in 1995, which took very little convincing.[13] However, Fordice's request to eliminate the income tax "marriage penalty" took a lot more effort to persuade the legislature. In Fordice's FY 1996 EBR, he requested an increase in the personal exemption for married persons from $9,500 to $14,000. The personal exemption for married persons was $9,500, and $6,000 for single persons. Fordice believed that the tax law penalized married couples because they could exempt only $9,500 of their income, while two single persons together could exempt $6,000 each, for a larger total exemption of $12,000. Fordice explained that "[t]his exemption increase would end the state's penalty on married taxpayers."[14] The legislature initially rejected Fordice's marriage penalty tax cut proposal, killing all eight bills introduced on the subject during the 1996 legislative session.[15]

Fordice renewed his plea to eliminate the income tax marriage penalty in his FY 1997 EBR.[16] To pay for the tax cut, the governor's budget office limited executive agency spending requests, and while that savings alone did not cover the cost of the entire tax cut, the legislature elected to phase in the elimination of the marriage penalty in personal exemptions by the year 2000, as well as the elimination of the marriage penalty in the standard deduction by the year 1999. The legislature did not raise the personal exemption for married persons to $14,000 as the governor had requested, but it did raise it to $12,000, which was equal to the total amount of exemptions for two single people.[17]

Fordice's final fiscal accomplishment, and perhaps the most impressive, was encouraging the legislature to increase the state's savings. Fordice was the first governor to benefit from the Working Cash-Stabilization Reserve Fund, informally known as the "rainy day fund." He expressed his satisfaction with the fund in his EBR, stating: "At June 30, 1993, the General Fund had a fiscal year ending balance of $175.3 million. With these funds available, the State was able to transfer $86.7 million to the Working Cash-Stabilization Reserve Fund to bring this fund to its statutory limit of $160.3 million (7.5 percent of general fund appropriations). This emergency fund, created in 1992, will be available in the future to offset revenue shortfalls and prevent devastating budget cuts."[18] The Joint Legislative Budget Committee (JLBC) stated that the purpose of the fund was to "set aside [. . .] projected revenue as an unappropriated contingency against a revenue shortfall."[19] Although many thought at the time that the task of holding the legislature to its own 2 percent set-aside requirement would not be difficult, future legislatures were successful in voting to suspend the set-aside requirement in order to appropriate 100 percent of collected revenue. So, Fordice should indeed receive credit for constantly reminding the legislature of the importance of following its own "98 percent rule."

The rainy day fund grew significantly as a result of adhering to the 2 percent set-aside requirement. The rainy day fund increased by more than $70 million from FY 1993 to FY 1999.[20] Furthermore, the fund increased every year that Fordice was in office, and he proudly reported in his final EBR:

> The financial condition of the State of Mississippi remains solid. General fund revenue increased $187.1 million in Fiscal Year 1998 to $3.0494 billion. The general fund ended the year with a surplus of $101,301,583. The Working Cash-Stabilization Fund [rainy day fund] began Fiscal Year 1999 with a balance of $230,387,041, providing the State with protection against revenue shortfalls.[21]

Although Fordice was very pleased with the rainy day fund serving as a safeguard against unexpected revenue drops, he also cautioned the legislature against becoming too optimistic about a continuation of positive revenue growth, explaining that the growth rates that have been enjoyed for a number of years "will not extend in perpetuity."[22]

Financial Environment under Fordice

Fordice took office in January 1992, following a national recession, and he instructed State Fiscal Officer Ed Ranck to cut budgets the very next month. Prior to ordering the budget cuts, Governor Fordice attended a briefing at the State Capitol on tax revenue projections and collections. He mentioned after the briefing that he would have closed Fordice Construction Company within forty-nine hours if the budget had ever resembled the state figures that he saw that day. "I find it alarming that the people in charge of government can sit around with such ease and digest numbers like this," explained the governor.[23] Fordice ended up ordering Ranck to reduce the total FY 1992 budget by $75,843,085.[24]

Ranck, who also served as the executive director of the Department of Finance and Administration (DFA), announced that only four agency budgets would avoid the maximum cut of 5 percent allowed by law and would instead be cut by only 2.5 percent. Those four agency budgets were the Minimum Education Program fund, the Department of Economic and Community Development, the Highway Patrol, and the Bureau of Narcotics. Fordice explained in his budget cut statement:

> The education of our children, the creation of jobs, the protection of our citizens—these are the needs we must fight to preserve. Even with the limited flexibility left to me by the huge budget mess I inherited, I have ordered my financial advisers to limit the cuts to classroom education, jobs and law enforcement to no more than half that imposed on every other agency in state government. If the law allowed, I would have made the cuts deeper in other areas and provided even greater protection to these key needs."[25]

The governor's budget cuts were not popular, but they had to be made. Arguments were made that Gov. Ray Mabus should have made the budget reductions before leaving office, because revenue began falling short of estimates in the fall of 1991, while he was still governor. Deputy Tax Commissioner Lester Herrington explained that tax collections from July through December of 1991 fell short of projections by approximately $3.3 million, and the shortages occurred in individual income tax payments and sales tax on goods purchased outside the state and shipped inside. Furthermore, Herrington explained that he expected the shortfall to widen and that the state economy would have to grow between 6 and 8 percent each month until June to reach projections, which he thought was doubtful.[26]

Fordice's 1992 budget cuts must have been on the legislature's mind when they adopted the sine die revenue estimate for the FY 1993 budget.[27] Even with a sluggish economy during the latter half of the Mabus Administration, the JLBC continued to adopt a higher revenue amount each year. But for the first time in multiple years, the legislature was pessimistic about revenue and expected a smaller amount to be generated in FY 1993 compared to FY 1992. The pessimism likely came when State Economist Phil Pepper stated that the revenue expectations for the state might have to be lowered if the national economy did not improve soon. Pepper explained that it is "hard to expect revenues to pick up . . . if the economy is not picking up."[28]

The FY 1993 general fund revenue estimate, compiled by the JLBC in May 1992, dropped to $1,992,900,000 from $2,000,397,000 the previous fiscal year.[29] Of the estimated revenue, 68.72 percent was expected to come from sales and individual income taxes. Sales and individual income taxes were expected to generate $853,200,000 and $516,400,000, respectively, for FY 1993. Although individual income was expected to increase year over year, the largest revenue generator, sales tax, was expected to decrease by $46,800,000 in FY 1993.[30] Sales and individual income taxes were, and still are, two categories that are affected greatly during recessions. The early 1990s recession was declared over in March 1991,[31] but Mississippi continued to endure the consequences of the recession. Mississippi was especially vulnerable to the down economy because of its dependency on sales and individual income taxes, which accounted for nearly 70 percent of the budget. Fordice's first EBR took into consideration the lack of revenue needed to cover current expenditures and was therefore pretty uneventful.

Fordice's first budget recommendation, for FY 1994, was submitted in November 1992, which was only a few months after he was forced to make budget cuts. Although the budget cuts were attributed to the sluggish economy, over appropriating by the legislature was also thought to have played a role. Fordice's first budget recommendation was very conservative, and of the $2,065,750,436 available to be appropriated, he recommended setting aside just under $42 million as a cushion.[32] The economy improved significantly after Fordice's first term, and he continued to recommend setting aside 2 percent of revenue every year while in office. After being forced to cut the FY 1992 budget, Fordice did not have to make any more budget cuts during his administration because revenue quickly rebounded, resulting in robust growth throughout his tenure.

The total funds available for Fordice's last fiscal year to propose a budget, FY 2000, had ballooned to a whopping $3,459,387,036, which included a 2 percent set-aside of just over $68 million.[33] The total funds available for appropriations increased by nearly 63 percent while Fordice was in office. During that same time period, general fund revenues had an average yearly growth of just over 7 percent.[34] In addition to Mississippi benefiting from general economic growth that was experienced nationwide, a portion of Mississippi's growth was attributed to the emergence of revenue generated by gaming.[35] By the mid-1990s, nearly 10 percent of general fund revenue came from a combination of gaming taxes and gaming-related increases, in both sales and individual income taxes.[36]

The significant revenue increase was accompanied by a substantial expenditure increase in expenditures by the legislature, although Fordice was against it. Fordice made it clear in all of his budget recommendations that he wanted to limit the growth of recurring expenditures and decrease debt service payments by limiting borrowing for capital projects. Between FY 1992 and FY 2000, during Fordice's eight years as governor, total general fund appropriations grew from $2,001,553,038 to $3,459,991,640, an increase of $1,458,438,602, or 73 percent.[37] Government spending ended up being a subject on which the governor and the legislature refused to compromise. The issue was not complicated; the governor wanted to spend less, and the legislature more, and there was no middle ground of compromise.

Struggles with the Legislature

The legislature disregarded Fordice's conservative low-tax, low-spend agenda from the start and responded to it by actually raising taxes, proposing more spending, and issuing more debt for capital projects—all during Fordice's very first legislative session in 1992. Fordice reacted by vetoing the tax increase bill (S.B. 3120) and the bond bill for capital improvements (S.B. 3057).[38] The legislature overrode both gubernatorial vetoes without hesitation, within one day.

During the 1993 legislative session, the governor decided to exercise his gubernatorial veto authority again by partially vetoing two more bond bills, H.B. 1613 and H.B. 1502,[39] along with twenty-seven appropriation bills. The legislature sent the bills to Fordice within five days of the sine die adjournment, which gave the governor fifteen days to sign or veto them. Fordice returned the bills to the legislature within fifteen days with a message that he had vetoed parts of twenty-nine bills. Many questioned the constitutionality of the governor's partial vetoes and viewed the move as an attempt to expand gubernatorial veto authority, because the manner in which he struck out or rewrote language in the bills was not authorized under existing judicial decisions.

A few legislators vowed to file a lawsuit against the governor to have his partial vetoes declared unconstitutional. When Fordice was notified that legislators were filing a lawsuit against him, he responded, "That's not the Legislature. That's Hob Bryan. Let's be truthful. I don't think the Legislature as a body has any stomach for it."[40] Sen. Hob Bryan was in fact largely behind the suit.

Senator Bryan and two other legislators filed their promised lawsuit in the First Judicial District of the Hinds County Chancery Court on August 6, 1993,[41] and Judge Chet Dillard heard the case. The legislators argued that Fordice overstepped his constitutional authority when he reduced the number of projects from the bond bills by striking them out and amended the language of the appropriation bills. They argued that bond bills may be vetoed or approved in their entirety but are not subject to partial vetoes, like appropriation bills are.[42] Although the legislators agreed that appropriation bills were subject to partial vetoes, they did not agree that the bills could be amended.[43] Fordice argued that bond bills obligated state money, similar to appropriation bills, so he had the power to reduce the amount using his partial veto authority. However, the court interpreted the matter in a different way: "In this court's opinion, there is no question that the bond bills were bond bills and the appropriations bills were appropriations bills, if for no other reason than the Legislature said so."[44]

The chancery court granted summary judgment in favor of the plaintiffs and declared all of the partial vetoes invalid. *Fordice v. Bryan* (1995) made it to the Supreme Court of Mississippi, resulting in the higher court upholding the lower court's decision on January 12, 1995.[45] Things did not get much better for Fordice during the 1995 legislative session when he vetoed two more revenue bills (S.B. 2945 and S.B. 3236)[46] and again had them quickly overridden by the legislature.

Matters got more frustrating for Fordice during his second term in office after state senator Ronnie Musgrove was elected lieutenant governor and selected Hob Bryan to chair the Senate Finance Committee. Already having experienced a defeat at the hands of Senator Bryan in court, Fordice was defeated again after he vetoed a revenue bill (S.B. 2649) authored by Senator Bryan during the 1997 legislative session and his veto was overridden.[47] Senator Bryan delivered another blow to Fordice during the 1999 legislative session when he refused to bring a tax reduction bill, which successfully passed the house, to a vote in the Senate Finance Committee—causing the bill to die.[48] Fordice decided to call legislators back for a special session a few months later to have them reconsider a reduction to the individual income tax. The house deferred action until the senate made its decision, and Senator Bryan again refused to bring the bill to a vote in his committee, which resulted in both chambers adjourning without passing any bills.[49]

It is safe to say that Fordice was unsuccessful in getting the legislature to adopt his major agenda items. He failed to get a substantial tax reduction and failed to curtail spending. However, he did use all executive authority available to him to try to control the legislature's excessive spending, especially when he partially vetoed the bond and appropriation bills, as a last resort, which was nothing short of an open invitation for court intervention.

Separation of Powers Revisited

In Fordice's attempt to curb legislative spending, he sparked a "separation of powers" debate that rivaled that of the landmark *Alexander v. State of Mississippi by and through Allain (1983)* case, which was argued over a decade earlier. Fordice knew that court intervention was inevitable after he partially vetoed the bills. He viewed the conflict between the legislature and himself as nothing more than a difference of opinion on the interpretation of the constitution. Fordice did not believe that the legislature should be the one to determine if he had the authority to partially veto legislation. Fordice was correct in assuming that the judicial branch, not the legislative branch, should determine the constitutionality of his actions. The *Alexander* case stated the following:

> The executive, legislative and judicial departments of the state all serve the same constituency and are, of course, subject to and bound by the terms of the same state constitution. The interpretation of the constitution becomes the duty of the judicial department when the meaning of that supreme document is put in issue.[50]

Many legislators discounted Fordice's actions from the beginning and believed that he did not have a chance to succeed in court, but the supreme court's job is to take all separation of powers cases seriously. The supreme court justices understood the importance of the case and described what they were asked to do as the "most difficult and delicate duty that ever falls to the lot of the court of last resort."[51] Unlike many legislators, the justices did not write the case off as a foregone conclusion but instead anticipated a complicated case.

The argument can be made that *Fordice v. Bryan (1995)* was more complex than the *Alexander* case, because all nine supreme court justices in the *Alexander* case joined in a unanimous opinion when rendering the decision, whereas the justices in the *Fordice v. Bryan* case were divided in their analysis and reasoning. Fordice appealed the chancery court's decision in favor of the legislators, arguing that he was properly exercising his partial veto power under Article 4, Section 73 of the Mississippi Constitution of 1890. However, the supreme court ultimately disagreed and affirmed the chancellor's decision.

Eight of the nine justices concurred in the majority opinion, affirming the summary judgment, finding the governor's attempt to partially veto H.B. 1613 and 1502 a nullity.[52] The supreme court also reviewed the twenty-seven partially vetoed appropriation bills, although Fordice did not appeal them. Writing in the majority opinion, Justice James Roberts Jr. justified why the supreme court reviewed the appropriation bills, explaining that "public policy and the magnitude of the importance of these issues requires this Court to review the Governor's actions with respect to the twenty-seven appropriations bills as such actions may continue to be repeated and forever escape review by this Court."[53] Chief Justice Armis Hawkins disagreed with the need to review the appropriation bills, and three other justices agreed that the reviews were unnecessary.[54] "In short, the Governor did not address the matter of the 27 appropriation bills in his brief, and neither should we," explained Justice Hawkins.[55] Whether or not the supreme court should have reviewed the appropriation bills was truly secondary in the big scheme of things. The primary point of the case was determining whether the governor could partially veto bond bills using Section 73 of the constitution, and all of the justices except for Justice James Smith Jr. believed that he could not.

Not only did Justice James Smith Jr. disagree with his colleagues, he said that they were flat-out wrong. Justice Smith stated in his dissenting opinion: "Governor Fordice has the constitutional right to properly exercise a line item veto as well as a responsibility to do so if and when he deems it to be in the best fiscal interest of the taxpaying citizens of this state. That is a governor's prerogative as chief executive officer of this state."[56] Fortunately for the legislature, a majority of the justices believed that Fordice overstepped his executive authority and encroached on legislative authority.

The justice with the most contempt for Fordice's actions was clearly Justice Chuck McRae. In his concurring opinion with the majority, Justice McRae wrote, "For almost one hundred years, no other governor has ever shown such contempt for the other two branches of government as Governor Fordice." He went on to say, "Fordice's actions and arguments surrounding these twenty-nine bills in question expose his disdain for the legislative and judicial branches of Mississippi government."[57] Matters appeared to get personal when McRae stated, in his opinion, "Perhaps, if Governor Fordice desires to write law or to offer amendments to proposed laws, then he should hang up his spurs as Governor and run for a position in the Legislature."[58] Responding to McRae's written opinion, Justice Smith stated that "there is no need to express views towards Governor Fordice, or any sitting Governor for that matter . . . Such comments are uncalled for, unnecessary and serve no purpose whatsoever."[59] The governor's office also weighed in on Justice McRae's statement, mentioning how it "sounds more like a statement of a supreme politician than a Supreme Court justice."[60]

Fordice v. Bryan was a very important separation of powers case that received some negative attention because of what seemed to be a personal attack on the governor by Justice McRae; however, that small hiccup did not take away from the significance of his separate written opinion. Regardless of Justice McRae's tone, he presented legal evidence defending his opinion and truly believed that Fordice's actions were unconstitutional. Apart from McRae's negative rhetoric, his separate opinion was in line with a majority of the other justices.

Justice Roberts explained in the majority opinion that the high court's job was to interpret various provisions of Mississippi's constitution, in order to declare the boundaries beyond which executive action may not pass and to determine the limitations on executive veto authority. Although the *Fordice v. Bryan* case was unique, the basic concept of the case was not. The supreme court was simply being asked to determine whether the governor was usurping legislative authority. Justice Roberts pointed out that the supreme court had already addressed the usurpation of executive authority by the legislative branch in the *Alexander* case. The final outcome of the *Alexander* case was in favor of the executive branch, whereas the court ruled in favor of the legislative branch over a decade later in *Fordice v. Bryan*. In both cases, the supreme court showed consistency and proved to be an independent mediator. The *Alexander* case was actually referenced quite a bit in the *Fordice v. Bryan* decision.

Both cases show the benefits of having an independent judicial system to assure that neither the legislature nor the governor oversteps their constitutional powers. As recognized by the courts, checks and balances are very important for a healthy democracy. Justice Roberts stated:

> The legislature's and the governor's power are not unlimited. The Governor is a check upon the spending power of the legislature within our established system of checks and balances. Therefore, the legislature may spend as it sees best just as the Governor may veto bills under [Section] 73 and [Section] 72 as he sees best, but both must still operate within the constitutional parameters established by the drafters of our constitution.[61]

It is not unusual for one branch of government to challenge another branch if one believes that the other is not following the constitution, and it is the judicial branch's job to act without delay when the constitutionality of an issue is presented. Justice Roberts mentioned in his concluding statement that the "Court, as the third branch, recognizes that the other two branches [...] were and are motivated by the best of intentions and good faith as each performs necessary acts of governance. For those necessary acts of governance to continue, disputes involving separation of powers must be resolved as they arise."[62]

Expenditure Limitations

Fordice believed that "state government expenditures should not be driven exclusively by increasing revenue" and that recurring general fund expenditures should be capped.[63] Fordice consistently preached the need to limit the growth of government during his first couple of years in office and decided to go a step further in his FY 1996 budget recommendation when he proposed a Taxpayers Bill of Rights (TABOR) initiative, which he referred to as the most important component of his budget recommendation.[64] The primary reason that Fordice wanted to limit the growth of government was to use the savings to reduce taxes.

The TABOR initiative proposed by Fordice consisted of reducing Mississippi's individual income tax, along with multiple fiscal recommendations that Fordice referred to as the Mississippi Fiscal Responsibility Act of 1995. The tax reduction plan proposed was to reduce the individual income tax by $77.6 million over a three-year period by increasing the personal exemption for all filing categories, especially the "married" category that penalized married couples. The fiscal responsibility act comprised multiple suggestions for improving Mississippi's long-term financial health, but the primary purpose was to limit future expenditures. "By placing real limits on spending and employment growth, this proposal would focus state government on priority setting, program review and increased efficiency," stated Fordice.[65]

Enhanced expenditure limits and state employee limits were two components of the act that would have resulted in the most savings for the state. The enhanced expenditure limits recommended that the legislature uphold the existing 98 percent limitation on appropriation of general funds, and it also included a formula-driven method for limiting annual growth. According to the plan, annual growth in total general fund appropriations was not to exceed an expenditure growth limit calculated as the prior three-year average of: (1) the inflation rate plus the percentage change in the state's population and (2) the percentage change in the state's total personal income. The other cost-saving measure suggested capping total state government employment at the FY 1996 level for three fiscal years. At the conclusion of the three-year period, yearly growth in employment would be prohibited from exceeding the greater of the average percentage change in the state's population for the prior three years or 1 percent.

The legislature rejected the Mississippi Fiscal Responsibility Act of 1995[66] in its entirety, with the exception of adhering to the 98 percent limitation. Seeing that there was no appetite in the legislature for his suggestions, Fordice did not recommend the act the next year. However, he did take a few ideas from the act and incorporated them into his 1996 Fiscal Legislative Agenda. Fordice realized that he could not force the legislature to put in place a limitation on expenditures, but he did have control over executive agencies. At the beginning of the FY 1998 budget process, Fordice imposed general fund budget request mandates on his executive agencies for the purpose of initiating limits on expenditure growth in state government.[67] Fordice's proactive decision to initiate executive branch expenditure limitations was successful, resulting in a general fund savings that contributed to the legislature's decision to phase in the elimination of the income tax marriage penalty by year 2000.

Expenditures for Capital Needs

Fordice believed that capital projects should be funded with general fund appropriations and not with proceeds from general obligation bonds. "I continue to be concerned about the growth of Mississippi's bonded indebtedness and feel that the State should fund capital expenditures with existing revenue whenever possible," explained Fordice in his EBR for FY 1995.[68] The governor's request was not too much to ask for, considering that the legislature had expressed the same sentiments only a few years earlier. Fordice's plan to use existing revenue for capital projects was not a new concept; it was actually the method used by the legislature to fund capital needs, especially repairs and renovations, prior to the Ray Mabus Administration.

The legislature lost its way when revenue began to decline in the late 1980s, and Mabus's recommendation to issue general obligation bonds for capital needs seemed to be the best solution at the time. The legislature passed S.B. 3192 during the 1990 legislative session, which provided for a total general obligation bonding authority of $69,485,000.[69] At the beginning of the bill, the legislature provided a statement pointing out how it had historically funded repairs and renovations to state-owned buildings with general funds and not bonds. The statement went on to justify the need for the bond bill by explaining that available general funds were inadequate to cover the capital project needs. The legislature expressed its intent that the bond funds issued for the capital needs were to be only a short-term solution and not a recurring practice. The following is the legislature's statement in S.B. 3192:

WHEREAS, the Mississippi Legislature has historically funded repairs and renovations to state-owned and other properties by General Fund appropriations and not with the proceeds from general obligation bonds; and

WHEREAS, the Mississippi Legislature is aware that there has been inadequate funding for repairs and renovations in recent years and now desires to make the repairs and renovations reasonably required . . . ; and

WHEREAS, the Mississippi Legislature hereby expresses its intent that future and recurring repairs and renovations shall be paid only from current funds or by a diversion of funds from the General Fund into a special fund for repairs and renovations to be appropriated only pursuant to law except that repairs and renovations that are substantially equal after renovations to new construction with a life expectancy of a new facility or that extend the useful life of the facility

for a period of time at least equal to the term of the bonds may be funded by
proceeds of a general obligation bond issued of the State of Mississippi: NOW,
THEREFORE,[70]

The above statement was to express the legislature's concerns with the recommendation made by Governor Mabus to finance capital needs in order to free up general funds to be spent on his priority agenda items. The point can easily be argued that Fordice was actually encouraging the legislature to follow its own advice from 1990.

Fordice's EBRs proved that capital improvements were a priority of his, and he provided the legislature with many capital improvement ideas. Fordice's FY 1995 EBR included $57.9 million for capital projects, and he specifically requested that the projects be funded with general fund appropriations as opposed to general obligation bonds.[71] His FY 1996 and FY 1997 recommendations both proposed the creation of a Capital Improvement Fund (CIF) that would be funded through a new end-of-the year distribution formula. After the rainy day fund was fully funded at 7.5 percent of the total general fund appropriations for the current fiscal year, 20 percent of the excess general fund balance would have been deposited into the CIF under his proposal.

Fordice was consistent in all of his EBRs when he requested that the legislature appropriate funds for capital improvements, instead of authorizing borrowing through the issuance of general obligation bonds. However, the legislature did not heed his advice and continued to finance capital projects, and debt service payments continued to grow and grow. The appropriation for debt services, which pays the state's principal and interest on bonds issued, increased from $22,253,413, or 1.1 percent of general funds appropriated in FY 1992, to $158,815,473, or 4.6 percent of general funds appropriated in FY 2000.[72] Excluding interest payments, the state's general obligation bonded indebtedness for principal alone grew from $634,933,000 in FY 1992 to $2,014,076,000 in FY 2000, a whopping increase of 217 percent.[73]

Gubernatorial Vetoes

"Gov. Kirk Fordice will be remembered for a number of things in Mississippi history books, particularly his vetoes—both the number and magnitude. The state's first Republican governor this century has never been shy about wielding his veto pen," reported the Associated Press in 1998.[74] Fordice was unfortunately a Republican tasked with working with a legislature that had been heavily dominated by Democrats for over one hundred years. At the time Fordice was elected, Democrats controlled 94 of 122 house seats and 39 of 52 senate seats.[75] With a supermajority in both chambers, the Democrats had the power to override any of Fordice's vetoes and put a stop to any of his taxing and spending ideas that ran counter to the legislature's ideas.

A number of Fordice's vetoes were attempts to control spending. Fordice vetoed more spending-related bills than the total number of bills vetoed by his predecessor Gov. Ray Mabus. Fordice vetoed twenty-five spending-related bills alone—thirteen appropriation bills and twelve revenue bills. Fordice vetoed or partially vetoed a total of 107 bills during his time in office, which does not include the twenty-nine partially vetoed bills (two bond bills and twenty-seven appropriation bills) passed in 1993 that were ruled null by the courts.[76] The partial vetoes of the twenty-nine spending bills were not recognized in the General Laws of Mississippi of 1993 by Secretary of State Dick Molpus, who later unsuccessfully challenged Fordice for governor in 1995, on the basis of a May 11, 1993, attorney general's opinion stating that the attempted partial vetoes were null and void.[77] Although the partial vetoes were not recognized in the law books, 1993 was still the year that Fordice vetoed the most bills, having vetoed twenty-two. It is no surprise that Fordice vetoed more bills than Governors Allain and Mabus combined, because he was a Republican working with a legislature dominated by Democrats. Allain and Mabus were both Democrats working with a Democratic legislature, but they both still vetoed bills. Allain vetoed a total of thirty bills, and Mabus vetoed a total of twenty-three.

Although political affiliation contributed to Fordice vetoing so many bills, a lack of relationships likely played a larger role. The governor's "construction boss" approach to interpersonal relationships limited his ability to influence legislators in either party. Additionally, Fordice typically removed himself from the legislative process and made little effort to influence bills, and then he would surprise the legislature with his unannounced vetoes.[78] Things began to get a little better for Fordice in his second term, when he vetoed fewer bills. Of the 107 total vetoes, only thirty-seven came during Fordice's second term.[79]

Chapter 7

A Progressive Approach to Budgeting under Musgrove

Ronnie Musgrove was very familiar with Mississippi's budget-making process when he was elected governor,[1] having served two four-year terms in the Mississippi Senate and one four-year term as lieutenant governor. Musgrove served on the Senate Appropriations Committee while a member of the legislature, and later as chair of the Joint Legislative Budget Committee (JLBC) while serving as lieutenant governor. Despite his budget knowledge and experience with the budget-making process, Musgrove had a desire to reform the process. "I am recommending a progressive approach to budgeting as a first step toward reforming the budgeting process," explained Musgrove in his executive budget recommendation (EBR).[2] What Musgrove meant by budget reform was that he wanted more executive involvement and agency autonomy.

Musgrove understood that the executive branch had very little control over the legislatively dominated budget-making process and knew that in order for him to accomplish his fiscal goals as governor, he would have to be included more in the budget process. The lack of executive power over the budget process allowed Musgrove to accomplish his fiscal goals while serving as lieutenant governor. Musgrove realized that in order for him to continue with the success that he started as lieutenant governor, he would have to shift some of the power away from the legislative branch to the executive branch. He would later find out that shifting power away from the legislature would be much more challenging than he expected.

Musgrove's goals and experiences in office closely mirrored those of former Gov. Ray Mabus. Both of them intended to change government drastically, especially in the area of education. At the top of both of their agendas was to raise teachers' salaries. Mabus was successful in getting a substantial teacher pay raise; however, he fell short of meeting his goal of getting the salaries to the "southeastern average." Musgrove too wanted to raise teacher salaries to the southeastern average, and he was successful. Another similarity between Musgrove and Mabus was that both wanted to increase the largest general fund expenditure, K–12 public education, but neither of them wanted a major tax increase. Like Mabus, Musgrove experienced a national recession that negatively affected revenue while in office, which lasted eight months.[3] In Musgrove's case, the recession was at the beginning of his term, and not in the middle as with Mabus, so revenue had time to somewhat rebound. However, revenue did not rebound enough to keep pace with expenditures, which forced Musgrove to cut budgets in FY 2002 by approximately $54 million, and again in FY 2003 by another $54 million.[4]

Governor Musgrove was successful in obtaining more funding for public education throughout his term in office, but the argument can be made that the legislature wanted to increase funding too and would have done so anyway. Musgrove campaigned on improving education, which contributed greatly to him being elected governor. Individual legislators understood that Mississippians had an appetite for increasing K–12 public education funding, and realized that their own legislative seats could be in jeopardy if they denied what was clearly in demand. Legislators likely did not view increasing funding for education as a win for Musgrove, as much as they viewed it as giving the people what they wanted. Nevertheless, the public did view the education increase as a win for the governor, and Musgrove's contributions to the discussion did influence the outcome. The legislature allowed Musgrove to be a part of the education decision making, which resulted in multiple wins for the governor. However, the legislature refused to increase executive involvement in budget decision making or give up any of its legislative budget authority, not even for an old legislative colleague. Before Musgrove's fiscal accomplishments are addressed, this chapter first discusses how Musgrove attempted to alter the budget-making process by inserting himself more into that process.

Unconventional Budget Proposals

Musgrove came into the governorship under unusual circumstances, being that he chaired the JLBC responsible for constructing the FY 2001 legislative budget recommendation (LBR). Because of his involvement in the legislative recommendation, he did not see a need to submit a FY 2001 EBR and elected to use the LBR in its place. This had never been done before, because Musgrove was the only governor who had served as lieutenant governor since the creation of the JLBC in 1984. The FY 2001 LBR was typical, and it used the revenue figure jointly adopted by the JLBC and the governor, which was nearly $200,000,000 over the revised FY 2000 figure. The actual revenue amount adopted was $3,632,500,000 in general fund receipts, or 5.8 percent over the previous fiscal year.[5] The law that requires the governor to submit an EBR does not specify whether the LBR can be used as the EBR, but it must have not been a problem, because the legality of the action was not challenged.

Legislators seemed to have accepted Musgrove's unorthodox recommendation (or lack thereof) for FY 2001, but they were not pleased with the approach taken by the governor when submitting his FY 2002 EBR. Musgrove took the legislature completely by surprise when he submitted his EBR on September 7, 2000, and made an unprecedented budget presentation revealing his recommendation. The biggest problem with the early submission of Musgrove's FY 2002 EBR was that it was released before the joint revenue estimate was adopted. Musgrove came up with his own revenue estimate for FY 2002, and the executive estimated amount assumed a growth of 5.3 percent over previous fiscal years.[6] Musgrove's predecessors likely never used this practice because it was clearly against the law.

Musgrove intended for his FY 2002 EBR to be different from other executive recommendations—he wanted his document to be useful to the legislature. He explained in his letter of transmittal:

Following this letter, you will find my budget recommendation for the Fiscal Year 2002. The format is significantly different from years past, and the content is organized differently in an effort to make the executive budget more useful and more accessible. From the table of contents to the index and glossary, you will find information designed to illuminate the budgeting process and clarify this administration's priorities.[7]

Musgrove's FY 2002 EBR was also very detailed and proposed many things, some of which were typical and others atypical. He proposed reducing some agency budgets, which was not unusual or different from other governors' proposals. The aberrant recommendations came when Musgrove suggested securitizing settlement funds expected from American Management Systems (AMS), a Virginia-based software company, and legislative approval for "lump sum" spending authority for agencies.

Musgrove referred to his recommended budget reductions as his 5 percent "budget reserve" plan, and he projected a savings of $81 million.[8] His plan exempted a few priority areas, such as education, Medicaid, and highway patrol. Musgrove's plan for agency heads to receive lump sum spending authority was to give them more flexibility in prioritizing agency spending. It was well within Musgrove's authority to request his 5 percent budget reserve plan and his lump sum plan, but the latter received lots of criticism from the legislature. House Speaker Tim Ford, who also chaired the JLBC that year, said that the 5 percent budget reserve plan might work but not the lump sum spending authority. Ford explained that agencies would "put monies in personnel and then come back and say we need more for equipment."[9] Longtime JLBC member Sen. Jack Gordon, who chaired the Senate Appropriations Committee at the time, believed that Musgrove's request for lump sum spending authority was a way to encroach on the legislature's authority. "What this does is attempt to take all the appropriation authority from the Legislature into the governor's office," explained Senator Gordon.[10]

Regardless of how the legislature felt about Musgrove's recommendations to adopt his 5 percent budget reserve plan and the request for lump sum spending authority in his FY 2002 EBR, no legislator questioned the legality of him making those requests. However, some legislators did question whether the governor could use the proposed savings from securitizing the AMS settlement in his EBR. To securitize settlement payments is to sell the future payments to investors for a reduced upfront sum. State Tax Commission chairman and Commissioner of Revenue Ed Buelow told lawmakers that the total settlement would be approximately $185 million, and the payments would be paid out over multiple years beginning in 2001.[11] The governor's office believed that securitization of the assets would bring the state $93,935,730.[12] Some legislators believed that this practice was a violation of state law, because revenues considered in the EBR and the LBR were supposed to be those that were currently available under existing law and not what would be available if proposed laws were enacted.[13]

Musgrove must have been informed later that governors are prohibited from using additional funding sources in an EBR, other than what is jointly adopted with the JLBC, because a supplemental budget recommendation accompanied his FY 2003 EBR. Musgrove's FY 2002 EBR plan to securitize future settlement payments was very unusual, and things got even stranger in his FY 2003 EBR. In order to make his budget work, the governor proposed using tobacco settlement revenue (the law directed the settlement payments to the Health Care Trust Fund), electronic fund transfers of accelerated tax collections, plus a diversion of state aid road revenue in a supplemental budget recommendation. The supplemental summary read:

In accordance with Section 27-103-139 of the MS Code, these supplemental recommendations are made separately from the executive budget recommendation.

Funding is recommended with tobacco settlement revenue ($209,029,286 annual payment received 12/01, $53,368,197 expendable fund balance forward, and $144,250,000 annual payment 12/02), net of $69,622,207 FY 02 appropriations plus $100,000,000 in electronic funds transfers plus a diversion of $48,000,000 of state aid road revenue.

The Governor recommends $100,000,000 of electronic funds transfers and the $48,000,000 state aid road revenue to address the FY 02 Medicaid deficit ($148,000,000—see Executive Budget Recommendation—Statement I). The Governor recommends the balance of the two referenced tobacco settlement annual payments ($283,657,079) be dedicated to Medicaid and the expendable balance ($53,368,197) be dedicated to Mental Health as shown in the supplementary recommendation.[14]

Musgrove's proposal received mixed reviews, many of them critical. Senator Gordon explained that Musgrove's proposal to use tobacco settlement revenue was not a new one, because Sen. Hob Bryan suggested diverting tobacco settlement funds before the Health Care Trust Fund was established in 1999. Furthermore, Gordon mentioned that he doubted Musgrove's plan would go anywhere because of the large amount of funds proposed by the governor. "I think it's going to be very difficult. Politically, the Legislature has chosen not to go into the trust fund. I think we will be looking to divert some of the money on a one-time basis to try to compensate our people more bearably," said Gordon.[15] In reference to the Health Care Trust Fund, Rep. Steve Holland, who worked closely with the Medicaid executive director on the Medicaid budget shortfall, said, "There will be great philosophical debate. Some feel it (the trust fund) is very sacred. I'm one of those."[16]

From the beginning, revenue experts found flaws in Musgrove's recommended $100 million in electronic fund transfers of accelerated tax collections. When asked about the governor's budget plan to escalate tax collections to generate $100 million, Commissioner Buelow stated, "It's not going to work."[17] Not only was Buelow knowledgeable about revenue, he was also very familiar with the budget-making process. Prior to being appointed chairman of the State Tax Commission in 1992, Buelow served in the legislature and was a member of both the House Appropriations Committee and the JLBC. Being very experienced with revenue and budgets, Buelow notified the governor's office that Musgrove's budget plan was flawed before the governor released it, but to no avail.

Buelow informed Musgrove's chief of staff, Bill Renick, that tax collection escalations would bring in only about half of what the governor anticipated. The governor based his proposal on the premise of electronic fund transfers of tax payments being made weekly by 4,200 Mississippi companies that pay more than $20,000 monthly in state sales and use taxes rather than the present monthly collections. "Only one of those 4,200 taxpayers is using electronic transfers presently. It would cost the Tax Commission $450,000 to get equipped to handle electronic transfers from these taxpayers at 100 percent compliance," said Buelow.[18] Buelow went on to explain that as a practical matter, conversion to a weekly capture of taxes would actually result in the commission collecting three weekly payments per month instead of four. The commission "would collect only about 75 percent of what the governor is estimating," explained Buelow. "We told them that."[19] Furthermore, the $100 million figure referenced by Musgrove was for gross tax collections that did not take into consideration a myriad of statutory tax diversions.[20]

It is ironic that Musgrove did not take the diversions into consideration when constructing his tax acceleration plan, because he, similar to Buelow, had previously served on the Appropriations Committee and on the JLBC and was very familiar with the revenue diversion process. There must have been some merit to Musgrove's acceleration tax plan, because the legislature passed a bill that did something very similar. The legislature passed H.B. 1379 during the 2002 legislative session,[21] which accelerated tax collections for a portion of revenues collected for income withholdings, sales taxes, and use taxes. The bill also revised the insurance premium tax payments. The legislature directed the FY 2003 accelerated tax collections to the Budget Contingency Fund,[22] created a year earlier, which could receive funding from any funding source. The anticipated amount that H.B. 1379 was thought to generate was $119,200,000.[23]

Musgrove's FY 2003 supplemental budget recommendation, minus federal funds, totaled $337,025,276.[24] His FY 2004 supplemental budget recommendation totaled $492,171,470, which included the following: $270,171,470 cash on hand; $102,000,000 of the December 2003 annual tobacco settlement payment; $60,000,000 in bond proceeds; $50,000,000 from the Working Cash-Stabilization Reserve Fund; and $10,000,000 of interest earned on the Health Care Trust Fund.[25] A majority of the supplemental revenue recommended in FY 2003 and FY 2004 was for Medicaid, which totaled $283,657,079 and $271,179,540, respectively.[26] The legislature did not follow Musgrove's plan to fund Medicaid, but it did find ways to keep the agency afloat without having to increase the funding levels significantly.

The legislature tolerated Musgrove's unusual budget recommendations but ended up rejecting most of his peculiar proposals. Although Musgrove intended for his EBRs to be useful in the budget-making process, the legislature treated his recommendations similar to the way that it had treated previous governors' recommendations, which was largely to ignore them. However, business as usual was not an option for constructing the budget in the early 2000s, because of the revenue situation. Governor Musgrove was not afraid to think outside the box to come up with solutions to the budget problem, regardless of whether the legislature elected to use his ideas or not. The legislature had to make hard budget decisions throughout the Musgrove Administration, but one such decision, which had a lasting effect on fiscal policy in Mississippi, was the decision to suspend the 2 percent set-aside requirement in order to appropriate 100 percent of anticipated revenue collections. Sen. Jack Gordon was the principal author of S.B. 2542, passed during the 2003 legislative session, which allowed the legislature to appropriate 100 percent of anticipated revenue for FY 2004 only.[27] Unfortunately, FY 2004 would not be the last time the legislature would suspend the 2 percent set-aside requirement in order to make the budget work.

Musgrove's Attempt to Strengthen Executive Budget Authority

Mississippi's constitution clearly favors the legislative branch of government in the budget-making process, and there are two ways for a governor to be more involved in that process. The first way is to reform the process, and the second way is to work in collaboration with the legislature. Although many governors attempted to reform the budget-making process in a way that provided more power to the executive branch, no action was more beneficial to the executive branch than when Bill Allain as attorney general filed a "separation of powers" case that forced legislators to vacate their seats on executive boards and commissions.[28] Gov. Ray Mabus, to a lesser extent than Allain, was also successful when he lobbied to establish the Department of Finance and Administration (DFA). Governor Fordice was not able to change the budget-making process to favor the executive branch, and neither was Governor Musgrove—but Musgrove sure did attempt to.

After being elected governor, Musgrove never hid the fact that he wanted to reform the budget-making process so that the executive branch could have more say in it. "A budgeting process that includes both the governor and the Legislature provides a greater opportunity at allowing both . . . to accomplish their purpose," he explained.[29] It seems ironic that Musgrove, in such a short period of time, became such an advocate for more executive inclusion in the budget-making process, seeing that he never volunteered to relinquish legislative budget authority when he served as a legislator or when he presided over the senate as lieutenant governor. Governor Musgrove never requested being a part of the appropriation process, but he did want to give his office a stronger role in shaping budget priorities. "The Legislature has the responsibility and the duty to appropriate dollars," and the "governor and the executive branch have the responsibility of [. . .] producing the vision and matching the budget to meet that vision," explained Musgrove.[30] Musgrove's concept of the executive branch being responsible for producing a vision did not seem to have applied to former Governor Fordice's low-tax, low-spend vision, because it appeared that then-Lieutenant Governor Musgrove, at the time, wanted the legislature to appropriate funds while also producing the vision.

Legislators responded to Musgrove's request to be more involved in the budget-making process in the same way that they responded to previous governors—by rejecting it. The Appropriations Committee chairmen in both the house and senate agreed that Musgrove's idea was a bad one. "We're certainly not going to turn the budget process over to the governor," explained House Appropriations Committee chairman Charlie Capps.[31] With similar sentiments, Senate Appropriations Committee chairman Gordon said that the legislature was not about to "hand over budget-writing powers to a governor."[32]

Musgrove's Fiscal Accomplishments

Musgrove's fiscal accomplishments consisted of the following: (1) encouraging the legislature to significantly increase funding for public education, (2) calling a special session to remove the link between the K–12 teacher pay raises and economic growth, and (3) forcing the legislature to prioritize public education funding over all other state agencies. Musgrove campaigned on raising teacher salaries to the southeastern average and was successful at getting the legislature to provide the funding. The legislature heeded his advice and increased teacher salaries by amending H.B. 1134, passed during the 2000 legislative session, to include teacher pay raises, but the pay raises were tied to 5 percent economic growth.[33] The total five-year teacher pay increase was $337,916,316, and was set to begin in FY 2002.[34] The governor was not happy about the economic growth trigger and called a special session to have it removed the next year. The legislature passed H.B. 1 during the First Extraordinary Session of 2001, which removed the growth requirement.[35] Musgrove was also successful in getting the 2003 legislature to appropriate funds for total education (K–12, community and junior colleges, and institutions of higher learning) at the beginning of the 2003 legislative session, instead of at the end, before funding the rest of state government.

Funding for K–12 Public Education

Musgrove made it clear—when he served as a legislator, lieutenant governor, and gubernatorial candidate—that education was his top priority. Although education on all levels benefited from Musgrove's leadership, K–12 public education benefited the most. Prior to being elected to statewide office, Musgrove served in the Mississippi Senate and chaired the Senate Education Committee. Musgrove chaired the committee during a time when education was highly prioritized. Not only was education appropriated more funding during that time, the sales tax was also increased (by S.B. 3120, passed during the 1992 legislative session) by 1 percent, with a majority of the proceeds going to K–12 public education.[36] Although S.B. 3120 (known as the "Education Bill") came out of the Senate Finance Committee, and not the Senate Education Committee, Musgrove was instrumental in getting funds directed to K–12 public education.

K–12 public education experienced even more success after Musgrove was elected lieutenant governor. Not only was education being funded at historic levels, the senate under Musgrove's leadership also passed S.B. 2649 during the 1997 legislative session, which revised the funding formula for the Mississippi Adequate Education Program (MAEP) to achieve stable and sufficient funding of public schools.[37] The bill also provided for the issuance of state bonds for specific educational purposes. Musgrove's pro-education agenda and vision as lieutenant governor further increased his reputation as a major proponent of education.

Musgrove's vision as lieutenant governor carried over to his vision as governor, and at the top of his fiscal agenda was even more funding for public education. Since Musgrove used the LBR as his EBR for FY 2001, his first official EBR was submitted for the FY 2002 budget, which recommended funding total K–12 public education at $1,525,868,918 in general funds.[38] Although the legislature funded public education a little lower than Musgrove's EBR, it was still a significant increase over the previous fiscal year. The legislature's FY 2002 general fund appropriation for total K–12 public education was $1,491,006,940, which was just over $48 million above the amount appropriated in FY 2001.[39] The next EBR submitted by Musgrove was for FY 2003, in which he recommended that K–12 public education be funded at $1,583,127,037 in general funds.[40] The legislature again denied Musgrove's total request but did fund education at a much higher level than in the previous fiscal year. The legislature's FY 2003 general fund appropriation for total K–12 public education was $1,518,881,763, which was nearly $28 million above FY 2002.[41]

The total appropriation for K–12 public education accounted for approximately 39 percent of general funds appropriated when Musgrove first took office; the amount appropriated for FY 2000 was $1,368,117,338.[42] By the time Musgrove left office in 2004, after a failed reelection bid, K–12 public education had a total appropriation of $1,519,596,940.[43] Total K–12 public education increased by $151,479,602, or 11 percent during the Musgrove Administration, and Musgrove left office with K–12 public education accounting for just over 44 percent of appropriated general funds.[44]

Governor Musgrove's inability to get the exact amount requested for K–12 public education was insignificant in the big scheme of things; the significant educational accomplishment came when Musgrove persuaded the legislature to increase K–12 teacher salaries to the southeastern average, plus getting the economic growth trigger removed during a special session.[45] The teacher pay schedule, according to HB 1134, required the following estimated funding levels: $23,072,568 in FY 2002; $67,197,821 in FY 2003; 68,365,551 in FY 2004; $89,506,854 in FY 2005; and $89,773,522 in FY 2006.[46] There was very little controversy between the governor and legislature regarding the teacher pay increase. The controversy came when the legislature, led by Lt. Gov. Amy Tuck, added the provision that teacher pay increases would not take place in any fiscal year in which general fund revenue did not increase by at least 5 percent.

H.B. 1134 did not originally include a 5 percent growth trigger. The trigger was added when Sen. Mike Chaney along with Sen. Alice Harden offered an amendment that eventually passed, which stated that the teacher pay increase will go into effect "[p]rovided, however, that in the event the sine die general fund revenue estimate increase for fiscal year 2002 is at least five percent (5%), as certified by the Legislative Budget Office to the State Board of Education."[47] Musgrove signed H.B. 1134 into law, but he publicly criticized the legislature, after the legislative session ended, for adding the 5 percent trigger. Musgrove explained during a news conference that "because of the legislators' actions, our teachers are not guaranteed a pay raise in the future. The Legislature has played games with our teachers . . . our children's education [and] with all of us."[48] After receiving lots of political pressure, House Speaker Tim Ford and Lieutenant Governor Tuck held a news conference announcing their support for removing the pay increase trigger. Musgrove called a special session the next year for the sole purpose of removing the 5 percent trigger, and the legislature passed H.B. 1, removing the trigger.[49] Musgrove's lobbying efforts paid off in getting the trigger removed, and K–12 public education benefited greatly from the governor's constant support. However, Musgrove's success in securing additional funding for K–12 public education came at the expense of other state agencies, including public higher education. Because of the depressed economy, which caused revenue to decline, there was no way to increase K–12 public education funding without cutting most of the other agencies.

Musgrove Prioritizes Total Public Education

Higher education, which includes the public community and junior colleges, along with the public universities, did not benefit from Musgrove's pro-education agenda as K–12 public education did. Total higher education received less year-over-year funding a majority of the time that Musgrove was in office. Furthermore, higher education was also subject to the governor's budget cuts. This is not to say that Musgrove and the legislature did not support higher education; there was simply not enough revenue available to increase teacher salaries and increase funding for higher education, because of the sluggish economy. However, Musgrove placed more of an emphasis on higher education than he placed on other state agencies and proved this by calling on the legislature to fund total education before funding the rest of government for FY 2004. He also wanted a larger percentage of appropriations to go toward total education. Musgrove wanted kindergarten through senior college funded at 62 percent of general and supplemental funds appropriated.[50]

All appropriation bills are typically passed at the end of the legislative session, so one could imagine the surprise of the 2003 legislature when Musgrove announced during his January 9 State of the State address that he wanted education to be prioritized as one appropriation bill and handled as the first line of business. "Pass that appropriation bill, put it on my desk and I will sign it—and I'm not talking about the third week of March, I'm talking about the third week of January," said Musgrove.[51] Legislators were doubtful that the governor would actually get his request. For example, outgoing House Speaker Tim Ford dismissed Musgrove's idea saying that if the legislature "fund[s] education early, it leaves other agencies in need."[52] The result was that the 2003 legislature followed Musgrove's advice by passing one appropriation bill early in the session, which funded total education at nearly 62 percent of the state's $3.5 billion general fund budget, for the first time in the state's history.[53] The actual amount of general funds appropriated for kindergarten through higher education (including university agricultural educational units) was 61.4 percent of general funds appropriated.[54] Unfortunately, the approximately 62 percent funding level, which was mentioned in Musgrove's FY 2004 EBR as well as the State of the State address, was all that he received from the legislature pertaining to his pro-education initiative that year. The rest of his recommendation was a bust.

Musgrove's FY 2004 EBR proposed a bold recommendation for higher education. The governor proposed the "Mississippi Brain Trust," which would have provided $200 million over ten years for higher education—$20 million annually beginning in FY 2004. The FY 2004 supplemental budget recommendation discussed earlier totaling $492,171,470 set aside $20 million for higher education—$15 million for universities and $5 million for community colleges. This plan showed that Musgrove prioritized higher education, as well as K-12, but the legislature rejected Musgrove's Mississippi Brain Trust plan in its entirety. Higher education actually received a year-over-year decrease in FY 2014.

Education Reserves

Education reserves have been utilized in Mississippi to provide additional funding for educational purposes since the late 1980s. H.B. 601, passed during the 1988 legislative session, created the Education Reserve Fund, and the bill provided that any unencumbered general fund cash remaining at the end of the fiscal year was to be transferred to the newly created fund until the fund had a balance of $50 million.[55] S.B. 3120 repealed the Education Reserve Fund in 1992, and that same bill created the Education Enhancement Fund.[56] The Education Enhancement Fund took the place of the Education Reserve Fund in the diversion process. Diverting unencumbered general fund cash balances at year's end to education reserve accounts was a long practice accepted by both the executive and legislative branches of government in Mississippi. Things drastically changed during the 2001 legislative session when the legislature proposed abolishing the diversion to the Education Enhancement Fund from the unencumbered year-end general fund cash balance.

Rep. Herb Frierson proposed H.B. 776 during the 2001 legislative session, which recommended amending the law to delete the diversion provision that required 50 percent of the unencumbered year-end general fund cash balance to be transferred into the Education Enhancement Fund. Under the new proposal, the 50 percent of the unencumbered cash balance that was currently going to the Education Enhancement Fund would now go to the general fund. The bill stated, "Unencumbered cash in the General Fund may be used for new year cash flow needs and may also be used for deficit appropriations or regular appropriations."[57] The action taken by the legislature was in response to the down economy. H.B. 776 passed both chambers and went to the governor, and Musgrove vetoed the bill on March 30, 2001. In Musgrove's veto message for H.B. 776, he explained that he was returning the bill without his approval and stated:

> Education is the priority of the administration. The state must ensure that K–12 education is adequately funded to provide an effective education to our students. Rather than providing secure and responsible funding sources for K–12 education, House Bill No. 776 simply shuffles existing revenue sources to address Fiscal Year 2001 deficits and Fiscal Year 2002 expenses. The Legislature's diversion of existing resources for our teachers, our classrooms and our students does not ensure adequate funding.[58]

After Musgrove vetoed H.B. 776, the veto was returned to the legislature, and the house and senate both voted to override the governor's veto. H.B. 776 was only one of many spending-related bills that Musgrove vetoed, and it was not the only veto overridden by the legislature. A majority of Musgrove's spending related vetoes were overridden.[59] The sluggish economy likely contributed to the fiscal disagreements between the governor and the legislature, and the relationship might have been better if the economy had been better.

Poor Economic Conditions and an Untimely Recovery

Neither Musgrove nor the legislature were able to fund priority items the way they wanted because of the weak economy. The national economy went into a recession in March 2001, and Mississippi went into recession soon after. The national recession lasted from March 2001 to November 2001.[60] Even after the national recession had concluded, Mississippi's revenue remained sluggish, making it very challenging for the governor and lawmakers to find ways to increase government spending without increasing revenue. Not only did the governor and legislature disagree on funding priorities after the recession, they also disagreed on revenue estimating.

Musgrove agreed with the legislature on revenue estimates prior to the recession, because both sides were very optimistic about expected growth. For the FY 2001 budget, both the governor and the JLBC accepted the revenue estimating committee's recommendation of $199 million, or 5.8 percent anticipated over the revised revenue estimate for FY 2000.[61] As mentioned earlier, FY 2002 was the year for which Musgrove made the unprecedented move to release his EBR in September 2000, prior to a joint revenue estimate being adopted with the JLBC. Although Musgrove's FY 2002 EBR projected revenue to grow to $3,754,787,400 in general fund receipts, or 5.3 percent,[62] he concurred with the estimate adopted by the JLBC of $3,634,500,000 on November 10, 2000.[63] By March 2001 Musgrove realized that the jointly adopted FY 2002 revenue estimate of 3.7 percent was too high as well, and he pleaded with the legislature to consider appropriating funds using a smaller revenue estimate. In an explanation of why he thought that the revenue estimate was too high, Musgrove stated:

> Yesterday the U.S. Department of Commerce reported that the U.S. economy grew at an annual rate of just 1% in the fourth quarter of 2000, the weakest performance in five years. Estimates for the first quarter of 2001 suggest 0% growth. Business investments have been sharply reduced. State revenues for March are projected to be $15–$18 million below estimates, a 7% fall off. Forecasts for the coming year call for sluggish growth. These clear signals demand fiscal prudence by our state leadership.[64]

Although the Department of Commerce's report referenced by Musgrove was quite convincing as to why the FY 2002 revenue estimate adopted was likely too high, one could have come to the same conclusion by looking at what happened to Mississippi in FY 2001. The JLBC was forced to adopt a revised estimate for FY 2001 of $3,505,500,000, which was a decrease of $144.9 million from the FY 2001 sine die general fund revenue estimate; the revised FY 2001 estimate reflected a growth rate of 3.9 percent over FY 2000, which was much lower than the original projected growth rate of 5.8 percent.[65]

Musgrove not only insisted that the legislature lower the revenue estimate, he also warned that he would veto any appropriation bills based on the current revenue estimated for FY 2002.[66] Musgrove stated, "This year's legislature seems to want to ignore the downturn in our economy and asks that we swallow a budget pill that is too big. We simply will not take in the dollars necessary to fund these bills. Considering together, the budget bills total $3.541 billion in general fund dollars."[67] The legislature did not heed the governor's advice and passed the appropriation bills using the inflated revenue figure, and Musgrove responded by vetoing forty-two appropriation bills during the 2001 legislative session. The legislature voted to override all forty-two vetoes. Musgrove also vetoed five more spending-related bills that legislative session, and the legislature overrode those vetoes as well.[68]

Musgrove and the legislature obviously did not agree on the best way to solve the FY 2002 budget problem, and a major reason was the lack of agreement concerning the amount of revenue that the state would collect. The JLBC remained confident in the 3.7 percent revenue growth that was recommended by the revenue estimating committee back in October 2000. Unfortunately for the JLBC, the committee had no choice but to revise the FY 2002 revenue growth estimate downward by 0.7 percent. State Fiscal Officer Gary Anderson, under the governor's direction, reduced budgets in FY 2002 by $53.7 million because of revenue shortfalls.[69] The FY 2002 budget cuts still did not prevent withdrawals totaling $97.2 million from the rainy day fund.[70]

The revenue battle between the governor and legislature did not get any better in FY 2003. When Musgrove met with the JLBC to jointly adopt the FY 2003 revenue estimate, the revenue estimating committee recommended 4.3 percent expected revenue growth, which the JLBC agreed with. Musgrove thought that 4.3 percent was too high. Musgrove refused to concur with the optimistic revenue figure, so the JLBC adopted it without him. The FY 2003 revenue estimate adopted by the JLBC was $3,616,100,000, an increase of $149.4 million over the revised estimate for FY 2002.[71] Musgrove used a smaller revenue figure for his FY 2003 EBR; he projected revenue to be $3,456,570,649, or 2.65 percent growth.[72]

Musgrove's FY 2003 revenue pessimism landed him in a much better situation than the legislature, because the JLBC was again forced to revise the revenue estimate downward. The legislature did not adopt the JLBC's overly optimistic fall revenue estimate as the sine die general fund revenue estimate, but instead adopted a figure $41,500,000 lower for a total sine die general fund revenue estimate of $3,574,600,000. The economy continued to struggle, forcing the JLBC to lower the FY 2003 sine die general fund revenue estimate a few months later by $96.8 million, for a new FY 2003 revised estimate of $3,477,800,000.[73] Executive budget cuts for FY 2003 totaled $53,985,549.[74] Similar to the previous fiscal year, the FY 2003 budget cuts still did not prevent withdrawals from the rainy day fund totaling $99,559,388.

Revenue estimating for FY 2004 was not contentious, and a revenue estimate was jointly adopted. The revenue estimating committee recommended a FY 2004 increase of $104.3 million, or 3 percent over the revised estimate for FY 2003. The total amount recommended by the revenue estimating committee and eventually adopted as the sine die general fund revenue estimate was $3,582,100,000. The governor and the JLBC had reason to believe that FY 2004 would be better, because the state economy was starting to recover. When presenting the FY 2004 revenue estimate, as recommended by the revenue estimating committee, the state economist explained that "the economy is improving and will continue to improve through FY 2004. The economic indicators for Mississippi project a 4.8 percent increase in the gross state product."[75] Gross state product for FY 2003 was 3.7 percent, so the 1.1 percent gain was seen as a positive for both the JLBC and governor. Unfortunately, the optimism regarding revenue for FY 2004 did not prevent the JLBC from having to revise the FY 2004 revenue estimate downward. The JLBC ended up lowering the FY 2004 estimate down to $3,522,100,000, a decrease of $60 million from the FY 2004 sine die general fund revenue estimate.[76] A withdrawal from the rainy day fund was necessary once again for FY 2004, for an amount totaling $110,303,639,[77] but there were no budget cuts made during that fiscal year.

Gubernatorial Vetoes

Very few legislators anticipated the constant bickering between Musgrove and the legislature. Musgrove had worked with legislators in both chambers when he presided over the senate as lieutenant governor, and he was successful in getting the necessary votes in the senate to override many of Fordice's gubernatorial vetoes. Needless to say, the cooperative effort diminished once Musgrove became governor. The collaborative effort between then–Lieutenant Governor Musgrove and House Speaker Tim Ford attributed a lot to Musgrove's legislative accomplishments.[78] However, Speaker Ford got pretty frustrated with Governor Musgrove concerning his lack of communication with the legislature. Speaker Ford wanted a healthy working relationship with the governor, although many legislators were fed up with Musgrove. "He's got some mending to do with the general membership. I don't like arguing with the governor. I know the public wants us to work together," explained Ford, speaking about Musgrove.[79] Although Ford tried diligently to work with Musgrove, that did not stop him from siding with the legislature to override many of the governor's vetoes.

Many of Musgrove's vetoes were spending related, similar to those of his predecessor Kirk Fordice, who vetoed twenty-five spending-related bills—which seemed high at the time compared to previous governors.[80] Musgrove, on the other hand, vetoed more spending bills in 2001 alone than Fordice did in all eight years in office. He vetoed a total of fifty-eight bills that legislative session, and most of the vetoed bills were appropriation bills. The legislature overrode forty-seven of the fifty-eight vetoes during the 2001 session.[81] Musgrove vetoed a total of eighty-eight bills during his four-year term in office.

Some of the bills that Musgrove vetoed, which vetoes were eventually overridden by the legislature, would have drastically changed fiscal policy had his vetoes stood. One such bill was S.B. 2680, passed during the 2001 legislative session, which created the Budget Contingency Fund.[82] The Budget Contingency Fund was set up as a special fund that could receive funding from any funding source. However, S.B. 2680 specifically redirected the state's share of proceeds collected from oil and gas severance taxes to the Budget Contingency Fund. The bill stated that the funds deposited into the Budget Contingency Fund would then be used for the support of the Minimum Education Program or the MAEP, as successor to the Minimum Education Program, until FY 2006.[83]

S.B. 2680 passed out of both chambers and went to Musgrove for his signature. Musgrove believed that the creation of the Budget Contingency Fund was unnecessary and vetoed the bill. In his veto message, Musgrove explained:

> There is no need to create a Budget Contingency Fund. I agreed that we needed a bridge for higher education. This could have been accomplished without the creation of the fund. This action compounds the budget problem for the short and long term. Senate Bill No. 2680 provides for the creation of the Budget Contingency Fund. These funds are appropriated to 24 different state departments and agencies. No repealer of the Budget Contingency Fund has been provided for in Senate Bill No. 2680 potentially creating an uncontrolled Legislative fund. If this is indeed a bridge, there should be a repealer on the fund.[84]

Musgrove stated that he could not sign S.B. 2680 in good conscience without asking the legislature to reconsider their efforts. The legislature decided to override the veto the same day that Musgrove vetoed the bill. Musgrove's description of the Budget Contingency Fund as an "uncontrolled legislative fund" truly sums up the fund. The legislature was able to deposit funds into the Budget Contingency Fund from any funding source and expend the funds any way it saw fit. During the 2001 legislative session, the legislature appropriated millions in budget contingency funds and continued that practice for the remainder of the time that Musgrove was in office, and well after he had left.

Separation of Powers Revisited

The judicial branch was forced to intervene to solve another "separation of powers" issue less than a decade after a decision in *Fordice v. Bryan* (1995) was rendered. *Barbour v. Delta Correctional Facility Authority* (2004) came about because Governor Musgrove partially vetoed an appropriation bill (S.B. 3163, passed during the 2002 legislative session) for the Mississippi Department of Corrections (MDOC).[85] This case was different from the *Fordice v. Bryan* case, because a private entity sued the governor and not legislators. Additionally, House Speaker Tim Ford requested an official opinion from Attorney General Mike Moore on the legality of the partial veto. The attorney general had to interpret whether the governor's veto of a portion of S.B. 3163 amounted to a veto of an appropriation or merely a condition of an appropriation. A lawsuit was filed, and the chancery court heard the case, followed by the Mississippi Supreme Court, concerning the constitutionality of partially vetoing an appropriation bill.

S.B. 3163 appropriated $250,190,746 in total funds to the MDOC, and it passed both legislative chambers and was sent to Musgrove. The bill appropriated funds to the following major objects of expenditure: support, medical services, parole board, farming operations, private prisons, and regional facilities. The problem came with the funds that were allocated for private prisons. Section 3 of S.B. 3163 allocated $54,726,714 in general funds to private prisons. On April 9, 2002, Musgrove approved Sections 1 and 2 of S.B. 3163 and vetoed a portion of Section 3 that dealt specifically with private prisons. In his veto message, Musgrove stated:

> Once again the special interests and the special friends of the Private Prison industry won the day, funding fully private prisons and at a higher level than our state and regional facilities. This preferential funding by itself is sufficient reason to exercise a partial veto. Yet this full funding for the Private Prisons is integrated in

Section 3 of the bill with a protective provision against any transfer of any of the funds. This restriction against transfer joined with full funding serves to insulate the Private Prison industry from the cold budgetary winds that affect all other operations of the Department of Corrections, and of State government in general.[86]

Although funding played a part in the governor's veto decision, Musgrove's frustration with S.B. 3163 seemed to be fueled more so because of a disdain for favorable treatment being given to private prisons by the legislature, and the fact that private prisons would not be subject to governor's budget cuts based on how the language was drafted. Following the partial veto, Speaker Ford requested an official opinion from the attorney general on the partial veto. In response to Ford's request, Moore explained that the "question you present is not a new one. Governor Musgrove has tried to do the same thing that a previous governor tried to do (i.e., veto conditions of appropriations), [in] which the Supreme Court subsequently declared to be null and void."[87]

Attorney General Moore issued an official opinion characterizing the vetoed language as a condition and not an appropriation. Moore opined that the governor's veto of Section 3 "constitutes an improper exercise of his Section 73 veto powers."[88] After Moore pronounced the partial veto invalid, the legislature never tried to override the partial veto, because of the attorney general's position.[89] However, Governor Musgrove argued that his veto was valid and renegotiated contracts at four private prisons and ordered the closing of the Delta prison, all after the legislature adjourned.[90]

On August 2, 2002, Delta Correctional Facility Authority (Delta) filed a motion for a temporary restraining order (TRO) and a verified complaint in the Chancery Court of Leflore County to enjoin the MDOC and the governor from closing the Delta prison.[91] Delta contended that the governor and the MDOC's termination of its contract was invalid because Governor Musgrove's partial veto was unconstitutional. Judge William G. Willard Jr. granted the TRO on August 5, 2002, which required the prison to continue operating until a hearing took place. On August 22, 2002, Attorney General Moore intervened, without objection from the parties, to argue the constitutionality of the partial veto. A one-day trial was conducted four days later, and on September 3, 2002, Judge Willard ruled that the partial veto was unconstitutional. Two days later, the governor and the MDOC appealed. Delta did not appeal, because of the attorney general's intervention; Moore responded with a brief as the appellee to the governor and the MDOC's appeal. The case went to the Mississippi Supreme Court, and the court affirmed the lower court's decision.[92]

The supreme court was divided in its decision, with four justices concurring, two dissenting, and one justice not participating.[93] Writing in the majority opinion, Justice Charles Easley explained that the court found "that the executive branch of government through a governor's use of a partial veto may not thwart or sabotage the legislative intent." S.B. 3163 clearly expressed the legislature's intentions of funding private prisons. The governor has only a qualified function and never creative legislative power, explained Justice Easley. "Thus, we find that the Governor's veto here cannot inhibit the legislative intent of the bill, nor can his veto create new legislation."[94] The supreme court concluded that the partial veto of S.B. 3163 exercised by the governor was an unconstitutional veto of a condition of an appropriation bill as written and thus a nullity.

Chapter 8

Barbour, the Influential Executive

The executive branch of government played a minor role in the budget-making process for much of Mississippi's history, until Haley Barbour was elected governor in 2003. The Mississippi Constitution of 1817, the state's first constitution, intentionally established a weak executive branch of government.[1] Mississippi's framers were reluctant to give the governor too much power because they were suspicious of a strong executive.[2] The framers of the state's current constitution, the Mississippi Constitution of 1890, shared the original framers' reluctance to provide too much formal power to the executive branch, especially regarding budget making. The 1890 constitution placed a majority of the formal budget-making power in the hands of the legislature, and Barbour was fully aware of that fact. Barbour's ability to build relationships with powerful decision makers was unmatched by many and admired by most, regardless of political affiliation. "[A]s political insiders across the ideological spectrum can attest, Haley's understanding of the levers of power—and, as a result, his access to those levers—[is] unparalleled."[3]

Contrary to popular belief, Governor Barbour did not increase the formal power of the executive branch of government; however, he did increase the informal executive power significantly. The problem with increasing informal power is that it is not automatically transferable, so the next governor may not benefit from it. Legislative power was never weakened during the Barbour Administration; Barbour enjoyed more influence in the legislative process, especially regarding budget making, only because the legislature allowed it. Latitude was granted to Barbour by the legislature that had not been given to previous governors, and the political environment in Mississippi was beginning to change.

The 2003 election resulted in Haley Barbour defeating Ronnie Musgrove, the incumbent Democratic governor,[4] and Republicans being elected to the legislature in numbers not seen since the Reconstruction era. "In fact, it had been more than 170 years since a Republican governor had been elected with a 'veto proof' legislature. In Mississippi, a governor's veto can be overridden by a two-third's vote of both houses of the legislature. Or, to look at the equation another way, a governor needs only one-third of the members to sustain a veto."[5] (Actually, a governor needs only one-third plus one of the members of *one house* to sustain a veto.) Not only did Barbour benefit from Republicans picking up seats in the legislature, he also benefited from Lt. Gov. Amy Tuck switching to the Republican Party prior to the 2003 election and becoming an ally of his. "With Barbour in the Governor's Mansion and with seventy-one Republicans in the legislature, a political dynamic emerged at the [C]apitol that was unique in the state's history—issues were debated from a Democratic perspective and a Republican perspective."[6] To add insult to injury, a party switch by a senate Democrat after the 2003 election gave control of the senate to Republicans for the first time since Reconstruction, which intensified the political dynamic even more.[7]

This new political dynamic of viewing issues from a political party perspective shifted the mind-set of a number of legislators and had a huge impact on the budget-making process. The goal for some legislators shifted from preserving as much legislative power as possible to preserving political party control. Without a supermajority, Democrats did not have enough votes to override a gubernatorial veto, and senate Republicans voted with Governor Barbour instead of the Democratic house. For that reason, Barbour did not have a single veto overridden during his two terms in office. Furthermore, Governor Barbour called an unprecedented number of special sessions in order to control the agenda. Gubernatorial vetoes and the ability to call special sessions are both formal powers that contributed to Barbour's success as governor, but his adept use of informal power is what set him apart from previous governors.

Governor Barbour did not increase the executive power over Mississippi's budget-making process through the passage of legislation but instead used "party discipline to gain leverage over budget decisions."[8] Barbour used this informal power of political persuasion to insert himself into the "legislative approval" phase of Mississippi's budget-making process, which was not an easy task.[9] Opponents of Barbour believed that he meddled in legislative affairs too much and thought that no governor should have that level of power. As impressive as Barbour's success was in penetrating Mississippi's legislatively dominated budget-making process, his legacy will likely be his fiscal policies recommended during the Fifth Extraordinary Session of 2005 and his involvement in securing an unprecedented amount of federal funds to help the state recover from the devastation of Hurricane Katrina in August 2005.

Barbour's Fiscal Accomplishments

Haley Barbour accomplished a great deal as governor because he mastered the art of using personal and political relationships to be more involved in the budget-making process on both the state and federal levels. Barbour was able to influence the content of legislation because of his access to budget decision makers and his ability to compromise with his opponents. Barbour's fiscal success on the state level consisted of collaborating with legislative leadership in order to insert himself into the legislative process. Barbour also achieved a substantial amount of success on the federal level. He was successful in constructing a plan for Hurricane Katrina relief, endorsed by the Mississippi Congressional Delegation, which resulted in billions of dollars in federal aid being awarded to the state. Barbour's federal accomplishments included three major victories: First, he was able to secure an unprecedented amount of funds through two existing block grant programs, which included the Community Development Block Grant (CDBG) Program and the Social Services Block Grant (SSBG) Program. Second, he was able to get Congress to agree to a tax-incentive package for businesses, which came to be known as the Gulf Opportunity Zone Act of 2005 (GO Zone Act). Lastly, Barbour was able to get Congress to agree to a plan that provided Mississippi with nearly $600 million in Medicaid funding to cover the state's share of the Medicaid match for two years.

Budget Power through Political Relationships

Barbour had never been elected to public office prior to being elected governor, but he was well connected politically because of his Republican Party experience and his long career as a Washington, DC, lobbyist.[10] "Those connections and that experience would translate into a [gubernatorial] campaign that raised and spent $13.5 million, more than three times what any candidate had ever spent in a statewide campaign in Mississippi."[11] Barbour's job as a lobbyist became Musgrove's main attack during the 2003 gubernatorial election. However, a poll conducted by Barbour's campaign showed that most Mississippians thought that having an experienced lobbyist as governor would be more helpful than harmful.[12]

Party politics was becoming an important variable in Mississippi's budget-making process, and the newly elected governor was no stranger to party politics. "Not since William Winter had Mississippians elected a governor who had as deep a history in the affairs of his political party as Haley Barbour."[13] In 1968 Barbour dropped out of college at the University of Mississippi to work on Republican Richard Nixon's presidential campaign before later returning and receiving a law degree.[14] Barbour served as the Mississippi Republican Party's campaign director, at a time when there was very few Republican office holders in the state, and he worked to get multiple Republicans elected to office. An early campaign that Barbour worked on was Thad Cochran's first congressional bid in 1972, which blossomed into a long-term relationship that proved advantageous in the future.[15]

Barbour also built political relationships working for the federal government and the national Republican Party. In the mid-1980s, Barbour served as director of the White House Office of Political Affairs for President Ronald Reagan and later as the Republican National Committee (RNC) chairman, from 1993 to 1997. During Barbour's time as RNC chair, Republicans won control of both houses of Congress for the first time in forty years.[16] Furthermore, the number of Republican governors increased from seventeen to thirty-two during Barbour's tenure as RNC chair.[17] Barbour's unique experience in party politics assisted him greatly in inserting himself into the budget-making process on both the state and federal levels.

Governor Barbour's success in penetrating the legislatively dominated budget-making process was no small feat, and it was something that had likely not been done by any other governor. Two key budget makers with whom Barbour had a special relationship who significantly contributed to his success were Lieutenant Governor Tuck, on the state level, who presided over the Mississippi Senate, and Mississippi's senior US senator, Thad Cochran, who chaired the powerful Senate Appropriations Committee.

Tuck was helpful because, as president of the Mississippi Senate, she appointed committee chairs and controlled the flow of bills in the senate.[18] Bills that she wanted to come out of committee came out, and bills that she wanted to die in committee never saw the light of day. Furthermore, when Barbour vetoed a bill, there was enough party discipline in the senate among the Republicans to prevent an override. Senator Cochran was equally helpful, because he chaired the money committee in the US Senate and was willing to hold a defense spending bill hostage in order to get additional funding for Hurricane Katrina relief.[19] Not only did Cochran pitch in to assist Barbour with securing federal funding for Katrina, all of the other members of the Mississippi Congressional Delegation chipped in too. "For Mississippi to have been visited by such a horrendous and epic disaster, we were [as] well prepared to seek help from the federal government as we had been at any time in our state's history," explained Barbour.[20]

Barbour's collaboration with Tuck and Cochran was not unusual, because they were all Republicans. What was impressive, as well as unexpected, was Barbour's success in getting the Speaker of the Mississippi House, Billy McCoy, a Democrat whom Barbour referred to as his political nemesis, to bring an onshore gaming bill to the house floor during a special legislative session in September 2005.[21] Three months earlier Barbour and McCoy had been fighting over state spending priorities and Medicaid spending, which resulted in the adoption of a state budget during a special session only one month before the start of the new fiscal year. The new dynamics of partisan politics was a two-way street, and McCoy demanded party discipline from house Democrats to counter Barbour and Tuck. "How a legislator voted on education, health care, and taxes and spending was determined in large part by the party label appended to his or her name. This movement toward a distinctly partisan legislature was put on 'pause' on August 29, 2005."[22] This was the date that Hurricane Katrina made landfall on the Mississippi Gulf Coast.

2005 Fifth Extraordinary Session of 2005

Haley Barbour was not shy about calling special sessions; he called at least one special session every year during his two terms in office and called eighteen special sessions altogether. In 2005 Barbour called the legislature back into session a whopping five times. The most memorable special session during the Barbour Administration was the fifth and final special session called in 2005, in response to the devastation created by Hurricane Katrina. Included with Katrina's devastation was a severe hit to state revenue. Coast casinos had generated more than $105 million in gross gaming revenue in the month of August before the storm hit; however, for the next three months that figure was zero. Prior to Hurricane Katrina, total gaming revenue for FY 2006 was estimated to bring in $189.3 million in general funds, not including gaming-related sales taxes, hotel taxes, and income taxes on companies and their employees.[23] It was inevitable that state revenue other than gaming would also be affected negatively by the storm. However, the State Tax Commission estimated that the state could sustain revenue losses of $213 million to $272 million.[24] Although the state was capable of enduring a revenue hit of that magnitude, the governor and lawmakers wanted the revenue disruption resolved promptly.

On Tuesday, September 27, 2005, Barbour was escorted to the chamber of the Mississippi House of Representatives to address the joint session of the legislature to describe the changes to laws that he was hoping the legislature would pass in response to Hurricane Katrina. Although the Gulf Coast was affected the most by Katrina, the hurricane affected the state as a whole because of the loss in revenue that would have been generated had the event never occurred. Gaming on the Gulf Coast brought millions of people to Mississippi, and it had a large impact on tourism. The State Tax Commission explained that the state had the capacity to sustain revenue losses, but nobody knew exactly how revenue would be affected. Governor Barbour explained that "because our state revenue estimates were so uncertain at the time of the special session, the Legislature authorized the State Bond Commission to borrow up to $500 million to create a line of credit for the operations of state government."[25] This borrowing was authorized when the house and senate passed H.B. 43, which was noncontroversial.[26] The controversy came with the gaming legislation that Barbour proposed.

The highlight of the session, according to Barbour, was the move to give more flexibility to casinos by allowing them to be located onshore.[27] Gaming in Mississippi has always been a controversial topic, and it is one topic that had received bipartisan contempt. The general public would experience something during the Fifth Extraordinary Session of 2005 that they did not see much during Barbour's first term in office—for the first time, Lieutenant Governor Tuck and Barbour were not on the same page regarding major legislation. Tuck and other senators did not want the gaming bill to have a senate bill number, which was a huge problem for the governor.

Barbour had been informed early on that the Republican leadership in the senate did not want the gaming bill to originate in the senate, which meant that Speaker McCoy would have to allow the house to take the lead in order for the bill to succeed.[28] The speaker and governor had been in constant battle from the time that Barbour was sworn into office, and now Barbour needed Billy McCoy's help. Recalling the situation, Barbour explained, "I found Billy exasperated with the Senate and sharply critical of the lieutenant governor's unwillingness to bring the onshore gaming bill to the Senate floor first."[29] Despite his differences of opinion with the governor and his own personal opposition to gaming, McCoy allowed the bill to originate in the house to start the legislative process. Barbour explained:

> I will always admire Billy McCoy for his decision. He was personally opposed to gaming; support for the bill was not in his political best interest, and he was helping me, the guy with whom he had been battling for a year and a half. Yet he agreed to do what I thought was right and what he ultimately believed was in the best interest of Mississippi. . . .
>
> In spite of a Gulf Coast that lay in ruins, and in spite of a recognition that gaming provided a level of jobs that was virtually required to sustain any recovery, allowing casinos onshore was far from certain in the Mississippi Legislature. Not everybody was strong as Billy McCoy.[30]

Representative Bobby Moak chaired the House Gaming Committee and was the principal author of H.B. 45, which was the bill that included Barbour's recommendations, on behalf of the gaming industry, to jumpstart the Gulf Coast recovery efforts by allowing casinos to be moved onshore. The bill passed the house by a vote of 61–53 and went to the senate. Gaming was a major contributor to the Gulf Coast's economy, but that did not stop religious leaders from opposing all gambling legislation and encouraging legislators to oppose it too. Barbour was pleased to see the bill get out of the house and encouraged the senate to pass the bill without any amendments, so that it would not have to be returned to the house, where there would be a vote on concurrence or to send it to a conference committee. To Barbour's surprise and disappointment, Gulf Coast Sen. Billy Hewes offered an amendment that was adopted on Friday, just before the legislature adjourned for the weekend. After the amendment was adopted, Lieutenant Governor Tuck called for the senate to reconvene at two o'clock Monday afternoon, which gave Barbour and his team the weekend to convince Hewes to withdraw his amendment.[31]

That weekend the *Sun Herald* led with the headline "Casino Plan Stalls in Senate" and blamed Senator Hewes for the delay.[32] The work over the weekend to get H.B. 45 passed out of the senate without any amendments worked, because Hewes withdrew his amendment that Monday, and no other amendment prevailed. As a result, the bill passed the senate by a margin of 29–21. Barbour was one step closer to getting the bill sent to him for his signature when another roadblock emerged. Senate Appropriations Committee chairman Jack Gordon was not happy with H.B. 44, known as the Tidelands Bill, and decided to hold H.B. 45 on a motion to reconsider until H.B. 44 was written to his satisfaction. Gordon argued that H.B. 45 should not become law until the house and senate could agree on the state-owned land along certain parts of the coastline, known as tidelands, that was leased out. Gordon was convinced that moving the casinos onshore could potentially affect the funds generated from leasing the tidelands. Tuck supported Gordon's motion, and he eventually got what he wanted in regard to the Tidelands Bill. H.B. 44 and 45 eventually made it to Barbour for his signature, and he signed both bills into law.[33]

The *Sun Herald* explained, after the conclusion of the special session, "House leaders left claiming they had saved the Coast's tourism industry [and] Senate leaders claiming they had saved the tidelands funds."[34] Barbour had learned from lobbying and politics the importance of finding a way to give everyone involved in a fight a way to claim victory, and that sometimes "compromise is about finding a way to give somebody something rather than making someone else look like a loser."[35] The special session in general was considered a huge success, and Haley Barbour's leadership was thought to have significantly contributed to that success. Barbour's staff also received praise for their contribution to Hurricane Katrina relief, resulting in house Democrat Joe Warren authoring House Concurrent Resolution 9 commending Barbour's staff. In addition to benefiting from a staff that was truly committed to Katrina recovery, Barbour also benefited from private citizens and local governments that were glad to lend a hand. Governor Barbour took full advantage of this generosity and decided to use individuals in more of an official capacity.

Governor's Commission on Recovery, Rebuilding, and Renewal

Barbour needed to come up with a Hurricane Katrina recovery plan and decided to create a broad-scale commission—made up of business, community, and government leaders serving in an advisory role—to create a report of recommendations to the governor. The commission was called the Governor's Commission on Recovery, Rebuilding, and Renewal. Barbour selected retired CEO of Netscape Jim Barksdale to chair the commission, and he selected former governor William Winter, a Democrat, to serve as outside counsel.[36] Barbour made the decision that the local community and not Jackson or Washington, DC, would determine the issues that would be considered for implementation by the legislature and Congress. Barksdale decided that he would not exclude any recommendations generated by the commission from the report, causing the document to become more of a menu of suggestions that were not all created equal. Some of the suggestions were important and should have been implemented in the past, while others were seen as farfetched. Regardless of whether the suggestions were probable or improbable of adoption, Katrina provided an avenue for all of them to be considered.

The final report contained 238 recommendations. One thing that was true about almost all of the recommendations is that funding would be needed to implement them.[37] "To find the money to put the commission's recommendations into effect required one of the most comprehensive and strenuous lobbying efforts ever carried out in Washington," explained Barbour.[38] Lucky for Barbour, several of Mississippi's senators and representatives were in key leadership roles in Congress and were capable of making the plan a reality. Barbour made it a priority of his to keep Congress well informed on the commission's work and the possible costs associated with the recommendations. Barbour stated, "For much of the time the commission was developing its report, I was in Washington lobbying for funds to help turn many of those recommendations into concrete projects."[39]

No Symbolic Legislation Needed

In addition to getting the Mississippi Legislature to follow his lead regarding Hurricane Katrina relief, Barbour was challenged with stopping any symbolic legislation from passing out of the legislature that could jeopardize receiving the maximum amount of federal funds. The legislature wanted to be proactive by passing a housing plan to assist Katrina victims, which Barbour thought was a bad idea. He believed that the house and senate proposals were not enough to scratch the surface of the housing problems caused by Katrina, and believed that the federal government should lead in funding the recovery efforts. Barbour explained:

> The House had passed a $100 million proposal to spur housing, and the Senate had increased it to $500 million. With uninsured losses approaching $5 billion, I thought this amount of money was more symbolic than substantive—an effort to get political credit "for doing something." Moreover, my first priority was to obtain the billions we needed from the federal government, and I worried this legislative initiative would be used as an excuse by many in Congress and the administration to undermine our request for unprecedented assistance from Washington, D.C. As a result, the tough vote I was requesting was to do nothing, which is ultimately how it ended.[40]

Barbour was asking the Mississippi Legislature to place trust in his recovery plan, which was not easy for some legislators. He was asking the legislature to stand down so that the Mississippi Congressional Delegation could lead in funding the recovery efforts.

Federal Funding for Hurricane Katrina Relief

The entire Mississippi Congressional Delegation contributed to the Hurricane Katrina recovery efforts, but the individual in place to do the most was US senator Thad Cochran, because he chaired the Senate Appropriations Committee. Two days after Hurricane Katrina made landfall, Senator Cochran met Governor Barbour at the governor's mansion and stated, "Tell me what you need, and I'll do my best to deliver."[41] The one thing that the State of Mississippi needed more than anything else was additional federal funds, which Cochran was in the position to help with in a significant way. The first thing on Cochran's recovery agenda was to get an early infusion of money to the Federal Emergency Management Agency (FEMA), which faced multiple challenges. Cochran was aware that the federal government was one month away from the end of its fiscal year, which meant that there was likely not a sufficient amount of funds remaining in FEMA's disaster relief fund. Furthermore, Congress was out for its August recess. However, these small hiccups would not stop Cochran from getting the necessary funding.

Cochran and the congressional leadership responded to the first problem by conferring with the White House on the situation and getting President George W. Bush to submit a request for an initial appropriation of $10.5 billion—with $10 billion going to FEMA and the remaining amount going to the Pentagon.[42] The second problem was solved when Cochran and congressional leaders took advantage of US House and US Senate rules that allowed a few members to convene when Congress was out of session. When the full Congress was back in session a few days later, the special FEMA appropriation bill, H.R. 3645, passed out of the US House and US Senate and was signed by the president. The specific purpose of H.R. 3645 was to make an emergency supplemental appropriation to meet immediate needs arising from the consequences of Hurricane Katrina, for the fiscal year ending September 30, 2005.[43] Another $51.8 billion was approved for FEMA and the Defense Department when Congress passed H.R. 3673.[44] Congress also passed H.R. 3768, known as the Katrina Emergency Tax Relief Act of 2005, which provided emergency tax relief for persons affected by Hurricane Katrina.[45] The emergency supplemental appropriation and the emergency tax relief legislation solved some of the immediate problems caused by the storm, but another problem soon surfaced that required additional attention. The problem was that the federal disaster law, in its current format, was not sufficient to deal with Hurricane Katrina. The Federal Disaster Assistance Act, known as the Stafford Act, governs FEMA and other agencies' legal authority to respond to natural disasters, and it was designed for handling much smaller events.[46]

In spite of all of the known and unknown challenges resulting from Hurricane Katrina, Cochran did not have the luxury of just asking Congress for a blank check for the recovery efforts without justification. Therefore, he asked Barbour to put together a long-term plan of what was needed and how the funds would be expended. Barbour asked his policy director Jim Perry to write the plan, which consisted of three major components: (1) funding beyond what the Stafford Act would allow, with the bulk of the funds being appropriated through the CDBG and SSBG programs, (2) new tax incentives for businesses to return to the damaged areas, and (3) for the federal government to cover the state's matching share required for Medicaid to provide relief to the state budget. Senator Cochran took the lead on handling the funding beyond the Stafford Act in the Senate, while Rep. Roger Wicker assisted in the House, since he served on the House Appropriations Committee and was a senior member of the House Budget Committee. Sen. Trent Lott was called on to help with the tax legislation, because he served on the Senate Finance Committee.[47] Rep. Chip Pickering served as vice-chairman of the House Energy and Commerce Committee, which had jurisdiction over Medicaid-related legislation, and received a call concerning the Medicaid match exemption.[48] Governor Barbour's plan was in full play, and the next challenge would be to get the White House to buy into his proposal.

Mississippi was in a good position to receive the much-needed federal government support because of its influential congressional delegation, but there was one problem. The federal government does not allow for an executive and legislative budget proposal the way that the State of Mississippi does. Congressional leaders informed Barbour that it would be "much easier legislatively to expand a provision that was already in the president's plan, such as a block grant program."[49] This meant that Governor Barbour had to convince President George W. Bush that his plan was necessary. "Our first priority . . . was getting as much as possible of what we needed included in the Bush proposal to Congress," explained Barbour.[50] Barbour met President Bush at the White House to pitch his plan, but he was not pleased with how the president and staff received the plan. The president's staff did not want to set a bad precedent regarding disaster relief, and Bush did not receive the plan with open arms like Barbour anticipated. He actually rejected some important aspects of the plan but did eventually include line items for both the CDBG and SSBG programs. In summarizing the president's inclusion of the block grant programs in his executive budget proposal, Barbour explained:

> In late October, President Bush formally asked Congress for $17.1 billion for Katrina relief. One newspaper report included this detail: "In the reallocation of FEMA money request was a White House proposal that $1.5 billion be redirected to the CDBG program operated through [the Department of Housing and Urban Development] HUD." The president had also included a line item for SSBG spending. Cochran now had his vehicle.[51]

Barbour was pleased that the president included line item funding for the block grant programs, but he was disturbed about major omissions in Bush's proposal, especially assistance for homeowners outside of the flood zone. Furthermore, the amount proposed by Bush was not just for Mississippi but was also for other states affected by the disaster, and Barbour was afraid that Louisiana would get a larger proportion of the funds.

Barbour presented his formal plan for Mississippi to the president and Congress on Thursday, November 1, 2005. The total cost of the plan was $33 billion over ten years, with $24 billion needed for the next two years. In fear of some fiscal conservatives opposing the plan, because of the large price tag and the chance of setting a new funding precedent for disasters, it was decided that the plan should be attached as an amendment to what lobbyists refer to as "must-pass" legislation. Senator Cochran knew that President Bush had to have a new appropriation bill to continue funding the wars in Afghanistan and Iraq passed by the end of the year and decided to include the appropriation amendment in H.R. 2863, which was the Department of Defense bill.[52] Cochran and Barbour both thought that H.R. 2863 was "must-pass" legislation, making it an excellent vehicle for their plan. Barbour explained, "Using the Defense bill also gave us grounds for a great argument for those who wanted to oppose our plan: you are willing to spend hundreds of billions of dollars in a foreign country but unwilling to spend far less to rebuild your own country?"[53] It was quite remarkable that a Senate Republican would be willing to hold up an important appropriation measure needed by a Republican president.

The White House believed that the president's $17.1 billion proposal for Katrina relief was sufficient, but Barbour and the Mississippi Congressional Delegation did not think so. In opposition to the president's proposal, Cochran held up the defense bill until the president would agree to $35 billion. Additionally, Pickering and Wicker decided to become obstructionist in the House. "Until Katrina funding gets done, we will block any rule that would authorize debate on the House floor on any other measure. We have the votes to do it . . . ," they explained.[54] President Bush decided to increase his funding proposal to $24 billion. Republican Speaker of the House Dennis Hastert seemed to be helping the president but also realized that he had a House to run, so he and other House members approached Cochran with a compromise of $29 billion. Although that figure was not ideal, Cochran agreed to it.

Before accepting the $29 billion compromise, Cochran checked to see if Governor Barbour was okay with that amount. Barbour explained that he could live with that amount if Louisiana didn't get all of the block grant funds. Of the $29 billion expected in the final bill, $11.5 billion was to be allocated to the CDBG Program, and Barbour's plan called for just over $5 billion in the first year. However, the legislation did not specify how much each state would receive. To assure that Mississippi would receive its fair share, Cochran's staff included language in the bill that limited the amount of CDBG funding that any state could receive to 54 percent of the total amount appropriated. An Appropriations Committee staffer concluded that the added language was "the strongest language that we've ever written. Those few words. Probably over 90 percent would have gone to Louisiana without that provision. Mississippi would get a few scraps and Alabama and Texas a few things here and there. But putting that language in there is how we got our money. The devil is always in the details."[55] Barbour's plan called for $5.4 billion in CDBG funds and received $5.2 billion with the compromise, which was an amount that he was satisfied with. The lead story in *Congressional Quarterly Today* gave Senator Cochran and the Mississippi delegation the well-deserved credit for the unprecedented legislation, explaining:

> After months of lobbying, negotiating and sometimes pleading, Gulf Coast lawmakers are on the brink of winning a much-needed boost for their constituents—at least $29 billion from federal taxpayers [to aid] state and local governments. That state's lawmakers were helped in recent weeks by influential and frustrated Mississippi officials, who pushed Republican Congressional leaders to provide additional aid before year's end. After months when it appeared that Congress and the Bush Administration had lost interest in rebuilding areas devastated by Hurricane Katrina, appropriators at the last minute came up with legislation that would address many of the infrastructure problems. . . . That happened in part as a result of increased pressure from Mississippi lawmakers, particularly Senate Appropriations Chairman Thad Cochran, who has been dissatisfied with the Bush Administration's funding strategy for the rebuilding effort.[56]

Cochran contributed greatly to the Katrina relief effort, and Barbour had no doubt that he would have held out for the entire $35 billion. But Barbour knew all along that $29 billion would be sufficient for the time being. Barbour explained that he did not ask Senator Cochran to ask for everything that he originally requested because of something that he learned from Ronald Reagan, which was "[i]n a negotiation, do not require perfection to accept a good deal; if you get 75–80 percent of what you want, take it, and come back for the rest later."[57]

In addition to Senator Cochran and Representative Wicker working tirelessly to successfully get funding for Barbour's recovery plan, Senator Lott and Representative Pickering also found success in getting legislation through the process for the GO Zone Act and Medicaid matching payments, respectively. Lott worked hard to get Congress to pass H.R. 4440, which amended the Internal Revenue Code of 1986 to allow states hit by Hurricane Katrina to offer tax-exempt bonds to rebuild infrastructure or geographical areas most damaged by the storms.[58] Speaking about the importance of the GO Zone legislation, Barbour stated:

> The legislation contained a variety of other federal tax breaks that provided the kind of economic incentives businesses needed to rebuild and expand and create jobs that could fuel our recovery. While I have given more attention to

passing the appropriation bill, chiefly because it was by far the most controversial part of our package, I don't want to minimize the significance of the
GO Zone legislation and how much it contributed to our recovery. Although
it never garnered the public attention that a multi-billion-dollar housing grant
program could generate, the bill's many tax provisions fueled thousands of
individual decisions by Mississippi businesses that led to the kind of rebuilding effort we had to have.[59]

The Medicaid-related legislation that Pickering successfully worked on also
failed to gain the attention that the major appropriation bills received, similar
to the GO Zone legislation, but was very important and provided much-needed
budget relief to the State of Mississippi. At the time that Katrina hit, Mississippi's Medicaid match rate was approximately 25 percent, and the federal
government paid the remaining 75 percent. Governor Barbour was initially
hoping that Pickering could get the match rate down to 10 or 15 percent but
was pleased when Pickering suggested that Mississippi should go for a zero
percent match rate. The chairman of the Energy and Commerce Committee,
Joe Barton, who named Pickering as one of his vice-chairmen earlier in the
year, gave Pickering the authority to negotiate the Medicaid issue on behalf of
the entire committee.[60] With Pickering's leadership, the Medicaid provision
was attached to S. 1932, the Deficit Reduction Act of 2005, which appropriated
funding for Medicaid matching payments for Mississippi and Louisiana.[61]
Unlike the other bills passed in Barbour's plan, S. 1932 was actually passed in
calendar year 2006 instead of 2005.

Using his experience as a Washington lobbyist and working through the Mississippi Congressional Delegation, Governor Barbour successfully penetrated
the federal proposal and approval phases. Barbour's lobbying experience proved
beneficial when getting President Bush to include the block grant funding in
the president's budget proposal, and his personal and political relationships
helped him sell his plan to Mississippi's congressional delegation, which ultimately pushed it through the legislative process. After his time as governor had
ended and while remembering how everything played out, Barbour explained
that he remained "extraordinarily impressed by the way [the congressional]
delegation and staff worked the legislation through Congress."[62] Another great
thing that occurred for Governor Barbour was his level of discretion over the
federal block grant funds received by the state for Katrina relief. The Mississippi
Development Authority was the state agency that received the CDBG funds,
and it was an executive agency in which the executive director served at the
will and pleasure of the governor, giving the governor substantial influence
over the agency.

State Fiscal Policy under Barbour

Barbour successfully penetrated Mississippi's budget-making process, similar to the way that he did on the federal level, which allowed him to have influence during the legislative approval phase. The legislative branch is responsible for appropriating funds during the legislative approval phase, and the executive branch is typically not involved at all in this phase. Barbour's relationship with senate Republicans allowed him to have a say during budget negotiations, even at the legislative committee level.[63] Being involved in the budget-making process allowed Barbour to influence many of the revenue and spending decisions made by the legislature. While Republicans welcomed the governor's contributions to the budget-making process, Democrats thought of it as meddling.

One particular Democrat who thought that Governor Barbour was interfering was Rep. Cecil Brown. Representative Brown, who previously served as state fiscal officer under Gov. Ray Mabus, was a key budget negotiator during the Barbour Administration, and he disliked the governor's involvement in the budget-making process.[64] Brown served on the House Appropriations Committee and the Joint Legislative Budget Committee (JLBC) during the Barbour Administration. Brown was also a certified public accountant (CPA) at the time and was labeled by many as a budget expert.[65] The governor's staff was often present during house and senate negotiations, especially when budget discussions hit a snag. Recalling Governor Barbour's involvement in the budget process, Brown explained, "Haley was absent. Jim Perry was key; we dealt almost exclusively with Jim, and he was tough. The governor had given Jim authority to negotiation on his behalf."[66] Brown explained that it would have been much easier for house members involved in the budget process if they did not have to negotiate with two different bodies (that is, the senate and the governor's office). Furthermore, Brown believed that the senate was weak and allowed the governor's office too much influence over the budget-making process, which was unprecedented.

Not disputing Brown's assessment of the Barbour Administration's involvement in the budget-making process, Perry agreed that it was "probably the first time that the governor was intimately involved in the line item aspects of the budget and not just a big item (e.g., teacher pay raise)."[67] Perry did not consider the senate weak, and he disagreed with Brown's assessment of the senate's omission from budget decision making. On the contrary, he believed that Barbour "involved more rank and file members in the budget process."[68] Perry explained that Barbour did not try to control senators; he educated them on the budget and provided a holistic viewpoint. "Barbour helped legislators understand why it was in their best interest to go along with his budget plan, and he provided polling data to back up his argument. Legislators were predisposed to a roadmap for an option other than raising taxes," explained Perry.[69]

Barbour's inclusion in the legislative approval phase did not mean that he controlled it; he still had to compromise with the legislature on many fiscal policy issues, especially because of the declining revenue available to the state. Democrats in the legislature thought that more funding should be spent on government services, even if it meant raising taxes, while Barbour believed that too much was being spent on government. Governor Barbour believed that Mississippi could not afford the government that Democrats wanted, and he thought that state agencies should eliminate waste and become more efficient, thereby needing less funding. Barbour inherited a deficit when he came into office, and he refused to raise taxes to fix the problem. He believed that conservative fiscal policy would be a better remedy. Barbour's solution to the budget problems was to eliminate the use of one-time money by using recurring funds for recurring expenditures and by cutting government services to bring expenditures in line with revenue collections.

Barbour was confident that the deficit would vanish if the legislature would work with him to implement his fiscal goals. "I am committed to working with the Legislature to implement cost-saving measures so that we can move our state toward living within available revenue, while funding top priorities and not raising taxes," explained Barbour.[70] Having a say in the budget-making process increased Barbour's chances of achieving his fiscal goals, but he would soon learn why previous governors and the legislature used less-than-desirable tactics to balance the state budget.

Barbour learned early on that eliminating the use of one-time money was much easier said than done, because the legislature had grown quite dependent on it. In Barbour's first executive budget recommendation (EBR), for FY 2005, he expressed his concern with using one-time money, but also realized that he could not just up and stop the practice in his first year. Barbour stated in his FY 2005 recommendation:

> I agree with the assessment of the JLBC that budgets of the last two years have relied upon extensive use of one-time monies to fund recurring expenses. This and initiatives of previous years, which caused escalating long-term costs, have created a situation in which there is not enough current revenue to fund the programs of state government in their existing fashion. We must set the goal of not using one-time monies to fund recurring expenses; however, as I stated repeatedly during the recent campaign, we will not be able to accomplish this in one year. My hope is to accomplish this in two years.[71]

Barbour's FY 2005 recommendation included the use of $132 million in one-time transfers of special funds to the State General Fund, which was a reduction of the use of one-time money by nearly 50 percent and was thought by the governor to be a first step toward putting the state on the path to living within its means within two years. However, Mississippi's revenue problems did not improve by the time that Barbour left office, so he was not able to eliminate the practice altogether, as he had anticipated.

In addition to the continued practice of using one-time money to balance the state's budget, executive budget cuts were also necessary. Barbour cut budgets by $200 million in FY 2009 and nearly $500 million in FY 2010.[72] The first round of cuts were made to the FY 2009 budget just after the nation entered into the Great Recession.[73] Some legislators started pressuring the governor to consider increasing taxes in order to generate more revenue, but Barbour refused to do so, believing that he and the legislature could find a way to manage the state budget. A month after the nation went into a recession, Barbour stated that when he first took office, he and the legislature "worked together to dig out of a $720 million budget hole without raising anybody's taxes, at the same time rebuilding [the] rainy day fund."[74] The next round of budget cuts occurred after the recession had officially concluded, but revenue continued to underperform, which forced the legislature to adjust the FY 2010 revenue estimate downward. In his FY 2010 budget reduction letter to State Fiscal Officer Kevin Upchurch, Barbour explained why more budget cuts were necessary, stating:

> Today the Joint Legislative Budget Committee adopted a revised revenue estimate for Fiscal Year 2010, which will force me [to] reduce state spending for the current fiscal year in order to achieve a balanced budget. As you know, to date I have been forced to trim the Fiscal Year 2010 budget by approximately $458.5 million through four rounds of cuts as the state continues to experience the impact of this global recession.
>
> . . . Based on these newest revenue numbers, the Revenue Estimating Committee has revised the expected shortfall for the current fiscal year to $499.1 million, which is approximately $40.6 million more than previously estimated. Therefore, I am reducing state budgets by a corresponding amount in order to conform with the revised FY 2010 revenue estimate adopted today by members of the Joint Legislative Budget Committee.[75]

Governor Barbour's last round of budget cuts in FY 2010 brought the total reduction for most state agencies to 9.5 percent, which the governor thought was "necessary to balance the budget in accordance with state law and the Constitution."[76] Even with the drastic budget cuts, Barbour continued to reject the demand for any major tax increases (i.e., sales, individual income, or corporate taxes).

A lack of revenue growth caused most of the state's fiscal problems during the Barbour Administration, but spending also played a role. Both of Barbour's terms were plagued with arguments with Democrats concerning the appropriate funding levels for state government, especially funding for public education and Medicaid. Neither the governor nor the Democrats received exactly what they wanted when it came to spending; there was lots of give-and-take on both sides. As Rep. Cecil Brown explained, "We got as much as we gave. Haley did not get everything that he wanted. One only has to look at his EBRs to see that Democrats never gave in to much of what Haley requested. There were compromises made by the governor and the legislature."[77] One thing that occurred with much of the compromise is that total general fund appropriations continued to grow. The total amount of general funds appropriated in FY 2005 was $3,595,725,332 when Barbour first took office, and that amount grew to $4,494,767,060 in FY 2012 by the time he left office.[78] That was an increase of $899,041,728, or 25 percent.

Government spending likely would have grown at a much faster pace had Barbour not been governor, and he was convinced that government waste and inefficiency was contributing to the problem. Seeing that neither Democrats nor Republicans in the legislature really had an appetite for decreasing government spending, Barbour decided that he would instead try to make agencies more accountable for the funds appropriated to them. In order for Barbour to rid the government of waste and make government more efficient, he would need help from the legislature. Barbour attempted to accomplish this in his second term and recruited newly elected lieutenant governor Phil Bryant to lead the Commission for a New Mississippi. Bryant was more than qualified to lead the effort, having served as state auditor for over a decade prior to being elected lieutenant governor. One of the many duties of the state auditor included "conducting investigations into abuse of public funds and violations of law," along with providing best practices for "budgeting and reporting financial facts."[79] Delivering his plan for effective budgeting while also asking for legislative support of the plan, Barbour explained:

> In 2008, I asked Lieutenant Governor Phil Bryant to lead a task force to root out waste and inefficiency in state government. Over the course of the past year, the Commission for a New Mississippi has been working to develop a plan to achieve this mission, with final recommendations centering around three points: having a strategic, statewide plan that is well-communicated across governmental entities; reforming performance-based budgeting, and creating a state agency from

existing entities to provide continuous review and improvements of state government operations.

I urge the Legislature to consider adopting these meritorious proposals, which
I believe can have long-term implications for improving the current budgeting
process. Now, more than ever, we must think differently about the way state government is operated, including how the budgeting process relates to efficiency
and effectiveness in all of state government. I sincerely appreciate the Lieutenant
Governor and commission members for their thoughtful plan that addresses
these issues.[80]

If the legislature had adopted the commission's recommendation, it would have
added an informal review/reporting phase to Mississippi's formal budget-making
process. The house rejected the measure, so the commission's proposal never
came to fruition. Barbour's relationship with the senate leadership allowed
him to be included in the budget-making process, but that did not stop the
house Democrats from rejecting the commission's proposal. Adding a review/
reporting phase to Mississippi's budget process likely would have made agencies
more accountable, but it is hard to say whether it would have actually slowed
government spending.

Chapter 9

Legislative Joint Rules Change

One of the fundamental topics discussed in this book has been the power struggle between the legislative branch and the executive branch to control the budget. Significant gain of control over the budget process is sometimes thought to be a zero-sum game—that is, legislative gain over the budget usually comes at the expense of the executive branch, and vice versa. However, a legislative rules change in 2012 gave more budget power to the legislative leadership at the expense of the rank-and-file legislator. The specific change was Joint Rule 20A, which was added as a new joint rule when the house and senate adopted the joint rules at the beginning of the new four-year term. "House Speaker Philip Gunn, R-Clinton, and Republican Lt. Gov. Tate Reeves pushed through the rules change during the opening day of their tenure to prohibit any member from trying to increase the budget of any agency without stating from what agency the increase in funding would be taken."[1]

Joint Rule 20A was thought by some at the time to be "the most significant legislative rules change since the 1980s."[2] Opponents of the new rule saw the change as a way to restrict rank-and-file members, especially Democrats, from having access to state support funds and reserves, while proponents saw the change as nothing more than a way to keep aggregate appropriations spending in check. The key provision of Joint Rule 20A was subsection (2) (a), which provided that:

> When an amendment is offered to an appropriation bill on the floor of
> either house that would increase the amount of state support funds autho-
> rized for expenditure by the state agency, official or program being funded in

that appropriation bill, the amendment must also include a reduction in the amount of state support funds for one (1) or more other state agencies, officials or programs by a total amount that equals the amount of the increase in the amendment.[3]

An argument can easily be made that the controversial rules change simultaneously accomplished both what the opponents and proponents suggested. The effect of Joint Rule 20A limited the authority of rank-and-file members from offering amendments to appropriation bills on the house and senate floor that would have added more funds to the overall budget than the amount determined by the Appropriations Committee of each respective house. The sum of the appropriation bills that passed out of the house and senate Appropriations Committees were meant to be the only funds available for developing the budget when the bills were to be first voted on in each respective house. For example, if there is any unappropriated money in the State General Fund or in the Working-Cash Stabilization Reserve Fund (rainy day fund) when the appropriation bills are being considered on the floor, the rule prohibits a member from offering an amendment to the bill that uses any of those unappropriated funds, because it would increase the total amount of funds appropriated for the budget above the amount that was determined by the Appropriations Committee. By limiting the authority of individual members to offer those types of floor amendments, the rule increased the power of the Appropriations Committee to control the budget relative to the house and senate as a whole, whose power was therefore reduced.

Critics of Joint Rule 20A knew that the legislative leadership could purposefully exclude available funds during budget deliberations early in the session, electing instead to wait until the time that the final budget was resolved in conference committees, near the end of the session, to add revenue to the budget. The additional revenue could be unallocated funds, reserves, or any anticipated new revenue that resulted from raising the revenue estimate as recommended by the revenue estimating committee. It is not uncommon for the Joint Legislative Budget Committee (JLBC) to call the revenue estimating committee back during the session to reevaluate the revenue outlook, which typically results in the revenue estimate being raised if revenue is currently outperforming expectations. "Now, with new revenue in hand, House and Senate leaders . . . meet together, primarily behind closed doors, to develop a budget . . ."[4] At that point, the budget cannot be altered by rank-and-file members on the floor because conference committee reports cannot be amended. Each chamber has to approve the budget in a conference committee report for a bill or vote to send it back for additional negotiations between the house and senate conference committee members. "If they send it back for more than one day of negotiations, because of constitutional deadlines, it throws the session in chaos and extraordinary parliamentary maneuvers must be taken, requiring a two-thirds vote to pass a budget."[5] Because of the time constraints and restrictions on amendments, rank-and-file members have limited ability to impact the budgeting process at the end of the session. This is why voting to limit their authority at the beginning of the session was so crucial. "[T]he truth is that early in the session, when the framers of the state Constitution intended rank-and-file members to have the ability to have an impact, those same rank-and-file members said, thanks, but no thanks, we do not want to have an impact"[6] when they adopted Joint Rule 20A.

One of the leading media critics of Joint Rule 20A was the *Northeast Mississippi Daily Journal* capitol correspondent Bobby Harrison, who was critical of the rule from its inception. Harrison explained, "On the surface, the rules changes seem reasonable. If you want to increase the budget, say from where the money is being taken. But in reality, the rule gives Reeves and Gunn, and their appropriations lieutenants, more control over the budgeting process than perhaps any Mississippi Legislature's presiding officers have had in recent memory."[7] Harrison further expressed his concerns:

> The problem is that there are so many other pots of money available for legislators to tap into to amend the budget to provide more money for say education or public safety or any other function of government. The state has various reserve funds—totaling probably as much as $500 million. Perhaps, it is bad policy to tap into reserve funds. But should the average legislator—who is not a key member of the leadership's budget team—be prevented from offering that proposal to his colleagues during debate on the floors of the House and Senate?[8]

Harrison's concerns were legitimate, and legislators who belonged to the Democratic Party asked similar questions while also accusing Republicans Reeves and Gunn of playing politics when adopting the rule. Democratic legislators believed that the rules change was a way to limit Democrats from making amendments to the Republicans' budget, while Reeves and Gunn claimed that the change was a way to be more fiscally responsible with the budget. Regardless of motive, it would be hard to prove that the rules change was strictly to restrict rank-and-file Democrats from amending the budget, because the change also affected rank-and-file Republicans who did not serve on the Appropriations Committee. Furthermore, a similar rules change was proposed by Democratic members over two decades earlier, during the 1991 legislative session, which ultimately failed.

The 1991 proposed rules change was developed by Rep. Billy McCoy, a Democrat, who would become speaker of the house over a decade later, but authored by Rep. Bobby Moody, also a Democrat, with McCoy as a coauthor.[9] McCoy was already an influential member at the time of the proposal, but he still would have been considered a rank-and-file member. The proposed rules change, which was introduced as House Concurrent Resolution No. 48, would have required that amendments offered to both general bills and appropriation bills, in committee or on the floor, that would cause an expenditure of state funds, must include in the amendment a provision to provide funding for the increased expenditure in state funds. The similar provision that was included in both the 1991 resolution and the 2012 resolution that contained Joint Rule 20A dealt specifically with amending appropriation bills. The 1991 resolution read:

> Whenever an amendment is offered to an appropriation bill in committee or on the floor of the House or the Senate that would increase any sum appropriated or authorized to be expended by the bill . . . the amendment shall include a provision or provisions that will reduce a sum or sums appropriated or authorized to be expended . . . in the same bill or in any other appropriation bill or bills that still are under consideration in the house in which the amendment is offered, or in both the same bill and another bill or bills, by amounts so that the amendment will provide a total reduction in sums that is not less than the total increase in sums provided in the amendment.[10]

The concept of Representative McCoy's resolution is clearly similar to the concept of Joint Rule 20A in the 2012 resolution supported by Reeves and Gunn; however, nobody can accuse McCoy of proposing the rules change for partisan gain, because rank-and-file legislators in 1991 who would have been the most affected would have been those in his own political party. At the time of the proposed resolution, Democrats heavily controlled both the house and senate. McCoy should be given the benefit of the doubt that he orchestrated the resolution for no other reason than that he believed that it was good fiscal policy. For the same reason, Reeves and Gunn should also be given the benefit of the doubt that they both believed that the rules change was good fiscal policy as well, being that more rank-and-file Republicans would be affected by it than Democrats. The house and senate did not get the chance to vote on McCoy's resolution, because it died in the House Rules Committee without a vote, so we will never know what the legislature would have done with the proposal.

Democrats and Republicans both believed that the legislative leadership had the votes to successfully pass Joint Rule 20A when they adopted the joint rules in 2012, because both houses were controlled by Republicans, and the vote would likely be cast along party lines. However, this did not stop some legislators familiar with the budgeting process from trying to stop it. One of those legislators was Rep. Cecil Brown, who raised a point of order when the house was considering House Concurrent Resolution No. 33, which included Joint Rule 20A, asserting that the new rule was a violation of the house rules because it amended by reference (conflicted with) several of the house rules. Speaker Gunn ruled that Brown's point of order was not proper, because the "concept of amending by reference applies only to code sections, not to House or Joint Rules."[11] After making his unsuccessful point of order, Brown also attempted to amend House Concurrent Resolution No. 33 by striking "Section 20A . . . in its entirety."[12] Brown's amendment was defeated by a vote of fifty-four yeas and sixty-six nays, with the division being almost totally according to party.[13]

The successful adoption of Joint Rule 20A forced legislators, such as Representative Brown, to adjust to the change in order to have any influence on the budget. Brown found a loophole in the rule that prevented it from being as effective as it was envisioned—which was that the rule was not binding after the initial vote on the appropriation bills in the respective houses. If an amendment was adopted to increase one agency's budget and reduce another agency's budget by a corresponding amount, the other house or the conference committee could restore the funds to the agency whose funds had been reduced by the amendment. For that reason, a legislator could offer an amendment to increase an agency's budget by taking it from an agency that is large enough to absorb the reduction, plus important enough that the reduction would most likely be restored by the conference committee. This technique was used as a way to technically comply with the requirements of the rule but also to effectively get around the purpose of the rule by allowing amendments to be offered on any matter and for any amount that an individual wanted. Brown was the first representative to put this technique into practice, during the 2012 session, when he proposed reducing the budgets of the Division of Medicaid and debt service (payment of principal and interest on state bonds), which both met the previously explained criteria of size and importance.

The floor amendments offered by Brown would have increased the appropriation bills for K–12 education and the State Department of Health by $25 million and $4 million, respectively. H.B. 1593 was the appropriation bill for K–12 education, and Brown proposed to "amend [the bill] by deleting $1,831,559,102.00 and inserting in lieu thereof $1,856,559,102.00."[14] Brown's amendment to H.B. 1593 would have also decreased the amount appropriated in H.B. 1599, which was the appropriation bill for the Division of Medicaid, to cover the entire amount of the increase. Brown also proposed to amend H.B. 1613, which appropriated funds to the State Department of Health, "by deleting $23,477,939.00

and inserting in lieu thereof $27,477,939.00."[15] Brown's amendment to increase H.B. 1613 would have also decreased the amount appropriated in S.B. 3009 for debt service by a corresponding amount. Unfortunately for Brown, both of his amendments to increase the amounts in the two appropriation bills failed.

Representative Brown went from fighting to keep Republican Governor Haley Barbour out of the legislative budget-making process to fighting the Republican legislative leadership on keeping rank-and-file legislators included in the process. Regardless of the agenda behind passing Joint Rule 20A, it had an adverse effect on experienced budgeters like Cecil Brown, who no longer served on the Appropriations Committee or the JLBC and was now a rank-and-file member with little official power. Because of his loss of power and influence in the legislature, Brown decided not to run for reelection after sixteen years as a house member. Instead, he decided to run for Public Service Commissioner in 2015, and he was elected to that office. If Brown had remained in the legislature, he would have witnessed rank-and-file members vote yet again in support of Joint Rule 20A when they adopted the joint rules during the 2016 legislative session.

Chapter 10

Budget Control under Bryant

Gov. Phil Bryant never tried to penetrate the legislative approval phase the way that his predecessor did, believing that "it is the legislature's job to appropriate funds, not the governor['s]."¹ Executive and legislative duties in the budget-making process are clearly pointed out in statute, leaving little room for interpretation. Bryant's budgeting philosophy relayed to his staff was quite simple, "follow the law."² Bryant also held the legislature to the same standards. It came as a surprise to many when Bryant drafted a letter to the Senate and House Appropriations Committee chairmen, in his first year in office, encouraging them to stop the practice of issuing legislative intent letters for appropriation bills, which he believed to be unlawful.

During the 2012 legislative session, the Appropriations Committee chairmen added a section to the Mississippi Development Authority's (MDA) appropriation bill giving the agency a set amount of lump sum spending authority; however, the bill did not specify to the MDA how the funds were to be expended. After the appropriation bill passed both houses and was signed by the governor, the two Appropriations Committee chairmen then wrote an intent letter to the agency head explaining how the funds were to be spent. Bryant questioned whether two legislators could speak for the entire legislature, and he believed that the directive to expend the funds should have been specifically spelled out in the appropriation bill and voted on by the full house and senate. Bryant explained in his letter to the chairmen that "the law simply does not allow the expenditure of funds as you direct and places the agency head in the untenable position of possibly misappropriating public funds if he complies with your directive."[3] The end result was that the MDA did not spend the funds as directed in the intent letter.

So, Governor Bryant did not try to insert himself into the legislative approval phase, and he encouraged the Appropriations Committee chairmen to appropriate funds based on the appropriation bills and laws. However, this did not mean that Bryant approved of the budget system in its current format. On the contrary, he believed that the process did not work and needed revamping. Bryant advocated for performance-based budgeting when serving as lieutenant governor, and he continued to advocate for it as governor. In his argument for performance-based budgeting, Bryant explained:

> Mississippi's budget system is broken and must be fixed. Our state cannot be successful in the 21st century with a budget system from the 19th century. Instead of measuring outcomes and appropriating for success, our state budgets currently are set by two deciding factors: what was last year's budget number and who do you know at the Capitol. This practice is no way to treat tax dollars. We should work smarter, making spending transparent and designing budgets based on performance rather than politics.[4]

Bryant wanted the law governing the budgeting system changed, but he knew that it was the legislature's job to change it, not the governor's. Bryant clearly disapproved of the way that the legislature appropriated funds in the legislative approval phase, but as long as it was the law, he followed it.

Governor Bryant's philosophy to follow the law was not surprising, being that he previously served as a deputy sheriff. One could imagine Bryant's surprise when two legislators accused him of breaking the law by usurping the legislature's budget-making power, and filed a lawsuit to stop him from doing that. The two legislators claimed that when Bryant cut state agency budgets, he was actually interfering with appropriations, which is constitutionally a legislative function. This separation of powers case went to the Mississippi Supreme Court. Bryant believed that cutting agency budgets was a part of "budget control" and not "budget making," and the high court agreed. The supreme court ruled that budget control is an executive function, not a legislative function.[5] If the supreme court had sided with the two legislators, the legislative branch would have had nearly absolute control over the entire budget-making process.

Both the governor and the legislature had important roles to play in making the budget process work, while also improving Mississippi's fiscal condition. Bryant believed that budgeting based on evidence, along with other sound fiscal policies, contributed to improving the state's fiscal well-being. "The best measure of our success in governing responsibly is evidence that Mississippi is showing real improvements in its efficiency and fiscal health. This includes an increase in cash savings, stability or growth in the state's credit rating, and evidence that spending on state agencies and programs are [sic] generating results," explained Bryant.

Important benchmarks for measuring the state's fiscal success set forth by Bryant in *Opportunity Mississippi: Detailing the Roadmap to Success* included: (1) adopting and implementing legitimate performance-based budgeting standards; (2) maintaining or increasing the state's credit rating; (3) adhering to "the 98 percent rule," which limits the total state general fund appropriations to 98 percent of projected revenues; and (4) filling the Working-Cash Stabilization Reserve Fund ("rainy day fund") to its statutory limit. The specific benchmark that separated Bryant's fiscal policy from his predecessor Haley Barbour's was the push for performance-based budgeting, which was meant to take the politics out of the budget-making process. The argument can be made that Governor Barbour would have been ineffective in the budget process if politics had been removed from it during his time in office. Bryant not only talked about the importance of removing politics from budgeting but also asked for legislation to be introduced to make it law. He proposed the Smart Budget Act in his first executive budget recommendation (EBR), which the legislature rejected, but he was successful in getting other items on his fiscal agenda through the legislative process.

Governor Bryant was not successful in convincing the legislature to adopt meaningful legislation to change Mississippi's budgeting system to performance-based budgeting. Some legislators agreed with the governor that the current budget process was not perfect, but they did not want to change it and risk getting a process that might be worse. It was never Bryant's intent to weaken legislative power over the legislative approval phase, but removing politics from the appropriation process would have done just that. Although Bryant was not successful in getting performance-based budgeting passed in Mississippi, he did find success in other fiscal matters. What is impressive about Bryant's achievements is that he worked with the legislature to get fiscal legislation passed, meaning that those changes would remain unless the law was revised. By contrast, Barbour's influence on the budget process was due to his personal and political skills and relationships, which left the office of the governor when he did.

Bryant's Fiscal Accomplishments

Governor Bryant's fiscal accomplishments included using the executive authority provided to him by law to successfully manage the state's finances, while also getting meaningful legislation passed during special sessions that positively affected the state's budget and revenue. However, the former caused Bryant to be sued in 2017 by two legislators over the governor's statutory authority to reduce state agency budgets, claiming that it violated the state constitution. The case, *Representative Bryant W. Clark and Senator John Horhn v. Governor Phil Bryant et al.* (2018), made it to the Mississippi Supreme Court.[6] The State of Mississippi was applauded by the credit rating agencies for its statutory abilities to manage its finances during economic downturns; however, the rating agencies were highly concerned with the lawsuit brought by Clark and Horhn that challenged the governor's authority to control the budget. The lawsuit began with several executive agencies collaborating on the distinction between budget control and budget making in yet another separation of powers case. The courts ended up ruling in favor of the executive branch over the legislative branch, which was considered a huge win for Governor Bryant and future governors to come.

Important legislation was passed under Bryant's watch that positively affected his ability to manage Mississippi's finances. Such legislation included S.B. 2001, passed during the Second Extraordinary Session of 2016, which removed the $50 million rainy day fund transfer cap, for FY 2016 only, to allow for more executive flexibility to deal with budget deficits.[7] Furthermore, the legislature raised the transfer cap to $100 million, at the governor's request for FY 2017, when it passed S.B. 2649 during the 2017 legislative session.[8] Bryant recommended and was successful in getting the legislature to pass S.B. 2002, known as the Financial and Operational Responses That Invigorate Future Years (FORTIFY) Act, during the First Extraordinary Session of 2017, which was received positively by the credit rating agencies.[9] Perhaps the special session that gained Bryant the most acclaim was the First Extraordinary Session of 2018, which produced the passage of H.B. 1 and S.B. 2001, known as the Mississippi Infrastructure Modernization Act of 2018 and the Alyce G. Clarke Mississippi Lottery Law, respectively.[10] All of this legislation had a huge impact on Mississippi's finances and credit rating.

Bryant's Fiscal Management

Governor Bryant pledged his commitment to "honest budgeting based on real numbers and financial best practices."[11] Bryant knew that policy makers are judged on their ability to successfully manage the state's finances in good times and bad. He felt that it was his job as governor to protect the financial integrity of the state, pointing out that financial choices made by policymakers are critical to a state's financial health. Bryant's opinion was driven by credit rating agencies, as evident in the following statement:

As Moody's said in its U.S. States Rating Methodology, "Unlike economic factors, which are largely beyond the states' control, financial results are the product of many decisions and practices determined by state policymakers. While tax collections and expenditures reflect fiscal capacity, and they ebb and flow with economic cycles, the financial choices states make given the economic situations they face—at any point in the economic cycle—are critical."[12]

Bryant understood that he was not the only decision maker in the budget-making process and encouraged legislators to avoid bad fiscal habits, such as making unrealistic revenue estimates, deliberately underfunding major line items, and expending nonrecurring funds on recurring expenditures. He urged the legislature to avoid these practices, although they were "politically convenient."[13] Avoiding bad fiscal practices helped the state get through troubling times but did not prevent revenue slowdowns from occurring. Similar to all the governors discussed in previous chapters, Bryant experienced economic slowdowns that forced him to order the state fiscal officer to reduce state agency budgets to make up for revenue collections that failed to meet expectations.

FY 2016 and FY 2017 were by far the most challenging fiscal years during the Bryant Administration, resulting in executive budget cuts being made in both years. Governor Bryant believed that the state was well positioned to deal with declining revenue because of the funds set aside in the state's rainy day fund and the governor's statutory authority to reduce state agency budgets if revenue fell below expectations. "During my 2014 State of the State Address, I called on the Legislature to fill the Rainy Day Fund, and the Leadership responded by doing so for two consecutive years. There is no denying that the Rainy Day Fund prevented larger cuts in Fiscal Year 2016," explained Bryant in his FY 2017 EBR. Bryant decided to use much of the $50 million rainy day fund transfer authority in FY 2016, but he decided to reduce budgets more in FY 2017 so that he could save most of the rainy day fund transfer authority for the end of the fiscal year.

Governor Bryant had the state fiscal officer reduce state agency budgets for the first time in January of 2016 and ended up having to cut again in April, for a combined reduction of $64,791,417. He also directed that $45,208,583 be transferred from the rainy day fund to the State General Fund. "As Governor, I am required by state law to impose budget cuts when revenue collections do not meet our estimates. . . . I also have authority to transfer up to $50 million from the Working Cash Stabilization Reserve Fund, commonly known as the Rainy Day Fund, to the State General Fund to stabilize the budget when we are experiencing revenue shortfalls," stated Bryant.[14] Bryant's first round of budget reductions in FY 2016 was for $39,791,417, and he had $35,208,583 transferred from the rainy day fund for a combined January adjustment of $75 million. Bryant's second round of budget reductions that fiscal year came in April for an amount of $25 million, and he also directed a $10 million transfer from the rainy day fund.[15]

The FY 2016 budget adjustments for $110 million were not enough. After the governor cut state agency budgets in April, there was no room for more budget cuts. Any additional adjustments to the budget would have to be rainy day fund transfers to the general fund. The problem was that the governor had less than $5 million remaining in the rainy day fund transfer authority and did not know if that amount would be sufficient for finishing out the fiscal year. So, the governor called a special session and asked the legislature to remove the rainy day fund transfer cap for that fiscal year. The legislature responded by passing S.B. 2001, which authorized the executive director of the Department of Finance and Administration (DFA) to transfer rainy day funds to the general fund in an amount determined by the governor to alleviate any deficits at the end of FY 2016.[16]

FY 2017 proved to be as challenging as FY 2016, resulting in budgets being adjusted in September because of a legislative accounting error and being cut three times in January through March. Many governors are forced to have state agency budgets reduced when revenue underperforms. Governors usually wait before cutting budgets in order to give revenue an opportunity to recover; however, this was not done in FY 2017. Governor Bryant explained in a letter to State Fiscal Officer Laura Jackson, "Although it is too early in the fiscal year to determine how revenue collections will perform in FY 2017, budget adjustments in state government are necessary now to adjust for a $56,801,694 accounting error."[17] Some legislators believed that the governor's budget adjustments were premature, but Bryant disagreed, arguing that agencies could better plan for the cuts the sooner they knew about them.

In addition to the September adjustments, the governor had state agency budgets reduced by $50,974,616 in January, $43 million in February, and $20,446,237 in March. Total cuts from January through March were $114,420,853. Furthermore, Bryant also directed for transfers to be made from the rainy day fund to the general fund in January and February for $4,061,149 and $7 million, respectively.[18] Total adjustments and cuts in FY 2017 were $171,222,547, and total transfers from the rainy day fund were $11,061,149. Bryant was not happy having to cut agency budgets, but he believed that the reductions were necessary. In his next-to-last budget cut letter for FY 2017, Bryant defended his fiscal management actions, stating:

> It is tempting to leave things alone and hope for revenue collections to improve and offset the shortfall we are experiencing; however, I feel it is imperative that

we take action based on the best possible information available. If we postpone spending reductions until later, then state agencies must make relatively larger cuts and will have less flexibility/time to handle the necessary cuts.[19]

Bryant did not arbitrarily order state agency budget cuts for the sake of cutting budgets—he listened to the experts and made decisions accordingly. State Economist Darrin Webb's annual Legislative Economic Briefing clearly contributed to Bryant's decision to cut budgets in February. Webb explained in the briefing that Mississippi's economy was growing, but the growth was not translating into more revenue. Webb also stated that he did not foresee an uptick in revenue for the remainder of the fiscal year.[20]

Governor Bryant's office continued to monitor revenue collections for FY 2017 and was convinced that revenue would "not be adequate to support budget expenditures" for the remainder of the fiscal year.[21] Therefore, in addition to making his final budget reduction in March, Bryant explained the following to Jackson in the letter:

> I am authorizing you to transfer $39 million from the Working Cash-Stabilization Reserve Fund as needed, and I have requested legislation allowing you to access additional funds from the Working Cash-Stabilization Reserve Fund to prevent additional reductions before the end of the fiscal year. We will continue to closely monitor spending and to make fiscally conservative budget decisions.[22]

The legislature responded to the governor's request by passing S.B. 2649 during the 2017 legislative session, which raised the $50 million rainy day fund transfer cap to $100 million for FY 2017.[23] Bryant believed that all of the actions taken to manage the state's finances were necessary during the economic downturn. The credit rating agencies did not praise Bryant for the specific actions taken; however, the rating agencies did credit the State of Mississippi for having laws in place that allowed the governor to manage effectively during tough economic times.

Executive Authority Questioned

Judicial intervention has played a major role in shaping Mississippi's budget-making process, and it all started with the landmark *Alexander v. State of Mississippi by and through Allain (1983)* case.[24] Although the *Alexander* case forced a change to the legislatively dominated budget-making process, it was the legislature that determined what the process would be. The legislature responded to the *Alexander* decision by passing S.B. 3050 during the 1984 legislative session, known as the Mississippi Administrative Reorganization Act of 1984, which gave the DFA's predecessor the Fiscal Management Board the authority to carry out the budget control component of the budget execution phase.[25] It was the legislature that determined how the executive branch was to keep expenditures in line with revenue. Governors had followed the budget process prescribed by the legislature since 1984 without any issues, so one could only imagine Governor Bryant's surprise when, more than thirty years after the *Alexander* case, Rep. Bryant Clark and Sen. John Horhn challenged the governor's authority to reduce state agency budgets, claiming that it was a constitutional violation. Representative Clark and Senator Horhn's complaint stated:

1. This lawsuit seeks to enforce the Mississippi Constitution's separation of powers doctrine. In Mississippi, the Legislative Branch is responsible for making the budget, while the Executive Branch is charged with controlling the budget. These coequal branches of government are constitutionally prohibited from exercising the powers allotted to the other.

2. In violation of the separation of powers doctrine, Mississippi Code Section 27-104-13 gives the Executive Branch the power to make monthly "midyear budget cuts" when state general funds are not available to pay the state budget . . .

3. By allowing the Executive Branch to usurp the Legislature's budget-making power, Section 27-104-13 violates the separation of powers doctrine and must be permanently enjoined. If midyear budget cuts are to occur, they must be directed by the only body the Mississippi Constitution allows budget-making activity: the Legislature.[26]

Through spokesperson Clay Chandler, Bryant disputed the conclusion of the lawsuit, citing the *Alexander* opinion, where the supreme court ruled that once the taxes are levied and appropriations are made by the legislature, it is the duty of the executive branch to exercise "budget control" within the limits imposed on the governor by the legislature.[27]

Senior staff attorney Will Bardwell with the Southern Poverty Law Center represented Representative Clark and Senator Horhn. Bardwell argued that state agency budget cuts are part of the budget-making process and that the Mississippi Supreme Court has stated that the Mississippi Constitution says that "this is a power that can only be wielded by the Legislature."[28] Bardwell did not dispute the fact that Governor Bryant had the statutory authority to reduce state agency budgets, but he contended that the state law that gives the governor the authority to make cuts when revenue does not meet projections is a violation of the separation of powers clause of the Mississippi Constitu-tion.[29] The legislative branch of government, not the executive branch, must make any mid-year budget cuts, the lawsuit argued. "What [the governor] can't do is circumvent the legislature [and] deprive them of their constitutional authority to make budget making decisions, and [. . .] arbitrarily do it himself. Unfortunately, that's what he's been doing," argued Bardwell.[30]

Clark and Horhn filed their complaint on May 17, 2017, and on the same day filed a motion for a temporary restraining order (TRO) or preliminary injunction. Judging by both Clark's and Horhn's affidavits included with the plaintiffs' complaint, their grievances seemed to be more about Governor Bryant reducing the budget for the Mississippi Adequate Education Program (MAEP), rather than the governor usurping the legislature's budget-making power. The *Affidavit of Rep. Bryant W. Clark* explained the budget-making process, as he understood it, and expressed his thoughts on the most important component of the state budget. Clark's affidavit stated:

> I believe that the most important component of the state budget is the fund-ing for public schools, known as the Mississippi Adequate Education Program (MAEP). For the 2017 fiscal year, the budget allocated $2,036,556,667 to MAEP. This funding is critical because school districts need financial resources in order to educate our children adequately. In February 2017, Governor Bryant cut MAEP by more than $11.2 million. In March 2017, he cut MAEP by more than $8.6 mil-lion. These midyear budget cuts occurred without any input, oversight, or voting by the Legislature.[31]

A similar statement expressing the importance of MAEP funding was made in Senator Horhn's affidavit. Additionally, Senator Horhn stated, "I don't know why Governor Bryant cut MAEP by nearly $20 million. I also don't know what analysis was conducted that allowed the Governor to conclude that schools did not need this $20 million."[32]

The legislative leadership that served in the majority of both chambers never questioned the governor's authority to reduce budgets at the time of the lawsuit, which made it appear that the challenge was about politics. Republicans controlled both the house and the senate, and the governor was a Republican, while both of the challengers were Democrats. When asked about the lawsuit, Governor Bryant stated:

> The latest attempt by the Democrats and their allies to use the court system in a desperate grasp for relevance poses a genuine danger to Mississippi credit rating. Rating agencies have said time and again that executive authority to balance a state

budget is a primary determiner of credit worthiness. The Southern Poverty Law Center apparently holds Mississippi taxpayers in such low regard that it is willing to jeopardize the state's financial health for a meaningless academic exercise. We will vigorously defend responsible budgeting policies from this ridiculous lawsuit."[33]

The lawsuit appeared to be about partisan politics, but Attorney General Jim Hood, who was the only statewide elected Democrat at the time, still represented Republican Gov. Phil Bryant and the other defendants in the suit. More specifically, counsel for the state defendants were Krissy Nobile and Harold Pizzetta from the Office of the Attorney General's Civil Litigation Division.

The state defendants filed a response in opposition to the plaintiffs' motion for a TRO on May 30, 2017. Nobile and Pizzetta worked closely with the DFA to understand the budget-making process in its entirety and included the *Affidavit of Brian A. Pugh* (the deputy executive director of the DFA) with their response, which "explains in further detail the budget making and budget control functions in Mississippi."[34] The affidavit also addressed the MAEP concern raised by the two legislators, explaining:

> Neither MDE nor the MAEP is exempt from the State Fiscal Officer's budget control measures under Code Section 27-104-13. The Legislature has never exercised its discretionary authority to exempt MDE or the MAEP from mid-fiscal year budget reductions under Code Section 27-104-13 for any fiscal year, as it has with many other agencies and programs identified in that statute.[35]

Nobile went on to explain that the legislature not only has the discretion to exclude MAEP's appropriation but also "remains free to exclude any appropriation from the budget control measures of Section 27-104-13, preserving the legislature's final say on the appropriation."[36]

A primary source used by the DFA to explain the budget-making and budget control functions was the *Alexander* case. It is ironic that the defendants and plaintiffs both used the *Alexander* case to argue their point. In reaction to the plaintiffs' *Alexander* reference, Nobile pointed out, "In their complaint and motion for TRO, Plaintiffs primarily place their eggs in one legal basket: *Alexander v. State ex rel. Allain*. . . . The *Alexander* decision, though, does not carry Plaintiffs where they want to go. In fact, if anything, *Alexander* altogether closes the door on Plaintiffs' purported constitutional claim."[37] Nobile concluded that the plaintiffs' motion failed to maintain basic separation of powers principles, and the relief requested ran counter to law and clashed with the very purpose of a TRO. Therefore, the motion for TRO or preliminary injunction should be denied.[38]

Hinds County Chancery Court

Judge Patricia D. Wise of the of the Chancery Court of the First Judicial District of Hinds County heard the motion for a TRO or preliminary injunction on May 31, 2017. After reading the briefs, considering all of the evidence, and hearing the oral arguments made by Bardwell and Nobile, the court denied the motion for a TRO or preliminary injunction and dismissed the plaintiffs' complaint. Judge Wise used previous court cases to address the plaintiffs' constitutional challenge to the budget reduction statute, explaining that the plaintiffs "must 'overcome the strong presumption' that the Legislature acted within its constitutional authority" when it passed Section 27-104-13.[39] Furthermore, she explained that "the courts are without the right to substitute their judgment for that of the Legislature as to the wisdom and policy of the act and must enforce it, unless it appears beyond all reasonable doubt to violate the Constitution."[40] The Chancery Court's *Final Judgment and Order* found that the "Plaintiffs have failed to prove that they are entitled to any relief and that Section 27-104-13 is unconstitutional. Accordingly, Plaintiffs' complaint and all claims asserted in it should be finally dismissed with prejudice. The Court thus DISMISSES all of the Plaintiffs' claims."[41]

Supreme Court

Representative Clark and Senator Horhn appealed the chancellor's verdict to the Mississippi Supreme Court, and "the issue on appeal [was] whether a statute allowing the Executive Branch to make appropriations decisions violates the separation-of-powers doctrine under the Mississippi Constitution."[42] The executive branch maintained that Section 27-104-13 did not violate the separation-of-powers doctrine, and the supreme court agreed, stating:

> While we agree with the Executive that Section 27-104-13 is constitutional, we clarify that this case does not implicate separation of powers because the Executive was exercising its own core power under the Constitution. As the Legislators have failed to overcome the presumption that Section 27-104-13 is constitutional, we affirm the chancellor's dismissal of the complaint.[43]

All nine justices agreed with the lower court's decision, with two of the nine concurring in part.[44] If the courts had interpreted the *Alexander* case the way that the two legislators did with regard to budget control, there would have been no way for the executive branch to control the budget after funds were appropriated if revenue performed poorly. Therefore, a special legislative session would have to be called whenever revenue fell short of expectations when the legislature was out of session. If the court had ruled that Section 27-104-13 was unconstitutional, meaning that the governor would have lost the ability to control budgets, there is a good chance that the state's credit rating would have been downgraded by the credit rating agencies.

The FORTIFY Act

When Governor Bryant first took office, he set a goal in *Opportunity Mississippi: Detailing the Roadmap to Success* to maintain or increase the state's credit rating. Although this task may have appeared to be insignificant, it was actually no small feat. When Bryant first became governor, the State of Mississippi's credit ratings were AA+, Aa2, and AA by Fitch Ratings, Moody's Investor Services, and Standard and Poor's (S&P), respectively. The state maintained its credit rating from 2012 through 2015 with all three credit rating agencies. This all changed in 2016 when Fitch downgraded Mississippi from AA+ to AA. Although the other two rating agencies did not downgrade the state, Moody's revised the state's outlook to negative in 2016 and S&P made the same negative revision in 2017.

Prior to being downgraded by Fitch, the state was put on negative outlook. One contributing factor, among many, was the state's continued use of nonrecurring funds on recurring expenditures. Bryant expressed his frustration with the revised outlook in his FY 2015 EBR stating, "Mississippi received disappointing news last week, as Fitch Ratings changed the outlook on our bond rating from stable to negative. Among the primary reasons for this change was the State's continued reliance on one-time money to fund recurring expenses."[45] The state's downgrade and outlook revisions were not surprising to individuals on the governor's staff familiar with the situation, based on conversations and scorecard results from the credit rating agencies. Fortunately, the scorecard methodologies provided the governor's office with a guide for positive fiscal reform to prevent future downgrades.

Two months after the 2017 legislative session, Governor Bryant proposed the Financial and Operational Responses That Invigorate Future Years (FORTIFY) Act to the legislature as a way to utilize financial best practices in areas that the state could control.[46] The rating agencies' scorecards for the state pointed out things done well, and things done not so well. Unfortunately, the things that the state was penalized for had been problems plaguing the state for many years, such as having a relatively limited economy, stagnant population growth, below-average wealth and income indicators, etc.[47] Instead of focusing on those issues, Bryant decided to focus on improving areas where the state was already fairly strong.[48] The governor knew that he had to call a special session in 2017 because the legislature had failed to pass appropriation bills for multiple agencies during the regular legislative session, so he took that opportunity to propose the FORTIFY Act.

Senate Appropriations Committee chairman Eugene "Buck" Clarke authored S.B. 2002 during the First Extraordinary Session of 2017, creating the FORTIFY Act. Senator Clarke's bill included most of what the governor wanted, but it did not include everything. S.B. 2002 passed out of both the house and senate and was signed into law by Bryant, although it had been altered some. Items requested by the governor that made it into the bill included: naming the act; increasing the rainy day fund cap from 7.5 percent to 10 percent of general fund appropriations for the fiscal year; requiring the Legislative Budget Office (LBO) to produce a multi-year financial plan; no longer adding unencumbered cash to the revenue estimate when calculating the 98 percent limitation on appropriation of general funds; and revising the distribution of unencumbered cash at the end of a fiscal year to split between the rainy day fund and the Capital Expense Fund (CEF). One of the financial best practices, requested by the governor but omitted in Clarke's bill, would have taken away the legislature's vehicles for using nonrecurring funds on recurring expenditures. This would have been accomplished by amending the laws pertaining to both the Budget Contingency Fund (BCF) and the CEF.

There is no questioning that the BCF is considered nonrecurring, because there is no recurring funding source to deposit into the fund other than transfers made by the legislature. Former Gov. Ronnie Musgrove described the BCF, in his veto message of the legislation creating the fund, as an "uncontrolled legislative fund," which few budget experts disputed.[49] The legislature temporarily stopped appropriating from the BCF because the credit rating agencies frowned on the practice. Bryant recommended that the legislature abolish the BCF in the FORTIFY Act, but the legislature refused.[50] Instead of discontinuing the practice of spending one-time money altogether from the BCF, the legislature started funding recurring expenditures from the CEF.

The intended use of the CEF when it was established was for capital improvements and repair and renovations; however, broad language was included in the legislation that allowed the fund to be used for practically any purpose. The legislation provided that "[t]he Capital Expense Fund shall be used for capital expense needs, repair and renovation of state-owned properties and specific projects authorized by the Legislature."[51] The latter part of the sentence stating that the funds could be used for specific projects authorized by the legislature has been interpreted as whatever the legislature chooses to spend it on.

The CEF was created during the 2008 legislative session with bipartisan support when the legislature passed H.B. 1244, authored by House Appropriations Committee chairman Johnny Stringer, and signed into law by Gov. Haley Barbour. H.B. 1244 also added the CEF to the unencumbered cash balance distribution performed at the end of the fiscal year, which in theory provided a recurring funding source, assuming that there was any ending cash.[52] The problem was that the legislature had more wants and needs than the amount of money in the CEF. As a remedy to the problem, the legislature began to transfer funds from different funding sources into the CEF for one-time capital expense projects and recurring non-capital expense projects. Many policymakers approved of the CEF but disapproved of the way that it was being used. Then–Lieutenant Governor Bryant believed that the CEF should be limited to capital improvements only, and this belief carried over into his governorship. When speaking of the CEF in his FY 2016 EBR, Bryant stated:

> Once again, my budget calls for the proper uses of the Capital Expense Fund, which was established during my time as Lieutenant Governor. Each year a portion of ending cash should be set aside to address the capital needs, which results in a decreased need for bonding. Capital Expense Funds should be used for true capital expense needs such as renovation and repair. I will continue to advocate for proper fiscal management of this account.[53]

Unfortunately for Bryant, the legislature never heeded his advice and continued using the CEF for whatever they wanted. One specific request by Bryant in the FORTIFY Act was to require that the CEF be used for capital improvement needs only. The governor asked the legislature to remove the broad language that gave the legislature authority to use the fund any way it pleased. However, the legislature rejected Bryant's request, electing to keep its autonomy over the fund. Although the governor failed to persuade the legislature to revise the CEF language, it did not take away from the other positive gains made by the FORTIFY Act.

Governor Bryant was commended by the credit rating agencies for proactively managing the state's finances and for having the executive authority to do so. Passing the FORTIFY Act enhanced the governor's ability to manage the state's finances even more. After revising Mississippi's rating from negative to stable in 2018, Standard and Poor's (S&P) stated, "We consider Mississippi's financial management practices strong under its Financial Management Assessment methodology, indicating our view that practices are well embedded and likely sustainable."[54] Moody's also revised the state's outlook from negative to stable. The 2018 outlook revisions put the state on stable outlook by all three credit rating agencies, since Fitch already had the state's outlook as stable.

Budget Transparency and Simplification Act of 2016

The FORTIFY Act likely would not have come to fruition if it had not been for the legislature's failure to pass a consequential technical amendments bill for the Mississippi Budget Transparency and Simplification Act of 2016 during the 2017 legislative session, which forced the governor to call a special session for that purpose.[55] Since the legislature would already be in session for a technical amendments and appropriation bills, Bryant added the FORTIFY Act to the agenda of the special session. The technical amendments bill was the most controversial bill on the calendar during the First Extraordinary Session of 2017. Most of the objections to the technical amendments bill were a carryover of the same objections that were raised when the legislature passed S.B. 2362 during the 2016 legislative session, which created the Budget Transparency and Simplification Act.

S.B. 2362 was authored by Senate Appropriations chairman Eugene "Buck" Clarke, and it was portrayed by both the legislature and the media as a broad, sweeping budget reform act that would change most special fund agencies to general fund agencies so that they would have to fight for their piece of the budget "pie" of general funds.[56] On board with Senator Clarke was House Appropriations chairman Herb Frierson, who explained that after the passage of the act, special fund agencies would no longer have the luxury of "silo-ing that money.... They will have to come to us each year and justify their budget. They will be subject to fluctuations and the rise and fall of revenue, just like education is, just like mental health is."[57] However, the bill that actually passed was not nearly as broad or encompassing as it was portrayed, because it affected only sixteen special fund agencies out of around sixty-five, which was fairly insignificant in the grand scheme of the entire state budget.[58] The legislature anticipated that the general fund would receive $130,010,225 in new revenue resulting from S.B. 2362, which is not that much, considering that the legislature appropriated $2,300,633,016 in special funds a year earlier in FY 2016.[59] In addition to affecting only a small number of agencies, the bill was poorly drafted in several ways, which caused some of the funds transfers to not be made. In eight written official opinions and "several informal discussions" with agency heads, the Office of the Attorney General said that a total of $79.4 million in special funds could not legally be swept from the agencies into the general fund, because of problems under the Mississippi Constitution.[60]

Attorney General Jim Hood referred to S.B. 2362 as "legally and constitutionally flawed."[61] Hood pointed out conflicting language and other problems in the bill. He explained that the bill specifically stated that it "shall not apply to any trust fund account," but then it attempted to sweep funds from trust fund accounts into the general fund. Additionally, the bill abolished numerous special funds but failed to amend the laws that created them, which Hood said conflicted with a Mississippi Constitution section that prohibits the legislature from amending a law by reference. Other agency heads noticed similar inconsistencies in the bill and requested attorney general's opinions concerning the legality of the bill.

One of the first agencies to request an official opinion from the attorney general was the Mississippi Tort Claims Board, after being informed that its trust fund would be "abolished and all funds swept into the State General Fund."[62] Hood's office explained to the board in its opinion, "This office does not question the Legislature's authority to make statutory changes. The question here is did the Legislature, through S.B. 2362 and the amendments to Section 11-46-17, actually make these changes? It is the opinion of this office that the Legislature did not and that the language . . . of S.B. 2362 and the actual amendments to Section 11-46-17 do not abolish or authorize sweeping of the Tort Claims Fund."[63] Additionally, the opinion cited Section 61 of the Mississippi Constitution, which provides that "[n]o law shall be revived or amended by reference to its title only, but the section or sections, as amended or revived, shall be inserted at length."[64] Because of the legislature's failure to properly amend the necessary code sections, the newly appointed state fiscal officer and executive director of the DFA, Laura Jackson, followed the attorney general's opinion and did not sweep into the State General Fund the funds of the Tort Claims Board or those of any other agencies whose code sections were not properly amended. "Just as all past Executive Directors of the Department of Finance and Administration have done, we do plan to follow the opinions of the Attorney General," said Jackson.[65]

Jackson assumed the role of state fiscal officer after Kevin Upchurch's abrupt retirement in June 2016. Upchurch had tried to warn the legislature prior to the passage of S.B. 2362 that the bill failed to amend the necessary code sections to make it work, but the bill still passed, forcing him to request an attorney general's opinion for the DFA a few days before his retirement. Jackson accepted her appointment from Governor Bryant knowing that the first item on her agenda would be figuring out how to carry out the inconsistent and incomplete provisions of S.B. 2362. "Because the previous state fiscal officer had been so vocal in his opposition to the bill, it honestly would have been very difficult for him to implement. When I started this job on July 1, 2016, my mission was to implement the law, even though we were faced with agency heads who did not agree with the plan and numerous dissenting attorney general's opinions," explained Jackson.[66]

Governor Bryant knew that S.B. 2362 was unpopular with the agencies affected by it, but he believed that the decision to sweep special funds into the general fund was the legislature's to make, not the executive branch's. However, Bryant was not blind to the issues with the bill, so he called for a working group of budgeting experts, led by Jackson, to review and identify the perceived issues with the bill, so that they could be addressed at the beginning of the 2017 legislative session.[67] The working group analyzed the problems and made a recommendation to the legislature for a technical amendments bill to correct the flaws of S.B. 2362. The legislature received the working group's recommendation, and the house and senate passed S.B. 2625 during the 2017 legislative session, but the bill died in conference committee near the end of the session. The governor then called the legislature back for a special session to take up another technical amendments bill, S.B. 2001, and this bill passed and was signed into law.[68]

The effort to fix the flawed Budget Transparency and Simplification Act was long and tedious. In summing up the process, Jackson explained that "to be honest, it was a laborious process. The legislation would never have been successfully implemented had we not maintained an open line of communication with the legislative leadership and the sixteen agencies that were directly affected."[69] One of the working group's recommendations was to switch certain agencies back to being special fund agencies again. The legislature took nearly all of the working group's recommendations, which further diluted the scope of the act. During the three years after the act passed, several other agencies were removed from the act so that only eight of the sixteen agencies originally covered by the act remained as exclusively general fund agencies.

Despite its lofty name and ambitious purpose, the Budget Transparency and Simplification Act never came close to accomplishing what it was portrayed to be. The agencies that were affected by it were relatively minor agencies and collectively made up only a small part of the overall budget. Consequently, the act has made little significant impact on the budgeting process in Mississippi.

Saving as a Priority

Bryant paid close attention to the credit rating agencies' support of Mississippi's rainy day fund and its 98 percent limitation on appropriation of general funds. Similar to his predecessor Haley Barbour, Bryant called on the legislature to fill the rainy day fund to its statutory limit and to adhere to the 98 percent limitation. The legislature suspended the 98 percent limitation under both Barbour and Bryant, although being encouraged by the governors not to do so. Barbour and Bryant both wanted 2 percent set aside in order to be in a better position to fill the rainy day fund. The rainy day fund was filled to its statutory limit in FY 2008, while Barbour was governor and Bryant was lieutenant governor, and again in FY 2014 and FY 2015 while Bryant was governor. Bryant ended up taking the practice of saving to another level when he requested that the legislature raise the statutory rainy day fund limit cap from 7.5 percent of appropriated general funds to 10 percent, which became law when he signed the FORTIFY Act. The credit rating agencies saw the act as a move in the right direction and as a way to encourage more savings. Every dollar put into a reserve was a dollar not spent. Fitch explained that "maintenance of reserves provide[s] the state with ample capacity to address a moderate downturn scenario."[70]

In Bryant's FY 2020 budget recommendation, he highlighted how the state ended FY 2018 with just under a $120 million surplus, which allowed nearly $60 million to be transferred each to the rainy day fund and the CEF. The transfer to the rainy day fund brought the balance to approximately $350 million. Bryant stated that the transfers to both funds would not have been nearly as much if the FORTIFY Act had not passed. Bryant's budget recommendation also put forth a plan to get the rainy day fund balance to nearly $460 million by FY 2021.[71] Bryant's plan used general fund revenue estimates recommended by the revenue estimating committee, which had recommended a revision to the FY 2019 revenue estimate, and also made a FY 2020 recommendation to be jointly adopted for the executive and legislative budget recommendations. The Joint Legislative Budget Committee (JLBC) and the governor adopted the FY 2020 recommendation, but not the FY 2019 revised estimate. The revenue estimating committee had recommended raising the FY 2019 revenue estimate to $5.758 billion. Assuming that the revenue estimating committee was correct in its estimate, $102 million would have been available for the end-of-year distribution at the end of FY 2019. In discussing his plan, Bryant explained:

> Although the Joint Legislative Budget Committee (JLBC) and I elected to not revise the FY 2019 estimate, I agree with the revenue estimating [committee's] FY 2019 recommendation and believe that the additional funds should not be appropriated but put into reserves. By law, any excess cash from the close of FY 2019 would be directed to the Rainy Day Fund and Capital Expense Fund. The Rainy Day Fund balance will be just over $400 million after the transfer. Additionally, this EBR recommends spending only 98 percent of estimated revenue in FY 2020, which leaves $116 million available for the end of year distribution. After $750,000 is transferred to the Municipal Aid Fund, $57.6 million will be transferred to both the Capital Expense Fund and Rainy Day Fund. The Rainy Day Fund balance for FY 2021 will be approximately $458 million.[72]

If the revenue estimating committee's figures were to come to fruition according to Bryant's plan, the FY 2021 rainy day fund would have the highest amount ever in the account. If the FY 2021 general fund revenue estimate stayed exactly the same as the FY 2020 estimate of $5,802,200,000, and 2 percent was set aside, the general funds left to be appropriated would have been $5,686,156,000. The rainy day fund would have been full before passage of the FORTIFY Act with Bryant's savings plan. However, with the new cap at 10 percent of appropriated general funds, Bryant's FY 2021 rainy day fund plan would have needed approximately $142 million in additional funds to fill the account to its new statutory limit.

Critics of the FORTIFY Act mocked the move to increase the cap on the rainy day fund, saying that the state had trouble filling the rainy day fund when the cap was set at 7.5 percent, and believed that it would really struggle to fill the fund at 10 percent. However, to the surprise of many, revenue exceeded expectations at the end of FY 2019, only two years after the passage of the FORTIFY Act, which provided enough funds to fully fill the rainy day fund to its new statutory limit of 10 percent—resulting in the highest amount ever in the history of the rainy day fund. This is only the fifth time that the rainy day fund has been filled since its creation.

Mississippi Lottery

Mississippi lawmakers had been calling for a lottery for decades to no avail, ever since the legal pathway was cleared in 1992 after voters chose to remove the state's constitutional prohibition of a lottery. That all changed in 2018. Governor Bryant's FY 2018 EBR briefly mentioned a lottery but failed to offer a full endorsement. However, he did allude to being in favor of a lottery by referencing how well a state with similar demographics to Mississippi was doing with its lottery. Bryant explained that Arkansas received $80 million from its lottery and that Mississippi had the potential to generate more. "The Department of Revenue estimates that a state lottery would generate $88 million to $100 million annually for the state. Because of that, I am open to a general discussion about the implementation of a lottery in Mississippi," stated Bryant.[73] Bryant attempted to and was successful at changing the lottery narrative to one strictly about revenue. Bryant, who in the past opposed a lottery, now believed that the issue should at least be considered by the legislature. One thing that changed Bryant's mind was the fact that the state was losing revenue, because many Mississippians were traveling to neighboring states to purchase lottery tickets, which he stated was a strong argument for enacting a lottery.[74]

Knowing that Governor Bryant was open to having a lottery discussion appeared to cause the momentum for a lottery to grow; however, the legislature's two presiding officers, Speaker Philip Gunn in the house and Lt. Gov. Tate

Reeves in the senate, continued to oppose a lottery. Speaker Gunn explained, "I have been clear that I do not support a lottery. I have not changed my mind. I do not believe a lottery is based on sound economic policy, and it violates a number of conservative, Republican principles."[75] When Lieutenant Governor Reeves was asked in an earlier interview about the potential for a state lottery, he expressed concerns that a lottery might have an adverse effect on existing revenue. "If one's goal is to increase revenue to the state, the question that must be answered: Would any perceived increase in revenue from a lottery be offset by reductions in sales tax collections and gaming receipts?" Reeves said.[76] Furthermore, Reeves explained, "I personally am opposed to the lottery in Mississippi. . . . But I do believe a majority of Senators would like to vote to enact a lottery."[77]

Governor Bryant echoed Reeves's claim that a majority of senators preferred to enact a lottery, and he also believed that legislators in the house shared those same sentiments. Detecting a strong appetite for a lottery, Bryant called a special session in 2018 to address the issue. He wanted the funds generated from the lottery to go toward repairing Mississippi's crumbling roads and bridges. The principal author of the lottery legislation was Sen. Philip Moran, and it was assigned to the Senate Highways and Transportation Committee. The lottery legislation, S.B. 2001, passed during the First Extraordinary Session of 2018, created a state lottery that was to be administered by a corporation known as the Mississippi Lottery Corporation.[78] Explaining Mississippi new lottery, Bryant stated:

> The lottery will be administered by the Mississippi Lottery Corporation Board of Directors. The Lottery Corporation is a quasi-governmental entity that is intended to operate like a private corporation. It will not receive any state appropriation and will operate on its own revenues . . . The Corporation is charged with managing the lottery in a manner that will maximize revenue to the state . . . Until June 30, 2028, money deposited into the Lottery Proceeds Fund shall be paid into the State Highway Fund to provide funds to repair, renovate and maintain highway and bridges of the state. However, all such monies deposited into the Lottery Proceeds Fund over $80 million in a fiscal year shall be transferred into the Education Enhancement Fund for the purposes of funding the Early Childhood Learning Collaborative, the Classroom Supply Fund and/or other educational purposes.[79]

S.B. 2001 passed both houses with bipartisan support. One significant change to the lottery legislation was its name. The version of S.B. 2001 that was introduced by Senator Moran and passed the Senate was referred to as the "Mississippi

Lottery Law." However, the name was amended in the house, and included in the final bill, to be referred to as the "Alyce G. Clarke Mississippi Lottery Law" in honor of longtime House Democratic Rep. Alyce Clarke. Representative Clarke had been sponsoring lottery legislation each regular session since 2004, with no success.[80]

Governor Bryant received much praise for his involvement in the First Extraordinary Session of 2018, which was arguably the most successful session during his administration. In addition to getting the legislature to pass Mississippi's first lottery, he was credited with influencing the content of the Mississippi Infrastructure Modernization Act of 2018 (H.B. 1), which provided a steady stream of funding for current and future infrastructure needs and also provided $300 million in revenue bonds for infrastructure.[81] In summarizing the special session, the *Jackson Clarion-Ledger* reported that the special session "was an historic affair, and Mississippians should soon see better roads and lottery tickets for sale as a result. In all, Bryant got his special session agenda passed in five days, with few alterations. No easy feat."[82]

Conclusion

Major budget reform in Mississippi has occurred only twice in the last four decades, with the most significant reform occurring in the mid-1980s. No reform shaped Mississippi's budget-making process more than the Mississippi Administrative Reorganization Act of 1984 (S.B. 3050, passed during the 1984 legislative session), which was passed not voluntarily by the legislature but as a result of a court order. The drastic budget reform would have not occurred if it had not been for then–Attorney General Bill Allain's challenge to the structural makeup of the committee responsible for the budget-making process at the time, the Commission of Budget and Accounting. The state supreme court's decision in *Alexander v. State of Mississippi by and through Allain* (1983) led to the passage of the reorganization act. Although the *Alexander* case forced change to the legislatively dominated budget-making process, it was the legislature that determined what the new process would be.

The second major reform came about with no executive or judicial input, when the legislature passed the Budget Reform Act of 1992 (H.B. 505, passed during the 1992 legislative session). The Budget Reform Act was not intended to be sweeping budget reform but was instead passed to improve the budget-making process already in place. The Budget Reform Act created the Working Cash-Stabilization Reserve Fund, known as the rainy day fund, and prohibited the legislature from appropriating more than 98 percent of the estimated general fund revenue. The rainy day fund and the 2 percent set-aside benefited the executive branch a great deal, because both measures had the potential to positively affect budget control, which is an executive function, according to the *Alexander* case.

In addition to passing major reform that changed or improved the budget-making process, the legislature also passed budget reform laws that failed to meet expectations, such as the Mississippi Performance Budget and Strategic Planning Act of 1994 (S.B. 2995, passed during the 1994 legislative session) and the Budget Transparency and Simplification Act of 2016 (S.B 2362, passed during the 2016 legislative session). While the Performance Budget and Strategic Planning Act did implement performance budgeting and strategic planning for all agencies, beginning with the FY 1996 budget cycle, the legislature never used the information obtained to actually determine how funds were to be appropriated to state agencies. The Budget Transparency and Simplification Act was portrayed as a broad, sweeping budget reform act that would change most special fund agencies to general fund agencies, but in actuality only sixteen special fund agencies were affected by the act. Although both of these acts had the potential to drastically change the budget-making process, neither act came close to accomplishing what it was supposed to accomplish and therefore made an insignificant impact on the budgeting process in Mississippi.

Present-Day Budget-Making Process

The Mississippi Administrative Reorganization Act of 1984 revised the budget-making process (explained in more detail in Appendix I) so that it operated in a sequential pattern of organization, which included the following formal phases: budget preparation and proposal, legislative budget approval (budget making), and budget execution (budget control). The reorganization act created the Joint Legislative Budget Committee (JLBC) and its staff, the Legislative Budget Office (LBO). The act also created the State Fiscal Management Board (FMB), which was later replaced by the Department of Finance and Administration (DFA). Under the act the JLBC was required to submit a legislative budget recommendation (LBR), and the governor was required to submit a separate executive budget recommendation (EBR), which was prepared by the DFA's Office of Budget and Fund Management. The JLBC was given the responsibility of making recommendations regarding budget making to the entire legislative body, and the state fiscal officer, who also serves as the executive director of the DFA and is appointed by the governor, was given the authority to carry out budget control. The budget-making process that was put in place back in 1984 is still used today, with some minor changes having been made to the process over the years.

Budget Preparation and Proposal

Mississippi is one of a few states that include legislators in the budget preparation and proposal phase. Budget proposals in most states are strictly an executive function, similar to the federal government. Mississippi's governor had the sole authority of submitting a budget proposal from 1918 through 1955 after the legislature gave the governor that solitary power. Legislators got back into the business of proposing budgets in 1955 when the Commission of Budget and Accounting was created, which included the governor and legislators serving jointly on the commission. After the Commission of Budget and Accounting was deemed to be unconstitutional in the *Alexander* case in 1983, the legislature dropped the governor from the commission, and it became the JLBC and continued proposing budgets. The legislature actually tried to keep the governor from proposing budgets altogether and would have likely succeeded if Governor Allain had not threatened to veto S.B. 3050 because he wanted to have full control over the FMB. This is why Mississippi has two budget proposals, one from each branch.

Today, Mississippi's annual budget-making process starts when state agencies begin submitting their budget requests to the LBO and the DFA, which are typically due on or before August 1. The guidelines that agencies use to prepare their budget requests are developed by the JLBC, without any executive input. The agencies' requests are then used to prepare both the LBR and the EBR. Between September and November, except in the years following a governor's new term in office, the governor proposes his EBR to the legislature. In December the JLBC adopts and proposes its LBR to the entire legislative body, just before the start of the legislative session.

The LBR, not the EBR, serves as the starting point for budget discussions and appropriations subcommittee deliberations once the legislature is in session. Although this is uncommon in other states, it seems to work well for Mississippi because the legislative budget proposal consists of detailed figures broken down by major objects of expenditures. The governor's EBR does not contain the details of the LBR, because it is meant to be more of a policy document. As one would imagine, the legislature usually ignores the executive's proposal in its deliberations on the budget.

Legislative Budget Approval

The legislative budget approval phase is known simply as budget making, and this is the phase where the legislature appropriates funds to operate state government. The Mississippi Legislature convenes in January for its annual regular session and to create the next fiscal year's state budget, which begins on July 1, by passing appropriation bills that authorize the maximum amounts of funds that state entities and agencies may expend from state support funds and other funds. Mississippi does not have an omnibus appropriation process with one big budget bill, as many other states do, and the legislature passes well over one hundred appropriation bills each session. Once the appropriation bills are duly enacted through the legislative process, the legislature's budget-making duties are fulfilled, and its budget-making and appropriations authority expires. After the appropriation bills have been passed by the legislature, the governor can either sign or veto the bills. Once the legislative session is adjourned sine die, the legislature is no longer able to impose any new limitations, restrictions, or conditions on the expenditure of appropriated funds, which it can do only when the legislature is in session.

The appropriations process is usually straightforward, because budget making is solely the responsibility of the legislature under the state constitution, as declared in the *Alexander* case. However, Republican governors Fordice and Barbour were both accused of interfering in the process of budget making by Democratic legislators. Even if Barbour interfered in the legislative approval phase, he was never found to have violated any budget control statutes or the state constitution. Fordice, on the other hand, not only interfered in budget making but was also found by the courts to have overstepped his constitutional authority regarding the budget. This occurred when Fordice attempted to amend language in several appropriation bills, after first altering various projects in a bond bill, citing his constitutional authority to partially veto appropriation bills. Fordice was sued by Sen. Hob Bryan in *Fordice v. Bryan* (1995), a case that went to the Mississippi Supreme Court, and the court ruled in favor of Senator Bryan. Fordice's attempted partial vetoes of the appropriation bills and the bond bill were therefore declared to be invalid. The court's verdict was a warning to future governors to stay out of the legislative budget approval phase.

Budget Execution

Budget execution is the final phase of the budget-making process, and it is referred to as budget control. Budget control is typically noncontroversial, because most of the executive branch's authority regarding budget control has been statutorily given to it by the legislature. The reorganization act gave the state fiscal officer the authority to take necessary steps to ensure that the State and state agencies do not spend more revenue, within their operating budgets, than the amount of revenue that is collected over the course of the fiscal year. Additionally, the state fiscal officer (acting through the DFA's Office of Budget and Fund Management) reviews and approves each agency's submitted operating budget to ensure compliance with the agency's appropriation bill. Once the DFA approves an agency's operating budget, it is used for authorizing the agency's expenditure of funds throughout the fiscal year.

The state fiscal officer's budget control duties also include monitoring the fiscal year's official general fund revenue estimate that is adopted by the JLBC, and reducing agencies' operating budgets if revenues underperform expectations. If general fund revenue falls below 98 percent of the JLBC's adopted general fund revenue estimate, at the end of October, or at the end of any subsequent month during the fiscal year, the state fiscal officer is required by law to reduce eligible agencies' operating budgets or transfer funds from the rainy day fund to the general fund to supplement the general fund revenue. Reductions to agencies' operating budgets cannot exceed 5 percent for any agency until all eligible agencies' budgets have been reduced by that percentage. Once all eligible agencies' budgets have been reduced by 5 percent, then any additional budget reductions must be a uniform percentage reduction to all eligible agencies' budgets—a requirement that limits executive authority over budget control. More limitations on reducing agencies' budgets would have been placed on governors by the legislature in the late 1980s if Gov. Ray Mabus had not vetoed S.B. 2214 during the 1988 legislative session, which would have weakened executive discretion over budget cuts by mandating that the executive branch uniformly reduce agencies' budgets when revenue did not meet expectations. This would have taken practically all of the governor's budget reduction discretion away during budget control.

The all-important *Alexander* case held that budget control is an executive function. A difference of opinion regarding the interpretation of the *Alexander* case led to another separation of powers lawsuit, thirty-five years after the supreme court rendered its decision in the case, when two members of the legislature filed a lawsuit against the governor in *Representative Bryant W. Clark and Senator John Horhn v. Governor Phil Bryant et al.* (2018), which made it to the Mississippi Supreme Court. Representative Clark and Senator Horhn claimed that Governor Bryant was actually participating in budget making instead of budget control when he exercised his statutory authority to reduce agency budgets, which was a violation of the separation of powers clause of the state constitution. Gov. Phil Bryant dismissed the lawsuit as an "academic exercise" and asserted that budget reductions are clearly a function of budget control. It was somewhat surprising that both sides used the *Alexander* case to argue their point. The court ended up rejecting the legislators' claim and ruling in favor of the executive branch. If the legislators had won their argument, that decision would have completely changed the budget control phase of Mississippi's budget-making process.

Important Enhancements to the Budget-Making Process

The central features of the Budget Reform Act of 1992 dealt with (1) replacing two inferior reserve funds that were created a decade earlier with the rainy day fund, and (2) setting limitations on total annual appropriations from the general fund by requiring a 2 percent set-aside. The purpose of the rainy day fund is to set aside a portion of projected revenue as an unappropriated contingency against a revenue shortfall. At the time it was created, the fund was to be considered full when the balance equaled 7.5 percent of appropriated general funds for each fiscal year, but that percentage was increased to 10 percent in 2017. The rainy day fund has proven to be a valuable tool, because it allows governors to pull monies from the fund when revenue estimates are not met, instead of having to reduce agencies' budgets to the max.

The 2 percent set-aside was intended to serve as a cushion in case revenues fell short of expectations. Prior to the passage of the 1992 reform act, it was quite common for agencies to expect executive budget reductions to be made at some point during the fiscal year, because the legislature would usually appropriate 100 percent of the expected revenue, and the revenue estimate was oftentimes not on target. After the legislature started appropriating only 98 percent of anticipated revenue, it did not matter nearly as much when revenue estimates were slightly off. Additionally, with the 2 percent set-aside in place, it is more likely that there will be remaining funds at the end of the fiscal year, and a portion of those funds will be deposited into the rainy day fund, which makes saving much easier. One disadvantage of having funds sit idly in a savings account is the constant demand to appropriate the funds in order to fund government at a higher level. Spending from the rainy day fund is not a problem if the funds are expended on nonrecurring expenditures; however, many legislators want the funds to be spent on recurring items, which would create future budget problems. Credit rating agencies often penalize states for spending nonrecurring funds on recurring expenditures, making borrowing more expensive, which in turn makes funding government more expensive.

Kirk Fordice was the first governor to benefit from the Budget Reform Act after he practically forced the legislature to adhere to its own "98 percent rule." The rainy day fund grew significantly as a result, increasing by more than $70 million from FY 1993 to FY 1999. However, the future amount in the fund would likely have been lower if Senate Finance Committee chair Hob Bryan had not refused to bring Fordice's tax cut bill, which had successfully passed the house, to a vote in the Senate Finance Committee, causing the bill to die during the 1999 legislative session. A tax cut would have affected the state's savings because the house and senate had proven that they had no appetite for cutting expenditures. If Fordice's tax cut had passed, and the legislature continued its refusal to cut expenditures, the savings would have slowly been spent down and likely created a deficit for the next governor.

To avoid cutting expenditures, the legislature has sometimes suspended the 2 percent set-aside requirement in order to appropriate 100 percent of the anticipated revenue. Appropriating all of the expected revenue is considered to be bad fiscal policy, because it sometimes forces agencies to cut budgets in midyear or closer to the end of the fiscal year, rather than up front. It is much easier for agencies to plan for budget cuts at the beginning of a fiscal year, rather than near the end of it.

The Budget Reform Act contributed greatly to the idea of savings because of the optimistic goal of filling the fund at 7.5 percent of appropriated general funds. The bar was raised even higher when Governor Bryant proposed the Financial and Operational Responses That Invigorate Future Years (FORTIFY) Act during the First Extraordinary Session of 2017, which increased the rainy day fund cap from 7.5 percent to 10 percent of general fund appropriations for the fiscal year. The legislature passed the FORTIFY Act into law, which enhanced the governor's ability to manage the state's finances even more. Critics of the FORTIFY Act claimed that raising the fund was pointless, since it was rarely ever filled when the statutory amount to fill it was 2.5 percent lower.

Assessing the Mississippi Budget-Making Process

Major budget reform in Mississippi has not occurred more regularly because it is hard to accomplish. Critics of the current budget-making process often fail to offer an alternative plan that could get the necessary support needed to actually change the process. The legislature preserved as much power as possible when it passed the Mississippi Administrative Reorganization Act of 1984, and is still reluctant to give up any of its power. Mississippi has traditionally had a weak governor, and most of the pro-reformers advocate for more executive power. The chance of the legislative branch giving up its budget power is unlikely. Instead of arguing for total budget reform that benefits the executive branch, a much more realistic request would be to relax some of the current limitations on the executive branch during the budget control phase. Limitations that currently exist in the budget control phase include certain agencies being exempt from budget reductions (e.g., regulatory special fund agencies) and requiring agency budget reductions to be made using a uniform percentage reduction after all eligible agencies have been cut by 5 percent.

The legislature can currently by statute exempt any agencies that it chooses from executive budget reductions, which further dilutes the executive branch's authority to manage the state's finances when there is an unexpected dip in revenue collections. For example, the legislature could amend the laws to exempt the Mississippi Adequate Education Program (MAEP) and the Medicaid program from budget reductions, which would take half of the general funds off the table. If revenue collections were to decline by 15 percent, which would force major budget reductions, and MAEP and Medicaid were exempt from the reductions, the rest of state government would have to be reduced at a level that would likely be unsustainable to many.

History has shown that when executives are equipped with more budget-control authority, the state is more likely to weather a financial crisis. For a state that has never trusted a strong executive, Mississippi was forced to give the governor more power during the Great Depression. In reaction to the economic depression, the legislature on May 5, 1932, passed H.B. 205 to create the Budget Commission, which was charged with promoting economy and efficiency in the management of the state's finances. The legislation designated the governor as ex officio director of the budget and the chairman of the State Tax Commission, who was appointed by the governor, as the assistant director. Included in the Budget Commission's power was the budget control authority to allow state agencies to exceed their appropriations during emergencies. Executives today obviously do not need the authority to allow agencies to exceed their appropriations, but this example shows that extreme times sometimes call for extreme measures. In the worst economic downturn in the history of the United States, the executive branch in Mississippi was given more budget control power to manage the state's finances, not less.

The State of Mississippi has been applauded by the credit rating agencies for its statutory abilities to manage its finances during economic downturns. Mississippi's budget-making process could be much stronger if the legislature allowed the governor to manage the state's finances after the legislature has adjourned sine die, without limitations. If the legislature thought that the governor was doing a poor job of managing the state's finances while it is out of session, it would always have the option to reverse any unwanted changes after the legislature returns. That being said, the legislature would still have the final say on the matter, as it should be.

Appendix

IN THE CHANCERY COURT OF HINDS COUNTY, MISSISSIPPI
FIRST JUDICIAL DISTRICT

REP. BRYANT CLARK AND
SEN. JOHN HORHN
                                                    PLAINTIFFS
VS.   CAUSE NO. G2017-722 S/2

GOVERNOR PHIL BRYANT,
STATE FISCAL OFFICER LAURA JACKSON,
THE MISSISSIPPI DEPARTMENT OF
EDUCATION, AND STATE TREASURER
LYNN FITCH   DEFENDANTS

AFFIDAVIT OF BRIAN A. PUGH

I, Brian A. Pugh, hereby state under oath that the following is based on personal knowledge and experience, and true and correct to the best of my knowledge and belief:

1. I am currently the Deputy Executive Director of the Mississippi Department of Finance and Administration (DFA), an executive branch agency of the State of Mississippi that possesses certain powers and duties prescribed by Mississippi law with respect to the State's fiscal affairs. I have been employed by DFA since July 2016.

At DFA, I am currently responsible for direct management and oversight of six of the 19 offices within the department. Those offices include: the Office of Budget & Accounting, the Office of Budget & Fund Management, the Bond Advisory Division, the Office of Fiscal Management, the Office of Financial Reporting and the Office of Financial Affairs. I work directly for the State Fiscal Officer, Laura Jackson, who was appointed by Governor Phil Bryant and serves as DFA's Executive Director.

2. Prior to my employment at DFA, I served as the Director of Finance for the Governor's Office and as a Budget Analyst for the Legislative Budget Office. My budget knowledge also extends to academia. I teach graduate courses in "State and Local Government Budgeting and Finance" for Jackson State University's Department of Public Policy and Administration. I also hold a Master's Degree and a Ph.D. in Public Policy and Administration.

3. "Budget control" and "budget making" are generally accepted and understood as mutually exclusive activities in the field of governmental fiscal management. "Budget control" is generally accepted and understood, when operating under a fiscal year-by-year balanced budgeting system, including monitoring governmental revenue receipts, comparing those receipts to budgeted revenue estimates and planned expenditures, and then taking corrective actions when necessary over the course of the fiscal year to eliminate the possibility of a budget deficit at the end of the fiscal year. "Budget making" is generally accepted and understood, when in the same context of operating under a fiscal year-by-year balanced budgeting system, as establishing a set of planned expenditures based on revenue estimates, which are then subject to budget control measures taken in the course of the budget's operation for the fiscal year. Legislative "budget making" concludes once the Regular Session adjourns *sine die* (which ends the legislative session) and executive "budget control" begins.

4. The State of Mississippi's current annual budget-making process is governed by Title 27, Chapter 103, Section 101 et seq. of the Mississippi Code. The budget-making process begins each June, when state agencies may begin to submit their next fiscal year's budget request to the Legislative Budget Office (LBO). LBO is the administrative arm of the Joint Legislative Budget Committee (JLBC). JLBC is a Legislative

Committee created by, and whose membership is defined by Code
Section 27-103-101.

5. Annual agency budget requests for the next fiscal year must conform
   to statutorily-prescribed (see Code Section 27-103-129) and other LBO
   requirements, and be submitted to LBO through the Online Budget
   Request System (OBRS) on or before August 1.
6. Between September and November, the JLBC conducts hearings,
   and collects and reviews data including agency budget requests, State
   revenue estimates, and other pertinent information. In November
   (except in years following the Governor's new term of office), the
   Governor submits a separate balanced state budget as required by
   Code Section 27-103-139. In
       December, JLBC adopts a Legislative Budget Recommendation
   for an overall balanced budget for the State for the next fiscal year, as
   required by Code Section 27-103-113, and that includes the contents
   required by Code Sections 27-103-123 through -127.
7. In January, the Mississippi Legislature convenes for its annual Regular
   Session and ordinarily effectuates the next fiscal year's State budget
   (which begins on July 1) by passing separate appropriation bills
   authorizing the maximum amounts of state funds that particular
   State entities and agencies may expend from general and special
   fund sources of revenue. Each appropriation bill must conform to
   Constitutional and other requirements for all legislation, as well
   as other particularized requirements, including, but not limited to:
   Constitution Sections 63 (maximum sum of state funds authorized
   to be expended), 64 (appropriations bills remain in force no longer
   than two months after the expiration of the next fiscal year), 68
   (appropriations bills not passed in the last five days of the session), and
   69 (appropriation bills may prescribe conditions and limitations on
   which funds may be withdrawn).
8. After an appropriation bill is passed by the Legislature, the bill either
   becomes effective when the Governor signs and returns the bill, or fails
   to sign and return the bill in the time frames set forth in Constitution
   Section 72. If the Governor vetoes the bill pursuant to Constitution
   Section 72, or vetoes parts of the bill pursuant to Section 73, then the
   bill or the vetoed portions of the bill may only become effective if the
   bill passes through the veto override process pursuant to Constitution
   Section 72. Appropriation bills that become effective ordinarily
   prescribe, pursuant to language in each bill itself, that the bill authorizes

expenditures beginning on July 1, which marks the beginning of the fiscal year following each Regular Session of the Legislature.

9. The Legislature ordinarily adjourns *sine die* sometime between late March and early May, depending on the length of the session. Once appropriation bills for state agencies are duly enacted through the process described above, the Legislature's budget-making duties are fulfilled, and its budget making and appropriations authority for the succeeding fiscal year expires. Once its Regular Session has adjourned *sine die*, the Legislature lacks authority to administer a duly enacted appropriation, and cannot impose any new limitations, restrictions or conditions on the expenditure of appropriated funds for the succeeding fiscal year when the Legislature is not in session. At that point, under Mississippi law (which statutorily requires the State to operate on a balanced budget system), it is the executive branch's duty and authority to exercise budget control measures which have the purpose of ensuring the State operates on a balanced budget during the fiscal year and thereby eliminates the possibility of a fiscal deficit at the end of the fiscal year, and may have the effect of reducing the actual amounts of state funds state agencies receive and expend over the course of the fiscal year.

10. The State Fiscal Officer and DFA have certain executive branch duties and authority over the State's fiscal affairs as codified at Title 27, Chapter 104, Section 1 et seq. of the Mississippi Code, separate and apart from the code provisions governing the State's annual budget-making process. The State Fiscal Officer's authority codified in Chapter 104 includes budget control measures first enacted in 1984 as part of the overall reorganization of the State government, and later revised from time to time. The budget control measures allow the executive branch officials involved to take necessary steps to ensure the State and state agencies do not spend more revenue within their operating budgets approved by the State Fiscal Officer than that amount of revenue which becomes available over the course of the fiscal year through taxes and other sources. The budget control measures, and the process for their implementation over the course of the fiscal year, also gives DFA and state agencies flexibility to adjust expenditures downward in response to fluctuations in each fiscal year's State revenue collections.

11. Under current budget control measures enacted in Chapter 104, after appropriations are enacted, but before the next fiscal year begins on July 1, pursuant to Code Section 27-104-9, each state agency must

submit an operating budget for the next fiscal year conforming to DFA requirements. The State Fiscal Officer reviews and approves each agency's submitted operating budget to ensure the budget complies with the agency's appropriations bill, and once approved by the State Fiscal Officer (acting through the DFA-Office of Budget and Fund Management) the operating budget is used for authorizing the agency's expenditure of funds throughout the fiscal year.

12. Pursuant to Code Section 27-104-11, during the course of the fiscal year, the State Fiscal Officer approves each agency's expenditures. In most instances, under the budget control authority of Code Section 27-104-11, no general or special funds may be expended by an agency until estimates of the amount required by the agency have been submitted to and approved by the State Fiscal Officer.

13. Pursuant to Code Section 27-104-13, during each fiscal year, the State Fiscal Officer's budget control duties and authority include the responsibility to monitor the fiscal year's official general fund revenue estimate adopted by JLBC at the conclusion of the Legislature's previous Regular Session. If at the end of October, or the end of any subsequent month during the fiscal year, the revenues received for the fiscal year fall below 98% of JLBC's adopted general fund revenue estimate, then the State Fiscal Officer is required by law to reduce allocations of general funds and eligible state-source special funds to the agencies' operating budgets (and a certain portion of the Mississippi Department of Transportation's (MDOT) operating budget) and immediately notify LBO. The amount of budget reductions ordered by the State Fiscal Officer must be the amount necessary to keep state agencies' expenditures within the sum of actual general fund receipts, including any transfers to the general fund from the Working Cash-Stabilization Reserve Fund (commonly known as the "Rainy Day Fund") for the fiscal year.

14. In the event of revenue shortfalls by the end of October, or the end of any subsequent month during the fiscal year, where the revenues received for the fiscal year fall below 98% of JLBC's adopted general fund revenue estimate, the State Fiscal Officer also has budget control authority to (1) transfer funds from the Working Cash-Stabilization Reserve Fund to increase the general fund, within an amount prescribed by statute, and (2) require certain state- source and special fund transfers to the general fund in an amount equal to the operating budget reductions of state agencies' eligible state-source special funds.

15. The required operating budget reductions ordered pursuant to the State Fiscal Officer's budget control authority for any one agency may ordinarily not exceed 5% of the agency's operating budget over the course of the fiscal year. However, in the event that all eligible general fund and special fund agencies' operating budgets, and a certain portion of MDOT's operating budget have been reduced by 5% over the course of the fiscal year, then any additional operating budget reductions for the fiscal year must be a uniform percentage reduction to the operating budgets of all eligible agencies.

16. Budget control measures taken under DFA's statutory authority do not reduce an agency's appropriations authorization. Rather, agency operating budget reductions implemented under the budget control process prescribed by Code Section 27-104-13 reduce the agency's authority to expend state funds under its DFA approved operating budget. Budget reductions under Code Section 27-104-13 thus do not constitute a reduction to an agency's maximum sum spending authorization established by its appropriations bill duly enacted prior to the fiscal year.

17. Once budget control measures are implemented to reduce an agency's operating budget during the fiscal year, Code Section 27-104-14 prohibits DFA or the Governor from rescinding or restoring any previously ordered budget reductions of any eligible agency.

18. At the end of the 2016 Legislative Session, the LBO reported an error in the preparation of the fiscal year 2017 budget in the amount of $56.8 million. The Governor made the budget control decision in September 2017 to reduce the general fund budgets in the amount of $56,801,694 to account for this error. In addition, as a result of revenue shortfalls, the budget control measures implemented by the State Fiscal Officer through fiscal year 2017 to date, as required by Code Section 27-104-13 have resulted in additional reductions to eligible agency operating budgets in January 2017, February 2017, and March 2017 in the respective amounts of $50,974,616 (January), $43,000,000 (February) and $20,446,237 (March).

19. At its 2016 Regular Session, the Legislature enacted an appropriation bill for the Mississippi Department of Education that was subsequently approved by the Governor. See 2016 HB 1643, true and correct copy affixed hereto as Exhibit "1." The bill appropriated MDE the maximum sum of $ 2,311,438,129, through a combination of estimated general fund and special fund revenues for fiscal year 2017, to be distributed to the State's more than 140 school districts

through the Mississippi Adequate Education Program. MDE, as required by Code Section 37-151-99, furnished preliminary estimates of the amount of MAEP funds to be distributed to the local school districts prior to the beginning of the fiscal year. As required by Code Section 37-37-1, MDE has formulated a uniform system of accounting for all local school districts which all districts are required to utilize in maintaining their financial records, including record keeping with respect to all funds expended each fiscal year.

20. After 2016 HB 1643 was approved by the Governor and the 2016 Legislature adjourned, and at the beginning of fiscal year 2017, as with prior years, DFA utilized MDE's data and information regarding monthly disbursement of funds to the State's more than 140 local school districts consistent with Code Sections 37-151-101 and 37-151-102, and consistent with the MDE's operating budget. During fiscal year 2017 (through the month of April 2017), MDE has accordingly received a monthly distribution of the funds to be disbursed to MDE under its operating budget, to be, in turn, disbursed by MDE (through the State's enterprise accounting system) to the more than 140 local school districts under the MAEP. Between July 2016 and April 2017, MDE received a monthly disbursement from the maximum sum of $ 2,311,438,129 originally authorized to be distributed for the MAEP amongst the State's more than 140 school districts.

21. Neither MDE nor the MAEP is exempt from the State Fiscal Officer's budget control measures under Code Section 27-104-13. The Legislature has never exercised its discretionary authority to exempt MDE or the MAEP from mid-fiscal year budget reductions under Code Section 27-104-13 for any fiscal year, as it has with many other agencies and programs identified in that statute.

22. The budget control measures taken by the State Fiscal Officer under Code Section 27-104-13 in January 2017 did not implement any MDE operating budget reductions as to the MAEP. In February 2017, however, required budget control measures implemented by the State Fiscal Officer in accordance with all requirements of Code Section 27-104-13 resulted in a reduction of approximately $ 11,207,191 to the MDE operating budget for the MAEP. Also in March 2017, a further required budget control measure implemented by the State Fiscal Officer in accordance with all requirements of Code Section 27-104-13 resulted in a reduction of approximately $ 8,601,764 to the amounts of funds authorized to be distributed for the MAEP (under MDE's operating budget), bringing the total fiscal year budget reduction to MAEP

to $19,808,955. MDE adjusted the calculation of MAEP funds to be distributed to the State's more than 140 school districts to account for the budget reductions to MAEP.

23. As mentioned previously, Code Section 27-104-14 prohibits the Governor or DFA from rescinding or restoring any reductions or revisions to an agency's operating budget once budget control measures of reducing an agency's or program's operating budget for the fiscal year have been implemented under Code Section 27-104-13. If DFA rescinds or restores all budget control measures implemented under Code Section 27-104-13 in September 2016, January 2017, February 2017, and March 2017 to reduce or revise all affected agencies' operating budgets (which would violate the law), then the approximate budget shortfall in the overall State budget at the end of the fiscal year would likely approximate $ 171,222,547.

DATED this the _____ day of May, 2017.

_____

STATE OF MISSISSIPPI
COUNTY OF HINDS

Sworn to and subscribed before me, this the _ day of May, 2017.

_____

NOTARY PUBLIC

My Commission Expires:

Notes

Introduction

1. The term "trias politica" or "separation of powers" was coined by Charles-Louis de Secondat, baron de La Brede et de Montesquieu, an eighteenth-century French social and political philosopher that published *Spirit of the Laws*, which is considered one of the great works in the history of political theory and jurisprudence. Furthermore, Charles-Louis's work inspired the Declaration of the Rights of Man and the Constitution of the United States. Under his model the political authority of the state is divided up into legislative, executive, and judicial powers, and he asserted that to effectively promote liberty, these branches must act independently. National Conference of State Legislatures (NCSL).

2. *Alexander v. State of Mississippi by and through Allain*, 441 So. 2d 1329 (Miss. 1983).

3. *Alexander v. State of Mississippi by and through Allain*, 441 So. 2d 1329 (Miss. 1983).

4. The thirty-six legislators illegally serving on boards and commissions included: William B. Alexander, Senator; Joseph L. Blount, Representative; Ellis B. Bodron, Senator; Thomas L. Brooks, Representative; Edward H. Buelow Jr., Representative; Thomas H. Campbell III, Representative; Archie L. Cates, Representative; Donald Ray Chambliss, Representative; Aubrey Mitchell Childre, Senator; Robert L. Crook, Senator; Algie Arnold Davis, Senator; Glenn S. DeWeese, Senator; Lawrence G. Dubaz Jr., Representative; W. Edward Ellington, Senator; Thomas A. Gollott, Senator; Carl J. Gordon Jr., Senator; J. K. Gresham, Senator; Richard E. Hall, Representative; R. G. Huggins, Representative; H. L. Merideth Jr., Representative; Theodore J. Millette, Representative; Joe Henry Mulholland, Senator; C. B. Newman, Representative; Charles Ray Nix, Senator; Edgar H. Overstreet, Senator; Emmett H. Owens, Representative; F. Edwin Perry, Representative; John William Powell, Senator; Don W. Richardson, Representative; James C. Simpson, Representative; George P. Smith, Senator; Q. Emerson Stringer Jr., Senator; W. Terrell Stubbs, Representative; John H. Waldrop, Senator; Thomas H. Walman, Representative; and Charles L. Young, Representative.

5. In addition to the Commission of Budget and Accounting, the other eight boards or commissions were: Board of Economic Development, Board of Trustees of the Public Employees' Retirement System, Central Data Processing Authority, State Personnel Board, Medicaid Commission, Capital Commission, Wildlife Heritage Committee, and Board of Corrections.

6. Edward Clynch, "Introduction," in *Budgeting in the States: Institutions, Processes, and Policies* (Westport, CT: Praeger, 2006), 2.

7. David Nice, "Public Budgeting" (Belmont, CA: Wadsworth/Thomson Learning, 2002), 38.

8. William Winter, *The Measure of Our Days: Writings of William F. Winter*, edited by Andrew Mullins (Jackson: University Press of Mississippi, 2006), 7.

9. Erle Johnston, "Long Ambition Realized; Winter Elected Governor," in *Politics: Mississippi Style* (Forest, MS: Lake Harbor, 1993), 301.

10. The "Boys of Spring" were young staff members who worked for Gov. William Winter. The other members included Dick Molpus, John Henegan, and Andy Mullins.

11. Prior to Kirk Fordice becoming governor, the state of Mississippi had not had a Republican governor since Reconstruction era governor Adelbert Ames, who served from 1874 to 1876.

Chapter One

1. "State of Mississippi," *Mississippi Republican*, August 13, 1817.

2. The Mississippi delegates were able to draft the Mississippi Constitution of 1817 so quickly because many of its provisions were adapted from constitutions of Kentucky, Tennessee, and Louisiana. Information from Mississippi Department of Archives and History's *Icons of Statehood*, presentation delivered at the 2017 Mississippi Historical Society Annual Conference.

3. For the original texts of Mississippi's four constitutions, see *The Constitutions of Mississippi as Originally Adopted* (University, MS: Bureau of Governmental Research, 1982).

4. Tip H. Allen Jr., "The Enduring Traditions of the State Constitutions," in *Mississippi Government and Politics, Modernizers versus Traditionalists* (Lincoln: University of Nebraska Press, 1992), 44.

5. David Sansing, *Mississippi Governors, Soldiers, Statesmen, Scholars, Scoundrels* (Oxford, MS: Nautilus, 2016), 11.

6. Sansing, *Mississippi Governors, Soldiers, Statesmen, Scholars, Scoundrels*, 35.

7. Porter L. Fortune Jr., "The Formative Period," in *A History of Mississippi*, edited by Richard Aubrey (Hattiesburg: University and College Press of Mississippi, 1973), 1:278–82.

8. *Journal of the Proceedings of the Constitutional Convention of the State of Mississippi* (1868), pp. 295–96, 519, 543; Mississippi Constitution (1868), arts. 4, 5, 6, 8, 10.

9. Mississippi Constitution (1890), arts. 4, 5, 7, 8, 15.

10. General Laws of Mississippi of 1918, Ch. 225

11. General Laws of Mississippi of 1918, Ch. 225; General Laws of Mississippi of 1932, Ch. 120; General Laws of Mississippi of 1952, Ch. 320.

12. Nannie Pitts McLemore, "The Progressive Era," in *A History of Mississippi*, edited by Richard Aubrey (Hattiesburg,: University and College Press of Mississippi, 1973), 2:61.

13. Sansing, *Mississippi Governors, Soldiers, Statesmen, Scholars, Scoundrels*.

14. Erle Johnston, "A White Suit and Red Necktie," in *Politics: Mississippi Style* (Forest, MS: Lake Harbor, 1993), 5.

15. Johnston, "White Suit and Red Necktie," 4.

16. Sansing, *Mississippi Governors, Soldiers, Statesmen, Scholars, Scoundrels*, 173.

17. Dennis J. Mitchell, "War, Depression, and Environmental Restoration," in *A New History of Mississippi* (Jackson: University of Mississippi Press, 2014), 312.

18. Mitchell, "War, Depression, and Environmental Restoration."

19. J. Oliver Emmerich, "Collapse and Recovery," in *A History of Mississippi*, edited by Richard Aubrey (Hattiesburg: University and College Press of Mississippi, 1973), 2: 97.

20. David Sansing, "A Democratic University," in *The University of Mississippi, a Sesquicentennial History* (Jackson: University of Mississippi Press, 1999), 198.

21. Emmerich, "Collapse and Recovery," 103.

22. Mitchell, "War, Depression, and Environmental Restoration," 322. Gov. Martin Conner resigned as speaker of the house to run for governor and was defeated in 1923 and 1927 before finally winning the gubernatorial election in 1931.

23. Emmerich, "Collapse and Recovery," 102; Mississippi House of Representatives, *House Journal* 1932, p. 786.

24. Emmerich, "Collapse and Recovery," 104.

25. Sansing, *Mississippi Governors, Soldiers, Statesmen, Scholars, Scoundrels*, 174.

26. Emmerich, "Collapse and Recovery," 104.

27. Westley F. Busbee, "The Depression Years," in *Mississippi: A History*, 2nd ed. (Malden, MA: Wiley Blackwell, 2015), 240.

28. Edward J. Clynch, "Mississippi's Taxing and Spending: Have Things Really Changed?," in *Mississippi Government and Politics, Modernizers versus Traditionalists* (Lincoln: University of Nebraska Press, 1992).

29. General Laws of Mississippi of 1932, Ch. 120.

30. Until the Mississippi Constitution of 1890 was amended in 1986, governors served four-year terms and were ineligible for immediate succession, while members of the State Tax Commission served six-year terms. Kirk Fordice was the first governor elected to successive terms when he was reelected for a second term in 1995, and he served for a total of eight years. The only other governor in the twentieth century, prior to Fordice, who served more than four consecutive years was Fielding Wright (1946–1952) because he filled the vacated governor's seat after the death of Thomas Bailey, who died in office in 1946.

31. "Ellis Becomes New Building Director," *Jackson Clarion-Ledger*, June 3, 1953.

32. Clynch, "Mississippi's Taxing and Spending."

33. General Laws of Mississippi of 1952, Ch. 320.

34. General Laws of Mississippi of the Extraordinary Session of 1955, Ch. 24.

35. Charles M. Hills, "Affairs of State," *Jackson Clarion-Ledger*, March 28, 1955.

36. Hills, "Affairs of State."

37. *Jackson Clarion-Ledger* and *Columbian-Progress*, May 27, 1955; *Jackson Clarion-Ledger* June 9, 1953.

38. *Jackson Clarion-Ledger* and *Columbian-Progress*, May 27, 1955.

39. Tim Parker, *Delta Democrat-Times* (Greenville, Mississippi), July 15, 1957.

40. Biennial Report of the State Budget Commission from July 1, 1955, through June 30, 1957.

41. "Golding Says Budgeteers Find Figures by Motions," *Jackson Clarion-Ledger*, May 2, 1958.

42. Mississippi Code of 1972, Annotated, Sections 27-103-125, 27-103-139, 27-103-211, and 27-104-13, available at http://www.lexisnexis.com. A professional revenue estimating committee consisting of the state economist, who is employed at the University Research Center, and the Department of Revenue predicts revenue estimates for the fiscal year and makes a recommendation to the legislature and governor to be jointly adopted by the Joint Legislative Budget Committee (JLBC) and the governor. Although Mississippi law gives revenue estimating authority only to the University Research Center and the Department of Revenue, three other agencies assist in this process, including the Legislative Budget Office (LBO), the Office of the State Treasurer, and the Department of Finance and Administration (DFA).

43. "Golding Says Budgeteers Find Figures by Motions," *Jackson Clarion-Ledger*, May 2, 1958.

44. The reviews and reports stage involves various people looking at a budget year to see what can be learned, and producing required and perhaps optional reports in connection with or independent of reviews. Parties internal and external to an organization conduct reviews.

45. Dall W. Forsythe, "Memos to the Governor: An Introduction to State Budgeting," 2nd ed. (Washington DC: Georgetown University Press, 2004), 65.

46. Clynch, "Mississippi's Taxing and Spending," 178.

Chapter Two

1. Edward J. Clynch, "Mississippi's Taxing and Spending: Have Things Really Changed?" in *Mississippi Government and Politics: Modernizers versus Traditionalists* (Lincoln: University of Nebraska Press, 1992), 178.

2. Cliff Treyens, "Allain's Legislators Suit Is Heard," *Jackson Clarion-Ledger*, November 16, 1982.

3. According to house legislative attorney Ronny Frith, Charles Young was not ousted from the legislature because he was already serving on the Board of Corrections before he became a member of the legislature. Because the other legislators became members of the executive boards and commissions after they were in the legislature, they vacated their office in the legislature by accepting their appointments in the executive branch. Mississippi Constitution of 1890 (Section 2).

4. *Alexander v. State of Mississippi by and through Allain*, 441 So. 2d 1329 (Miss. 1983).

5. Mississippi Code of 1972, Annotated, Section 27-10-13 (repealed). The successor provision for the Legislative Budget Office is found in Section 27-103-113, available at http://www.lexisnexis.com.

6. Commission of Budget and Accounting, State of Mississippi Budget Report for FY July 1, 1984, to June 30, 1985.

7. Mississippi Code of 1972, Annotated, Section 27-103-27 (repealed). The last sentence of the paragraph of the referenced section was used by the Commission of Budget and Accounting in 1984 to propose an alternative budget. The sentence read "the commission may recommend additional taxes or sources of revenue if in its judgment such additional funds are necessary to adequately support the functions of the state government." The successor provision for the Legislative Budget Office is found in Section 27-103-125, available at http://www.lexisnexis.com.

8. Commission of Budget and Accounting, State of Mississippi Budget Report for FY July 1, 1984, to June 30, 1985.

9. General Laws of Mississippi of 1984, Ch. 488.

10. General Laws of Mississippi of 1984, Ch. 488, Section 75.

11. General Laws of Mississippi of 1984, Ch. 488, Section 76; Clynch, "Mississippi's Taxing and Spending," 179.

12. General Laws of Mississippi of 1984, Ch. 488, Section 76.

13. Peggy Austin, "Two Government Units Arrive at Budget Proposals," *Jackson Daily News*, November 28, 1984.

14. Austin, "Two Government Units Arrive at Budget Proposals."

15. Clynch, "Mississippi's Taxing and Spending," 180.

16. General Laws of Mississippi of 1984, Ch. 488, Section 76.

17. General Laws of Mississippi of 1985, Ch. 525, Section 7. The current prevision is found in Mississippi Code of 1972, Annotated, Section 27-104-13 (2). Under that section, the sine

die revenue estimate is adopted by the Joint Legislative Budget Committee at the end of the regular legislative session. The end of the session is known as sine die adjournment.

18. Mississippi Code of 1972, Annotated, Section 27-104-13.

Chapter Three

1. Edward J. Clynch, "Mississippi's Taxing and Spending: Have Things Really Changed?" in *Mississippi Government and Politics: Modernizers versus Traditionalists* (Lincoln: University of Nebraska Press, 1992), 180.

2. Gov. Bill Allain, State of Mississippi Executive Budget for FY July 1, 1985, to June 30, 1986.

3. Commission of Budget and Accounting, State of Mississippi Budget Report for FY July 1, 1984, to June 30, 1985.

4. Bill Allain's written letter addressed to the legislature on November 15, 1984, which was included in his executive budget for FY 1985–1986.

5. Bill Allain's written letter addressed to the legislature on November 15, 1984.

6. According to the FY 1985 Budget Report, the Commission of Budget and Accounting was forced to cut over $240 million from legislative appropriations from FY 1981 through FY 1985 in order to be in compliance with the provisions of Chapter 466, Laws of 1979. The FY 1987 Executive Budget Recommendation stated that Allain had to cut $47.4 million from FY 1986.

7. Gov. Bill Allain, State of Mississippi Executive Budget for FY July 1, 1985, to June 30, 1986, p. 1 (opening letter).

8. Joint Proposals submitted by Gov. Bill Allain and the Joint Legislative Budget Committee, State of Mississippi Proposed Budget for FY July 1, 1987, to June 30, 1988, p. 26.

9. Edward J. Clynch, "Mississippi: Does the Governor Really Count?," in *Governors, Legislatures, and Budgets: Diversity across the American States* (Westport, CT: Greenwood, 1991), 129.

10. General Laws of Mississippi of 1984, Ch. 488, Section 75; Clynch, "Mississippi: Does the Governor Really Count?," 126.

11. Joe Atkins, "New Fiscal Board Takes Over Budget Duties Today," *Jackson Daily News*, July 2, 1984.

12. Clynch, "Mississippi's Taxing and Spending," i 180.

13. Atkins, "New Fiscal Board Takes Over Budget Duties Today."

14. Atkins, "New Fiscal Board Takes Over Budget Duties Today."

15. Fiscal Management Board, *Minutes*, July 1984 through June 1985.

16. Handbook of the Office of Administrative Services, *Mission Statement*, January 1985.

17. Gov. Bill Allain, Executive Order No. 526.

18. The cost allocation plan went into effect on February 5, 1985. The cost allocation plan, used to recoup costs and expenses of the Office of Administrative Services from the governmental units that were supported and served, was approved retroactive to July 1, 1984, by the Federal Region IV Department of Health & Human Services.

19. General Laws of Mississippi of 1985, Ch. 525, Section 35.

20. General Laws of Mississippi of 1985, Ch. 175.

21. General Laws of Mississippi of 1985, Ch. 525, Section 35.

22. Title IV of the Intergovernmental Personnel Act of 1970 (5 U.S.C. §§ 3371–3376).

23. Ed Ling's written letter to Gov. Bill Allain, July 15, 1985, updating him on the progress of the Governor's Office of Administrative Services.

24. Ed Ling's written letter to Gov. Bill Allain, July 15, 1985.

25. Ed Ling's written letter to Gov. Bill Allain, November 27, 1985, in response to the critical PEER Report on the Office of Administrative Services.

26. Gov. Bill Allain, State of Mississippi Executive Budget for FY July 1, 1985, to June 30, 1986, p. 157.

27. Gov. Bill Allain, veto message, April 9, 1986.

28. Gov. Bill Allain, veto message on April 9, 1986.

29. General Laws of Mississippi of the First Extraordinary Session of 1986, Ch. 12.

30. Gov. Bill Allain, A Proclamation by the Governor, May 28, 1986.

31. Mississippi Code of 1972, Annotated, Section 27-104-13, http://www.lexisnexis.com.

Chapter Four

1. State Auditor Ray Mabus, "Special State Financial Report Presented to the Mississippi Legislature," for the period July 1, 1984, through December 31, 1984. Published in Accordance with the Requirements of Section 7-7-45(b), Miss. Code Ann. (1972). January 1985.

2. The State of Mississippi Comprehensive Annual Financial Report for Fiscal Year Ended June 30, 1987. Published in Accordance with the Requirements of Section 27-104-4, Miss. Code Ann. (1972).

3. Andrew Mullins, "Little Action on Education in 1980 and 1981," in *Building Consensus: A History of the Passage of the Mississippi Education Reform Act of 1982* (Mississippi Humanities Council and the Phil Hardin Foundation, 1992), 20.

4. Joe O'Keefe, "Mabus Hits, Misses with Agenda Plans," *Jackson Clarion-Ledger*, May 8, 1988.

5. O'Keefe, "Mabus Hits, Misses with Agenda Plans."

6. Edward J. Clynch, "Government and Money in Mississippi," in *Politics in Mississippi*, 2nd ed. (Salem, WI: Sheffield, 2001), 137.

7. O'Keefe, "Mabus Hits, Misses with Agenda Plans."

8. General Laws of Mississippi of 1984, Ch. 488.

9. Governor Ray Mabus, veto message for S.B. 2214, May 24, 1988.

10. O'Keefe, "Mabus Hits, Misses with Agenda Plans."

11. Ray Mabus, "An Investment in Mississippi's Future: Priority Funding for Education," in *Ray Mabus 1988 Education Plan*, February 1988.

12. Mabus, "An Investment in Mississippi's Future."

13. Twelve southeastern states used to calculate average: Virginia—$28,020; Florida—$25,688; Georgia—$25,604; Tennessee—$25,129; North Carolina—$24,845; South Carolina—$24,467; Kentucky—$24,018; Alabama—$23,500; West Virginia—$21,446; Louisiana—$21,280; Arkansas—$20,951; and Mississippi—$20,750.

14. General Laws of Mississippi of 1988, Ch. 487.

15. O'Keefe, "Mabus Hits, Misses with Agenda Plans."

16. Education Reserve Fund: At the end of the fiscal year and prior to the required distributions to the General Fund Reserve and General Fund Stabilization Reserve, any unencumbered cash will be sent to the Education Reserve Fund. The amount transferred to the Education Reserve Fund shall not exceed $50 million. General Laws of Mississippi of 1988, Ch. 487, Section 13.

17. General Laws of Mississippi of 1988, Ch. 487, Section 13.

18. Joint Proposals submitted by Gov. Ray Mabus and the Joint Legislative Budget Committee, Volume I, State of Mississippi Proposed Budget for FY July 1, 1989, to June 30, 1990.

19. Joint Proposals submitted by Gov. Ray Mabus and the Joint Legislative Budget Committee, Volume II, State of Mississippi Proposed Budget for FY July 1, 1989, to June 30, 1990.

20. Ray Mabus, "Introductory Letter" for the Joint Proposals submitted by Gov. Ray Mabus and the Joint Legislative Budget Committee, Volume I, State of Mississippi Proposed Budget for FY July 1, 1990 to June 30, 1991 (November 1989), 26.

21. Lea Anne Brandon and Jay Eubank, "Mabus Calls for Education Reform II, Lottery," Jackson Clarion-Ledger, October 26, 1989.

22. Lea Anne Brandon, "Mabus Won't Look at Alternatives to State Lottery," Jackson Clarion-Ledger, December 8, 1989.

23. Brandon, "Mabus Won't Look at Alternatives to State Lottery."

24. Brandon, "Mabus Won't Look at Alternatives to State Lottery."

25. General Laws of Mississippi of 1990, Ch. 588 and Ch. 589.

26. General Laws of Mississippi of 1990, Ch. 589, Section 84 and Ch. 589, Section 56.

27. General Laws of Mississippi of the First Extraordinary Session of 1990, Ch. 45.

28. Joint Legislative Budget Committee, "Indicators of Financial Conditions of the States, FY 90, 91, & 92," in The Mississippi Budgeting Process: A Comparative Study Mandated by the Budget Reform Act of 1992 (December 1992), 27.

29. General Laws of Mississippi of 1988, Ch. 307. The Executive Branch Reorganization Study Commission appointed by Mabus consisted of the following members: Thomas Tann, chairperson, Jackson; Sen. Jack Gordon, Okolona; Rep. Leslie King, Greenville; Rep. Rick Fortenberry, Meridian; Leroy Brooks, Columbus; Carol Daily, Jackson; Michael Freeman, Indianola; John Harper, Starkville; Richard McRae Jr., Jackson; Dr. Paul Purdy, Jackson; Mary Russ, Gloster; Bennie Thompson, Bolton; Sen. Glen Deweese, Meridian; Sen. Alan Heflin, Forest; Rep. Tommy Walman, McComb; Bea Branch, Jackson; Harry Bush, Laurel; Lucy Denton, Biloxi; Milton Harper, Jackson; Jeanne Luckett, Jackson; Peggy Peterson, Jackson; Jacqueline Robinson, Cleveland; Shirley Terry, Natchez; and Jack Thompson, Gulfport.

30. Ray Mabus press release, March 9, 1988, titled "Governor Signs Government Reorganization Bill."

31. Ray Mabus press release, October 28, 1988, titled "Mabus Streamlining Plan Recommends 11 Major Departments, $32 Million Savings."

32. Ray Mabus press release, January 24, 1989, titled "Governor Praises House Reorganization Action."

33. General Laws of Mississippi of 1989, Ch. 544.

34. Ray Mabus letter titled "Reorganization Highlights: PEER Report" (1991).

35. Jeff Copeskey, "Lawmakers Give Cool Reception to Mabus' Proposals," Jackson Clarion-Ledger, January 4, 1989.

36. Ray Mabus' Five-Year Capital Budget Letter of Transmittal found in the "Joint Proposals submitted by Governor Ray Mabus and Joint Legislative Budget Committee," Volume I, State of Mississippi Proposed Budget for FY July 1, 1989 to June 30, 1990 (November 15, 1988), iii.

37. Ray Mabus' Five-Year Capital Budget Letter of Transmittal found in the "Joint Proposals submitted by Governor Ray Mabus and Joint Legislative Budget Committee." Volume I. State of Mississippi Proposed Budget for FY July 1, 1990 to June 30, 1991. (November 15, 1988), iv.

38. Edward J. Clynch, "Mississippi: Does the Governor Really Count?," in Governors, Legislatures, and Budgets: Diversity across the American States (Westport, CT: Greenwood, 1991), 133.

39. General Laws of Mississippi of the First Extraordinary Session of 1989, Ch. 2.

40. Ray Mabus Administration Analysis of Savings Related to H.B. 3, *Mississippi Capital Improvements Program / Calendar Year 1989-1990*. Document provided by Cecil Brown, former DFA executive director (1988–1990) and chief of staff (1990–1992) to Gov. Ray Mabus.

41. General Laws of Mississippi of 1990, Ch. 581.

42. Ray Mabus Administration Analysis of Savings Related to S.B. 3192, *Mississippi Capital Improvements Program / Calendar Year 1990-1991*. Document provided by Cecil Brown, former DFA executive director (1988–1990) and chief of staff (1990–1992) to Gov. Ray Mabus.

43. Lea Anne Brandon and Jay Eubank, "Mabus Calls for Education Reform II, Lottery," *Jackson Clarion-Ledger*, October 26, 1989.

44. Brandon and Eubank, "Mabus Calls for Education Reform II, Lottery."

45. "NBER Business Cycle Dating Committee—March 1991," in the *National Bureau of Economic Research*.

46. Thomas Nardone, Diane Herz, Earl Mellor, and Steven Hipple, "1992: Job Market in the Doldrums" *Monthly Labor Review*, Division of Labor Force Statistics, Bureau of Labor Statistics, February 1993.

47. Interview with Cecil Brown (state fiscal officer 1988–1990), October 12, 2017.

48. Cecil Brown, DFA Response Letter to PEER's Inquiry (January 17, 1991).

49. Brown, DFA Response Letter to PEER's Inquiry.

50. PEER Committee Report # 260 to the Mississippi Legislature titled *Deficit Spending in Mississippi Government* (February 18, 1991), 6–7.

51. Joint Legislative Budget Committee. "Indicators of Financial Conditions of the States, FY 90, 91, & 92," in *The Mississippi Budgeting Process: A Comparative Study Mandated by the Budget Reform Act of 1992* (December 1992), 43.

52. PEER Committee Report # 269 to the Mississippi Legislature titled *Deficit Spending in Mississippi Government: A Follow-Up Review* (November 7, 1991), 1.

Chapter Five

1. General Laws of Mississippi of 1991, Ch. 426.

2. General Laws of Mississippi of 1992, Ch. 484.

3. General Laws of Mississippi of 1994, Ch. 602.

4. Joint Legislative Budget Committee, "Introduction," in *The Mississippi Budgeting Process: A Comparative Study Mandated by the Budget Reform Act of 1992* (December 15, 1992), 1.

5. S.B. 2706 authors included Senators Paul Richard Lambert, Dick Hall, William Canon, Cecil Mills, P. Nevin Sledge, and Robert Dearing.

6. Bills were proposed in 1991 and 1992 to completely replace the Mississippi budget system with systems from other states, e.g., Arkansas. Two of the budget replacement bills were S.B. 2877 of 1991 and S.B. 2261 of 1992. Another bill proposed was S.B. 2568 of 1991, which would have required the implementation of zero-based budgeting. All of those bills died.

7. Joint Legislative Budget Committee, "Mississippi Financial Problems and Issues, Part III. Legislative Response to Fiscal Stress and Budget Problems," in *The Mississippi Budgeting Process: A Comparative Study Mandated by the Budget Reform Act of 1992* (December 15, 1992), 43.

8. Joint Legislative Budget Committee, "Introduction," 8.

9. General Laws of Mississippi of 1992, Ch. 484.

10. The Education Reserve Fund was created in H.B. 601 of the 1988 legislative session, the same bill in which teachers' salaries were increased under Gov. Ray Mabus. General Laws of Mississippi of 1988, Ch. 487, Section 13. The Education Reserve Fund was repealed in

1993 by H.B. 400. General Laws of Mississippi of 1993, Ch. 509, Section 6. Ironically enough, the Education Reserve Fund was also repealed in 1992 by S.B. 3120. General Laws of Mississippi of 1992, Ch. 419. In addition to repealing the Education Reserve Fund (Section 33), S.B. 3120 created the Education Enhancement Fund. The Education Enhancement Fund took the place of the Education Reserve Fund in the diversion process.

11. General Laws of Mississippi of 1982, Ch. 428.

12. Brian Pugh, "Promoting Budgetary Policy through Stabilization: The Impact of Spending Stabilization Rules on Service Delivery," PhD diss. (Jackson State University, 2014).

13. Pugh, "Promoting Budgetary Policy through Stabilization."

14. Joint Legislative Budget Committee staff memo to Rep. Charlie Williams (September 2, 1986).

15. Joint Legislative Budget Committee, "Introduction," 8.

16. General Laws of Mississippi of 1992, Ch. 484, Section 5.

17. Joint Legislative Budget Committee, "Introduction," in 5.

18. Joint Legislative Budget Committee, "Mississippi Financial Problems and Issues, Part III," 29.

19. Joint Legislative Budget Committee, "Mississippi Financial Problems and Issues, Part III," 149.

20. Joint Legislative Budget Committee. "Executive Summary and Recommendations, Part II," in *The Mississippi Budgeting Process: A Comparative Study Mandated by the Budget Reform Act of 1992* (December 15, 1992), 12.

21. Joint Legislative Budget Committee, "Executive Summary and Recommendations, Part II," 12–13.

22. Speaker of the Mississippi House Tim Ford, "Letter to Members of the Mississippi Legislature," in *The Mississippi Budgeting Process: A Comparative Study Mandated by the Budget Reform Act of 1992* (December 15, 1992).

23. Joint Legislative Budget Committee. "Mississippi Financial Problems and Issues, Part III," 49.

24. General Laws of Mississippi of 1992, Ch. 484, Section 5.

25. General Laws of Mississippi of 1994, Ch. 602.

Chapter Six

1. General Laws of Mississippi of 1992, Chapter 484.

2. Sarah Campbell. "Budget Process Needs Retooling, Governor Says," *Jackson Clarion-Ledger*, January 28, 1992.

3. Campbell, "Budget Process Needs Retooling, Governor Says."

4. David Sansing, *Mississippi Governors, Soldiers, Statesmen, Scholars, Scoundrels* (Oxford, MS: Nautilus, 2016), 233.

5. FY 1992 actual total budget was $5,117,474,159; FY 1993 appropriated budget was $5,868,456,232; and Fordice's FY 1994 recommended total budget was $5,964,374,644.

6. Kirk Fordice was the first Republican governor elected since the Reconstruction era, the period from 1863 to 1877. The legislature was dominated by Democrats at the time Fordice was elected governor and had been since the Reconstruction era.

7. Gov. Kirk Fordice, State of Mississippi Executive Budget Recommendation for FY July 1, 1994, to June 30, 1995.

8. Fordice, State of Mississippi Executive Budget Recommendation for FY July 1, 1994, to June 30, 1995.

9. Gov. Kirk Fordice, State of Mississippi Executive Budget Recommendation for FY July 1, 1999, to June 30, 2000.

10. Joint Legislative Budget Committee, State of Mississippi Budget Bulletin for FY 1992, Joint Legislative Budget Committee, State of Mississippi Budget Bulletin for FY 2000.

11. Fordice, State of Mississippi Executive Budget Recommendation for FY July 1, 1999, to June 30, 2000.

12. Sansing, *Mississippi Governors, Soldiers, Statesmen, Scholars, Scoundrels*, 233–34.

13. General Laws of Mississippi of 1995, Chapter 478.

14. Gov. Kirk Fordice. State of Mississippi Executive Budget Recommendation for FY July 1, 1995, to June 30, 1996.

15. Later during the 1996 legislative session, after all of those bills had died in committee, Rep. Phil Bryant, who later became governor in 2012, offered an amendment on the house floor to a bill (S.B. 2673, General Laws of Mississippi of 1996, Chapter 441) to phase in an increase in the standard deduction for income taxes in order to eliminate the marriage tax penalty that also existed with the standard deduction. However, his amendment was ruled out of order after a parliamentary objection, so the house never got to vote on it.

16. Gov. Kirk Fordice, State of Mississippi Executive Budget Recommendation for FY July 1, 1996, to June 30, 1997.

17. General Laws of Mississippi of 1997, Chapter 304.

18. Fordice, State of Mississippi Executive Budget Recommendation for FY July 1, 1994, to June 30, 1995.

19. Joint Legislative Budget Committee, "Introduction," in *The Mississippi Budgeting Process: A Comparative Study Mandated by the Budget Reform Act of 1992* (December 15, 1992), 8.

20. Gov. Kirk Fordice, State of Mississippi Executive Budget Recommendation for FY July 1, 1994, to June 30, 1995; Gov. Kirk Fordice, State of Mississippi Executive Budget Recommendation for FY July 1, 1999, to June 30, 2000.

21. Fordice, State of Mississippi Executive Budget Recommendation for FY July 1, 1999, to June 30, 2000.

22. Fordice, State of Mississippi Executive Budget Recommendation for FY July 1, 1999, to June 30, 2000.

23. Sarah Campbell, "Fordice Wrenches over State Budget Mess; More Cuts Possible," *Jackson Clarion-Ledger*, January 17, 1992.

24. Department of Finance and Administration Office of Budget and Fund Management, "Reductions to FY 1992 Appropriations."

25. Gov. Kirk Fordice's Budget Cut Statement, February 11, 1992.

26. Sarah Campbell, "More State Cuts Seen to Blot $30M in Red Ink," *Jackson Clarion-Ledger*, January 22, 1992.

27. The sine die revenue estimate is adopted by the Joint Legislative Budget Committee at the end of the regular legislative session. Section 27-104-13 (2) of the Mississippi Code of 1972. The end of the session is known as sine die adjournment.

28. Campbell, "Fordice Wrenches over State Budget Mess."

29. Joint Legislative Budget Committee, State of Mississippi Budget Bulletin for FY 1992; Joint Legislative Budget Committee, State of Mississippi Budget Bulletin for FY 1993.

30. Joint Legislative Budget Committee, State of Mississippi Budget Bulletin for FY 1993.

31. The National Bureau of Economic Research, "NBER Business Cycle Dating Committee Determines That Recession Ended in March 1991," https://www.nber.org/March91.html (Retrieved May 13, 2018).

32. Gov. Kirk Fordice, State of Mississippi Executive Budget Recommendation for FY July 1, 1993, to June 30, 1994.

33. Fordice, State of Mississippi Executive Budget Recommendation for FY July 1, 1999 to June 30, 2000.

34. Mississippi Department of Finance and Administration, *Mississippi Comprehensive Annual Financial Report for the Fiscal Year Ended June 30, 2000*, 156–57.

35. Casino gambling on vessels located on the Mississippi River and the Gulf of Mexico was legalized by the legislature in 1990, and the first casinos opened in 1992.

36. John Lee, "Economic Impacts of Casino Gaming," Mississippi Institutions of Higher Learning, Center for Policy Research and Planning, July 1994, 1–2.

37. Joint Legislative Budget Committee, State of Mississippi Budget Bulletin for FY 1992. Joint Legislative Budget Committee. State of Mississippi Budget Bulletin for FY 2000.

38. S.B. 3120, General Laws of Mississippi of 1992, Chapter 419; S.B. 3057, General Laws of Mississippi of 1992, Chapter 483.

39. H.B. 1613, General Laws of Mississippi of 1993, Chapter 571; H.B. 1502, General Laws of Mississippi of 1993, Chapter 564.

40. Mark Leggett, "Lawmakers File Promised Lawsuit against Fordice," *Daily Journal (Tupelo, Mississippi)*, August 7, 1993.

41. The three legislators that sued Governor Fordice were Sen. Hob Bryan, Sen. John Horhn, and Rep. Glenn Endris. Attorney General Mike Moore intervened as a party plaintiff on behalf of the people of the State of Mississippi.

42. Article 4, Section 73 of the Mississippi Constitution of 1980.

43. "Courts Will Have to Settle Controversy over Gov. Fordice's 'Line-Item' Vetoes," *Sun Herald*, May 1, 1993.

44. Lee J. Howard, "Judge Rejects Fordice Vetoes of Bond Bills," *Jackson Clarion-Ledger*, November 23, 1993.

45. *Fordice v. Bryan*, 651 So. 2d 998 (Miss. 1995).

46. S.B. 2945, General Laws of Mississippi of 1995, Chapter 518; S.B. 3236, General Laws of Mississippi of 1995, Chapter 628.

47. S.B. 2649 revised the funding formula for the Mississippi Adequate Education Program (MAEP) and provided for the issuance of state bonds for public schools. General Laws of Mississippi of 1997, Chapter 612.

48. H.B. 1665, 1999 Regular Session.

49. S.B. 2002, First Extraordinary Session of 1999.

50. *Alexander v. State of Mississippi by and through Allain*, 441 So. 2d 1329 (Miss. 1983).

51. *Fordice v. Bryan*, 651 So. 2d 998 (Miss. 1995).

52. The Supreme Court justices that affirmed the nullity of H.B. 1613 and H.B. 1502 were James Roberts Jr., Michael Sullivan, Edwin Pittman, Fred Banks, Chuck McRae, Armis Hawkins, Lenore Prather, and Dan Lee. The one dissenting vote was James Smith Jr.

53. *Fordice v. Bryan*, 651 So. 2d 998 (Miss. 1995).

54. The Supreme Court justices that dissented to reviewing the appropriation bills were Armis Hawkins, Lenore Prather, Dan Lee, and James Smith Jr.

55. *Fordice v. Bryan*, 651 So. 2d 998 (Miss. 1995).

56. *Fordice v. Bryan*, 651 So. 2d 998 (Miss. 1995).

57. *Fordice v. Bryan*, 651 So. 2d 998 (Miss. 1995).

58. *Fordice v. Bryan*, 651 So. 2d 998 (Miss. 1995).

59. *Fordice v. Bryan*, 651 So. 2d 998 (Miss. 1995).

60. Jerry Mitchell, "Court Strikes Line-Item Veto on Bond Bills," *Jackson Clarion-Ledger*, January 13, 1995.

61. *Fordice v. Bryan*, 651 So. 2d 998 (Miss. 1995).

62. *Fordice v. Bryan*, 651 So. 2d 998 (Miss. 1995).

63. Fordice, State of Mississippi Executive Budget Recommendation for FY July 1, 1994, to June 30, 1995.

64. Fordice, State of Mississippi Executive Budget Recommendation for FY July 1, 1995, to June 30, 1996.

65. Fordice, State of Mississippi Executive Budget Recommendation for FY July 1, 1995, to June 30, 1996.

66. H.B. 1358 and S.B. 2453, 1995 Regular Session. Neither bill made it out of committee. H.B. 1358 was introduced by Rep. Phil Bryant, who later became governor, in 2012.

67. Gov. Kirk Fordice, State of Mississippi Executive Budget Recommendation for FY July 1, 1997, to June 30, 1998.

68. Fordice, State of Mississippi Executive Budget Recommendation for FY July 1, 1994, to June 30, 1995.

69. General Laws of Mississippi of 1990, Chapter 581.

70. General Laws of Mississippi of 1990, Chapter 581.

71. Fordice, State of Mississippi Executive Budget Recommendation for FY July 1, 1994, to June 30, 1995.

72. Joint Legislative Budget Committee, State of Mississippi Budget Bulletin for FY 1992; Joint Legislative Budget Committee, State of Mississippi Budget Bulletin for FY 2000.

73. Mississippi Department of Finance and Administration, *Mississippi Comprehensive Annual Financial Report for the Fiscal Year Ended June 30, 2000*, 158.

74. Gina Holland, "Fordice May Be Best Remembered for Bills He Killed," Associated Press, April, 28, 1998.

75. Edward Clynch, "Mississippi: Changing Gubernatorial–Legislative Dynamics in Budget Decision Making," in *Budgeting in the States* (Westport, CT: Praeger, 2006), 259.

76. Veto count information compiled using the Legislative Services Bill Status Program.

77. Mitchell, "Court Strikes Line-Item Veto on Bond Bills."

78. Clynch, "Mississippi: Changing Gubernatorial–Legislative Dynamics," 260.

79. Veto count information compiled using the Legislative Services Bill Status Program.

Chapter Seven

1. The Mississippi House of Representatives was responsible for Musgrove becoming governor with a historic 86–36 vote that occurred after neither candidate Musgrove nor his opponent Mike Parker received a majority of the popular vote or a majority of the legislative districts during the 1999 election.

2. Gov. Ronnie Musgrove, State of Mississippi Executive Budget Recommendation for FY July 1, 2001, to June 30, 2002.

3. "NBER Business Cycle Dating Committee—March 1991," in the *National Bureau of Economic Research*; "NBER Business Cycle Dating Committee—March 2001," in the *National Bureau of Economic Research*.

4. Gary Anderson, Department of Finance and Administration executive director, letter to state agencies to reduce budgets. Budgets were reduced in FY 2002 and FY 2003.

5. Joint Legislative Budget Committee, State of Mississippi Proposed Budget for FY 2001.

6. Gov. Ronnie Musgrove, State of Mississippi Executive Budget Recommendation for FY July 1, 2001, to June 30, 2002.

7. Musgrove, State of Mississippi Executive Budget Recommendation for FY July 1, 2001, to June 30, 2002.

8. Musgrove, State of Mississippi Executive Budget Recommendation for FY July 1, 2001, to June 30, 2002.

9. Patrice Sawyer, "Musgrove Pitches Budget Proposal," *Jackson Clarion-Ledger*, September 8, 2000.

10. Sawyer, "Musgrove Pitches Budget Proposal."

11. Sawyer, "Musgrove Pitches Budget Proposal."

12. Musgrove, State of Mississippi Executive Budget Recommendation for FY July 1, 2001, to June 30, 2002.

13. Sawyer, "Musgrove Pitches Budget Proposal."

14. Gov. Ronnie Musgrove's Supplemental Recommendation for Fiscal Year 2003, State of Mississippi Executive Budget Recommendation for FY July 1, 2002, to June 30, 2003.

15. Patrice Sawyer, "Governor Eyes Tobacco Fund," *Jackson Clarion-Ledger*, July 27, 2001.

16. Sawyer, "Governor Eyes Tobacco Fund."

17. Sid Salter, "Governor Knew Tax Collection Scheme Flawed," *Jackson Clarion-Ledger*, January 30, 2002.

18. Salter, "Governor Knew Tax Collection Scheme Flawed."

19. Salter, "Governor Knew Tax Collection Scheme Flawed."

20. Those diversions not taken into consideration by Musgrove's plan included: Education Enhancement Fund, State Aid Road Fund, Fair Commission, telecommunications, automobile sales tax, ad valorem, municipal diversion, air and water grants, contractor's tax, boll weevil management, and the bad check reserve. The diversion list was found in Sid Salter's editorial "Governor Eyes Tobacco Fund," *Jackson Clarion-Ledger*, July 27, 2001.

21. General Laws of Mississippi of 2002, Ch. 539.

22. General Laws of Mississippi of 2001, Ch. 521, Section 2.

23. Joint Legislative Budget Committee, State of Mississippi Budget Bulletin for FY 2003.

24. Musgrove, Supplemental Recommendation for Fiscal Year 2003, State of Mississippi Executive Budget Recommendation for FY July 1, 2002, to June 30, 2003.

25. Gov. Ronnie Musgrove, Supplemental Recommendation for Fiscal Year 2004, State of Mississippi Executive Budget Recommendation for FY July 1, 2003, to June 30, 2004.

26. Musgrove, Supplemental Recommendation for Fiscal Year 2003, State of Mississippi Executive Budget Recommendation for FY July 1, 2002, to June 30, 2003; Musgrove, Supplemental Recommendation for Fiscal Year 2004, State of Mississippi Executive Budget Recommendation for FY July 1, 2003, to June 30, 2004.

27. General Laws of Mississippi of 2003, Ch. 507.

28. *Alexander v. State of Mississippi by and through Allain*, 441 So. 2d 1329 (Miss. 1983).

29. Emily Wagster, "Musgrove Wants in on Budget Process," *Jackson Clarion-Ledger*, September 13, 2000.

30. Emily Wagster, "Musgrove Joins Push for Power," *Jackson Clarion-Ledger*, September 24, 2000.

31. Wagster, "Musgrove Wants in on Budget Process."

32. Wagster, "Musgrove Joins Push for Power."

33. General Laws of Mississippi of 2000, Ch. 533.

34. Department of Finance and Administration internal document titled, "HB 1134 Summary and Analysis of Teacher Pay Schedule FY 2000–FY 2006.

35. General Laws of Mississippi of the First Extraordinary Session of 2001, Ch. 1.

36. General Laws of Mississippi of 1992, Ch. 419.

37. S.B. 2649 was known as the Mississippi Accountability and Adequate Education Program Act of 1997. S.B. 2649 was double-referred to both the Education and Appropriations Committees in both the house and the senate. General Laws of Mississippi of 1997, Chapter 612.

38. Musgrove, State of Mississippi Executive Budget Recommendation for FY July 1, 2001, to June 30, 2002.

39. Joint Legislative Budget Committee, State of Mississippi Budget Bulletin for FY 2002; Joint Legislative Budget Committee, State of Mississippi Budget Bulletin for FY 2003.

40. Musgrove, State of Mississippi Executive Budget Recommendation for FY July 1, 2002, to June 30, 2003.

41. Joint Legislative Budget Committee, State of Mississippi Budget Bulletin for FY 2003; Joint Legislative Budget Committee, State of Mississippi Budget Bulletin for FY 2004.

42. Joint Legislative Budget Committee, State of Mississippi Budget Bulletin for FY 2001.

43. Joint Legislative Budget Committee, State of Mississippi Budget Bulletin for FY 2005.

44. Joint Legislative Budget Committee, State of Mississippi Budget Bulletin for FY 2005.

45. The southeastern average of teacher salaries is always a moving target, because it goes up whenever any one of the states increases its teacher salaries. So, Mississippi teacher salaries did not stay at the southeastern average for long after Musgrove's historic increase. Nevertheless, because of his focus and perseverance, Musgrove was able to persuade the legislature to get the Mississippi teacher salaries to the southeastern average for the first time, achieving what none of his predecessors had.

46. Department of Finance and Administration internal document titled, "HB 1134 Summary and Analysis of Teacher Pay Schedule FY 2000–FY 2006."

47. Amendment No. 1 to Amendment No. 1 Proposed to H.B. 1134, http://billstatus.ls.state .ms.us/documents/2000/pdf/sam/HB1134_S_Amend_01_to_Amend_01.pdf/.

48. Ed Clynch interview with Judy Rhoades, Department of Education, June 2001.

49. H.B. 1, which removed the 5 percent trigger, was passed during the First Extraordinary Session of 2001, General Laws of Mississippi of the First Extraordinary Session of 2001, Ch. 1.

50. Musgrove, State of Mississippi Executive Budget Recommendation for FY July 1, 2003, to June 30, 2004.

51. Julie Goodman, "Job Training, Education Dominate in 'State of State,'" *Jackson Clarion-Ledger*, January 10, 2003.

52. "State's First Priority Is Education," *Jackson Clarion-Ledger*, September 7, 2003.

53. "State's First Priority Is Education."

54. Joint Legislative Budget Committee, State of Mississippi Budget Bulletin for FY 2004. Total K–12 public education funded at $1,519,596,940; total higher education funded at $535,108,542; and total higher education agricultural units funded at $55,415,006. Regular General Fund Appropriations for FY 2004 Budget: $3,434,911,661 (not including reappropriations from FY 2003 totaling $8,169,596 or general fund transfers to Budget Contingency Fund totaling $147,820,054).

55. Education Reserve Fund: at the end of the fiscal year and prior to the required distributions to the General Fund Reserve and General Fund Stabilization Reserve, any unencumbered general fund cash will be sent to the Education Reserve Fund. The amount

transferred to the Education Reserve Fund shall not exceed $50 million. General Laws of Mississippi of 1988, Ch. 487. Section 13.

56. The Education Reserve Fund was repealed in 1992 by S.B. 3120. General Laws of Mississippi of 1992, Ch. 419. In addition to repealing the Education Reserve Fund (Section 33), S.B. 3120 created the Education Enhancement Fund. Ironically enough, the Education Reserve Fund was repealed again in 1993 when the legislature passed H.B. 400. General Laws of Mississippi of 1993, Ch. 509, Section 6.

57. H.B. 776 also diverted Education Enhancement Funds that were allocated for the purchase of textbooks and for classroom supplies to the support of educational programs authorized by law. Additionally, the bill provided that state general obligation bonds may be issued for the purpose of providing funds for the payment of allocations of adequate education program funds to school districts for capital expenditures which have been pledged for debt. General Laws of Mississippi of 2001, Ch. 518, Section 1.

58. Gov. Ronnie Musgrove, veto message for H.B. 776, March 30, 2001.

59. Veto count information compiled using the Legislative Services Bill Status Program.

60. "NBER Business Cycle Dating Committee—March 1991," *National Bureau of Economic Research*; "NBER Business Cycle Dating Committee—March 2001," *National Bureau of Economic Research*.

61. Joint Legislative Budget Committee, State of Mississippi Proposed Budget for FY 2001.

62. Musgrove, State of Mississippi Executive Budget Recommendation for FY July 1, 2001, to June 30, 2002.

63. Joint Legislative Budget Committee, State of Mississippi Proposed Budget for FY 2002.

64. Musgrove, veto message for H.B. 776 on March 30, 2001.

65. Joint Legislative Budget Committee, State of Mississippi Proposed Budget for FY 2002.

66. Patrice Sawyer, "Musgrove: Legislative Discord Not Personal," *Jackson Clarion-Ledger*, July 12, 2001.

67. Musgrove, veto message for H.B. 776, March 30, 2001.

68. Veto count information compiled using the Legislative Services Bill Status Program.

69. Gary Anderson, director of the Department of Finance and Administration, budget cut letter to agencies titled "Revision of General Fund Budget Estimates for FY 2002," November 13, 2001.

70. Working Cash-Stabilization Reserve Fund balance provided by the Office of the State Treasurer.

71. Joint Legislative Budget Committee, State of Mississippi Proposed Budget for FY 2003.

72. Musgrove, State of Mississippi Executive Budget Recommendation for FY July 1, 2002, to June 30, 2003.

73. Joint Legislative Budget Committee, State of Mississippi Proposed Budget for FY 2004.

74. Gary Anderson, director of the Department of Finance and Administration (Consolidated Reduction) budget cut letter to agencies titled "Revision of General Fund Budget Estimates for FY 2003," February 18, 2003.

75. Anderson, "Revision of General Fund Budget Estimates for FY 2003."

76. Joint Legislative Budget Committee, State of Mississippi Proposed Budget for FY 2005.

77. Working Cash-Stabilization Reserve Fund balance provided by the Office of the State Treasurer.

78. Geoff Pender, "Former House Speaker Tim Ford Dies," *Jackson Clarion-Ledger*, February 27, 2015.

79. Sawyer, "Musgrove: Legislative Discord Not Personal."

80. Fordice's twenty-nine partially vetoed bills (two bond bills and twenty-seven appropriation bills) are not included in his total veto count, because he did not veto the entire bill.

81. Veto count information compiled using the Legislative Services Bill Status Program.

82. General Laws of Mississippi of 2001, Ch. 521, Section 2.

83. General Laws of Mississippi of 2001, Ch. 521, Section 2.

84. Musgrove, veto message for S.B. 2680, March 30, 2001.

85. General Laws of Mississippi of 2002, Ch. 135. Musgrove was unsuccessful in his 2003 reelection bid for governor, so his gubernatorial opponent Haley Barbour was named in the lawsuit brought by Delta Correctional Facility Authority by the time the case made it to the Mississippi Supreme Court.

86. Gov. Ronnie Musgrove, veto message for S.B. 3163 on April 9, 2002.

87. Attorney General's Opinion for "Attempted Partial Vetoes" requested by Speaker of the House Tim Ford, 2002 WL 1057921 (Miss. A.G.). Opinion No. 2002-0193, April 11, 2002.

88. Attorney General's Opinion for "Attempted Partial Vetoes" requested by Speaker of the House Tim Ford, 2002 WL 1057921 (Miss. A.G.). Opinion No. 2002-0193, April 11, 2002.

89. "Musgrove Partial Veto Wrong, Court Says," *Associated Press*, April 23, 2004.

90. "Musgrove Partial Veto Wrong, Court Says."

91. *Barbour v. Delta Correctional Facility Authority*, 871 So. 2d 703 (Miss. 2004).

92. *Barbour v. Delta Correctional Facility Authority*, 871 So. 2d 703 (Miss. 2004).

93. The Mississippi Supreme Court ruled on *Barbour v. Delta Correctional Facility Authority*, 871 So. 2d 703 (2004) on April 22, 2004. Justice Charles Easley wrote the majority opinion. Concurring were Justices James W. Smith Jr., George C. Carlson Jr., James E. Graves Jr., and Jess H. Dickinson. Dissenting were Justices Kay B. Cobb and William L. Waller Jr., and Justice Oliver E. Diaz Jr. did not participate. There was one vacancy on the court.

94. *Barbour v. Delta Correctional Facility Authority*, 871 So. 2d 703 (Miss. 2004).

Chapter Eight

1. The Mississippi Constitution of 1817 was signed on August 15, 1817, and it was a brief document, consisting of a mere eighteen pages.

2. Tip H. Allen Jr., "The Enduring Traditions of the State Constitutions," in *Mississippi Government and Politics, Modernizers versus Traditionalists* (Lincoln: University of Nebraska Press, 1992), 44.

3. Ricky R. Mathews, president of the NOLA Media Group, who wrote the foreword for Haley Barbour's book *America's Great Storm: Leading through Hurricane Katrina* (Jackson: University Press of Mississippi, 2015).

4. General Election Results for 2003: Haley Barbour (R) 470,404, or 52.6%; John Thomas Cripps (C) 6,317, or 0.7%; Sherman Lee Dillon (G) 3,909, or 0.4%; Ronnie Musgrove (D) 409,787, or 45.8%; and Shawn O'Hara (RP) 4,070, or 0.5%. Mississippi Blue Book. 2004–2008. Official and Statistical Register. Secretary of State: Eric Clark (2005).

5. Jere Nash and Andy Taggart, *Mississippi Politics: The Struggle for Power, 1976–2008* (Jackson: University Press of Mississippi, 2009), 308.

6. Nash and Taggart, *Mississippi Politics*, 308.

7. Mississippi state senator James "Shannon" Walley switched from Democrat to Republican in January 2007, which created a 26–26 tie in the senate between Democrats and Republicans. This tie gave Lt. Gov. Amy Tuck, who herself had become a Republican in 2002 after being elected as a Democrat in 1999, the tie-breaking vote. Two months after Walley's switch, state senator Tommy Gollott also switched parties, giving the Republicans an outright majority in the senate. Antoine Yoshinaka, *Crossing the Aisle: Party Switching by U.S. Legislators in the Postwar Era* (New York: Cambridge University Press, 2016), 87.

8. Edward Clynch, "Mississippi: Changing Gubernatorial–Legislative Dynamics in Budget Decision Making," in *Budgeting in the States* (Westport, CT: Praeger, 2006), 272.

9. Mississippi's budget-making process consists of three formal phases: budget preparation and submission, legislative approval (or simply adoption), and budget control. There is also an informal fourth phase, review/reporting.

10. He formed the Washington, DC, firm BGR Group with Lanny Griffith and Ed Rogers in 1987, which *Fortune* magazine eventually identified as the most influential lobbying firm in America.

11. Nash and Taggart. *Mississippi Politics*, 304.

12. Haley Barbour, with Jere Nash, *America's Great Storm: Leading through Hurricane Katrina* (Jackson: University Press of Mississippi, 2015).

13. Nash and Taggart. *Mississippi Politics*, 308.

14. David Sansing, *Mississippi Governors, Soldiers, Statesmen, Scholars, Scoundrels* (Oxford, MS: Nautilus, 2016).

15. Barbour, *America's Great Storm*.

16. Mississippi Blue Book. 2004–2008. Official and Statistical Register. Secretary of State: Eric Clark, (2005), 48.

17. Mississippi Blue Book. 2004–2008. Official and Statistical Register. Secretary of State: Eric Clark, (2005), 48.

18. Barbour, *America's Great Storm*.

19. Barbour, *America's Great Storm*.

20. Barbour, *America's Great Storm*, 134–35.

21. Barbour, *America's Great Storm*, 134–35.

22. Nash and Taggart, 309.

23. Joint Legislative Budget Committee, State of Mississippi Budget Bulletin for FY 2006.

24. Barbour, *America's Great Storm*.

25. Barbour, *America's Great Storm*.

26. General Laws of Mississippi of the Fifth Extraordinary Session of 2005, Ch. 12.

27. Since casinos were first authorized in 1990, those in the coast counties were required by law to be located on vessels on the waters of the Gulf of Mexico. Hurricane Katrina severely damaged or destroyed several of those vessels, so the casino industry wanted the ability to locate their facilities on land instead of water, to help prevent similar devastation to casinos in future hurricanes.

28. Barbour, *America's Great Storm*.

29. Barbour, *America's Great Storm*, 97–98.

30. Barbour, *America's Great Storm*, 97–98.

31. Barbour, *America's Great Storm*, 97–98.

32. Pender, Geoff, Melissa Scallan, and Tom Wilemon, "Casino Plan Stalls in the Senate," *Sun Herald*, October 5, 2005.

33. H.B. 44, General Laws of Mississippi of the Fifth Extraordinary Session of 2005, Ch. 15; H.B. 45, General Laws of Mississippi of the Fifth Extraordinary Session of 2005, Ch. 16.

34. Pender, Geoff. "Onshore Wins Standoff," *Sun Herald*, October 8, 2005.

35. Barbour, *America's Great Storm*, 101.

36. Governor's Commission on Recovery, Rebuilding, and Renewal: Barbour explained that he selected Jim Barksdale because he "wanted people to understand . . . that the commission chairmanship wasn't some political reward for a supporter. This appointment needed to be seen as the result of my effort to pick the 'best person available,' a serious and capable leader for a huge important assignment." Barksdale actually supported Barbour's opponent Ronnie Musgrove in the 2003 election. In explaining why he selected William Winter to serve as counsel to the commission, Barbour explained, "Governor Winter had a lot to contribute in terms of perspective and process, but he also gave the commission a bipartisanship that helped achieve its critical goal of giving 'hope and confidence' because he helped give us credibility and trustworthiness." Barbour, *America's Great Storm*, 106, 107.

37. Governor's Commission on Recovery, Rebuilding, and Renewal, http://www.mississippirenewal.com/documents/Governors_Commission_Report.pdf. (December 31, 2005).

38. Barbour, *America's Great Storm*, 130.

39. Barbour, *America's Great Storm*, 130.

40. Barbour, *America's Great Storm*, 99–100.

41. Barbour, *America's Great Storm*, 131.

42. Barbour, *America's Great Storm*, 133.

43. Public Law 109-61 (September 2, 2005).

44. Public Law 109-62 (September 8, 2005).

45. Public Law 109-73 (September 23, 2005).

46. Barbour, *America's Great Storm*.

47. Barbour, *America's Great Storm*.

48. The Chairman of the House Energy and Commerce Committee was Rep. Joe Barton, and he gave Rep. Chip Pickering the authority to negotiate the Medicaid issue on behalf of the entire committee—thus, effectively, for the entire House of Representatives, according to Haley Barbour.

49. Barbour, *America's Great Storm*, 144.

50. Barbour, *America's Great Storm*, 140.

51. Barbour, *America's Great Storm*, 147.

52. Public Law 109-148 (December 30, 2005).

53. Barbour, *America's Great Storm*, 150.

54. Barbour, *America's Great Storm*, 153.

55. Les Spivey was the number two staff member on the Senate Appropriations Committee and explained the strong CDBG language during an interview with Haley Barbour. Barbour, *America's Great Storm*, 151.

56. Barbour, *America's Great Storm*, 159.

57. Barbour, *America's Great Storm*, 160.

58. Public Law 109-135 (December 21, 2005). The GO Zone legislation, H.R. 4440, also benefited states hit by Hurricane Rita. Hurricane Rita was a devastating storm that hit the Gulf Coast less than one month after Hurricane Katrina.

59. Barbour, *America's Great Storm*, 157.

60. Barbour, *America's Great Storm*, 157.

61. Public Law 109-171 (February 8, 2006).

62. Barbour, *America's Great Storm*, 139.

63. Clynch, Edward. "Mississippi: Changing Gubernatorial-Legislative Dynamics in Budget Decision Making," in *Budgeting in the States*, (Westport, Connecticut: Praeger Publisher, 2006), 270.

64. Interview with former Rep. Cecil Brown, who was a former state fiscal officer (1988–1990) and former member of the Mississippi House of Representatives (2000–2016). Brown was invited to be a part of budget negotiations by Representative Johnny Stringer when he became Appropriations Committee chairman. Brown served on the Joint Legislative Budget Committee (JLBC) and the Appropriations Committee. (January 2, 2019).

65. Gordon, Mac. "'Go Ask Cecil': Imaging Mississippi Government without Cecil Brown," *Jackson Clarion-Ledger*, December 28, 2018.

66. Interview with former Rep. Cecil Brown. Brown explained that during Barbour's first term, he dealt with Jim Perry, who served has Governor Barbour's Policy Director. Perry eventually left the Governor's Office to work with Morgan Stanley. After Perry's departure, Brown explained that he worked with Paul Hurst (January 2, 2019).

67. Interview with Jim Perry (January 8, 2019).

68. Interview with Jim Perry (January 8, 2019).

69. Interview with Jim Perry (January 8, 2019).

70. Gov. Haley Barbour, State of Mississippi Executive Budget Recommendation for FY July 1, 2004 to June 30, 2005.

71. Barbour, State of Mississippi Executive Budget Recommendation for FY July 1, 2004 to June 30, 2005.

72. Budget cut information provided by the Department of Finance and Administration's Office of Budget and Fund Management. Total budget cuts ordered by Governor Barbour from all funding sources were $200,000,000 in FY 2009 and $499,100,636 in FY 2010.

73. U.S. Bureau of Economic Analysis. While the recession technically lasted from December 2007 through June 2009 (the nominal GDP trough), many important economic variables did not regain pre-recession (November or Q4 2007) levels until between 2011 and 2016.

74. Gov. Haley Barbour, State of Mississippi Executive Budget Recommendation for FY July 1, 2008, to June 30, 2009.

75. Gov. Haley Barbour's budget cut letter to State Fiscal Officer Kevin Upchurch, March 17, 2010.

76. Barbour's budget cut letter to Upchurch, March 17, 2010.

77. Interview with former Rep. Cecil Brown (January 2, 2019).

78. Barbour, State of Mississippi Executive Budget Recommendation for FY July 1, 2004 to June 30, 2005; Gov. Haley Barbour State of Mississippi Executive Budget Recommendation for FY July 1, 2011, to June 30, 2012.

79. *Mississippi Official and Statistical Register*. 2016–2020 Blue Book. Delbert Hosemann, Secretary of State. (2017), 84.

80. Gov. Haley Barbour, State of Mississippi Executive Budget Recommendation for FY July 1, 2010, to June 30, 2011.

Chapter Nine

1. Bobby Harrison, "Money Rule Constricts What Can Be Done with Funding," *Northeast Mississippi Daily Journal (Jackson Bureau)*, March 19, 2015.

2. Bobby Harrison, "Legislators Following Path on Budget Issue," *Northeast Mississippi Daily Journal (Jackson Bureau)*, March 16, 2017.

3. Joint Rule 20A, adopted for the 2012–2016 term in House Concurrent Resolution No. 33, Regular Session of 2012. General Laws of Mississippi of 2012, Chapter 2027. Subsection (1)(a) of the rule defines "state support funds" as "funds in the State General Fund and all state support special funds, which are funds in the Budget Contingency Fund, the Education Enhancement Fund, the Health Care Expendable Fund, the Tobacco Control Program Fund, and any other special funds that the Joint Legislative Budget Committee (JLBC) determines to be state support special funds."

4. Bobby Harrison, "More Money Found, but Members Gave Away the Right to Appropriate," *Northeast Mississippi Daily Journal (Jackson Bureau)*, March 16, 2014.

5. Harrison, "More Money Found, but Members Gave Away the Right to Appropriate."

6. Harrison, "More Money Found, but Members Gave Away the Right to Appropriate."

7. Harrison, "Money Rule Constricts What Can Be Done with Funding."

8. Harrison, "Money Rule Constricts What Can Be Done with Funding."

9. House Concurrent Resolution No. 48, Regular Session of 1991. The same legislative attorney, Ronny Frith, who drafted Joint Rule 20A in 2012, which successfully became a part of the joint rules, also drafted the proposed rules change in 1991, which did not get out of committee. Frith worked directly with Rep. Billy McCoy on the resolution in 1991 and explained that "even though the current Joint Rule 20A has no direct connection to the effort by McCoy twenty-one years earlier, the concept is very much related to what McCoy was trying to do in the resolution."

10. House Concurrent Resolution No. 48, Regular Session of 1991, proposing a new Joint Rule 20A; subsection (2).

11. Mississippi House of Representatives, *House Journal* 2012, February 13, 2012. Point of order raised by Rep. Cecil Brown and Speaker's Ruling, p. 152.

12. Mississippi House of Representatives, *House Journal* 2012, February 13, 2012, p. 153.

13. Mississippi House of Representatives, *House Journal* 2012, February 13, 2012, p. 153.

14. Mississippi House of Representatives, *House Journal* 2012, March 22, 2012. Rep. Cecil Brown's failed amendment to H.B. 1593, p. 596.

15. Mississippi House of Representatives, *House Journal* 2012, March 22, 2012. Rep. Cecil Brown's failed amendment to H.B. 1613, p. 601.

Chapter Ten

1. Comments made by Gov. Phil Bryant to his director of finance, Brian Pugh.

2. Prior to serving in public service, Phil Bryant's background in law enforcement played a major role in shaping his philosophy to simply "follow the law." Bryant began his service in statewide elective office and his path to becoming governor when he was plucked from relative obscurity as a five-year member of the Mississippi House of Representatives in November 1996 by Gov. Kirk Fordice, who appointed him to serve as state auditor after Democratic Auditor Steve Patterson resigned. Bryant was subsequently elected to a full term as auditor in 1999 and reelected in 2003. He was elected lieutenant governor in 2007 and then elected governor in 2011 and reelected in 2015.

3. Governor Bryant's letter to Senate Appropriations Committee chairman Eugene "Buck" Clarke and House Appropriations Committee chairman Herb Frierson concerning the Mississippi Development Authority's transfer of budget contingency funds to the Cleveland Music Foundation for the GRAMMY Museum in Cleveland, Mississippi. (June 20, 2012).

4. Gov. Phil Bryant. "Opportunity Mississippi: Detailing the Roadmap to Success." 2012, 26.

5. *Representative Bryant W. Clark and Senator John Horhn v. Governor Phil Bryant, State Fiscal Officer Laura Jackson, Mississippi Department of Education and State Treasurer Lynn Fitch*, No. 2017-CA-00750-SCT (Miss. 2018).

6. In addition to Gov. Phil Bryant being named in the lawsuit, State Fiscal Officer Laura Jackson was also sued along with the State Treasurer Lynn Fitch and the Mississippi Department of Education. *Representative Bryant W. Clark and Senator John Horhn v. Governor Phil Bryant, State Fiscal Officer Laura Jackson, Mississippi Department of Education and State Treasurer Lynn Fitch*, No. 2017-CA-00750-SCT (Miss. 2018).

7. General Laws of Mississippi of the Second Extraordinary Session of 2016, Ch. 1.

8. General Laws of Mississippi of 2017, Ch. 440, Section 3.

9. General Laws of Mississippi of the First Extraordinary Session of 2017, Ch. 6.

10. H.B. 1, General Laws of Mississippi of the First Extraordinary Session of 2018, Ch. 1; S.B. 2001, General Laws of Mississippi of the First Extraordinary Session of 2018, Ch. 2.

11. Gov. Phil Bryant, State of Mississippi Executive Budget Recommendation for FY July 1, 2018, to June 30, 2019.

12. Bryant, State of Mississippi Executive Budget Recommendation for FY July 1, 2018, to June 30, 2019.

13. Bryant, State of Mississippi Executive Budget Recommendation for FY July 1, 2018, to June 30, 2019.

14. Gov. Phil Bryant's budget cut letter to State Fiscal Officer Kevin Upchurch, January 20, 2016.

15. Bryant's budget cut letter to Upchurch, January 20, 2016.

16. General Laws of Mississippi of the Second Extraordinary Session of 2016, Ch. 1.

17. Gov. Phil Bryant's budget cut letter to State Fiscal Officer Laura Jackson, September 7, 2016.

18. Gov. Phil Bryant's budget cut letter to State Fiscal Officer Laura Jackson, January 12, 2017, February 21, 2017, and March 24, 2017.

19. Gov. Phil Bryant's budget cut letter to State Fiscal Officer Laura Jackson, February 21, 2017.

20. Bryant's budget cut letter to Jackson, February 21, 2017.

21. Gov. Phil Bryant's budget cut letter to State Fiscal Officer Laura Jackson. March 24, 2017.

22. Bryant's budget cut letter to Jackson, March 24, 2017.

23. General Laws of Mississippi of 2017, Ch. 440, Section 3.

24. *Alexander v. State of Mississippi by and through Allain*, 441 So. 2d 1329 (Miss. 1983).

25. General Laws of Mississippi of 1984, Ch. 488.

26. Rep. Bryant W. Clark and Sen. John Horhn's Complaint. In the Chancery Court of Hinds County, First Judicial District, made by Will Bardwell, Attorney for the Plaintiffs (filed on May 17, 2017), 1–2.

27. Bobby Harrison, "Lawsuit Questions Governor's Ability to Make Cuts," *Northeast Mississippi Daily Journal (Jackson Bureau)*, May 18, 2017.

28. Harrison, "Lawsuit Questions Governor's Ability to Make Cuts."

29. Harrison, "Lawsuit Questions Governor's Ability to Make Cuts."

30. Mark Rigsby, "SPLC Challenging Governor's Budget Cutting Authority," *Mississippi Public Broadcasting*, May 19, 2017, http://www.mpbonline.org/blogs/news/2017/05/19/splc -challenging-governors-budget-cutting-authority/ (accessed on June 1, 2017).

31. Affidavit of Representative Bryant W. Clark. (EXHIBIT 1). In the Chancery Court of Hinds County, First Judicial District. Case: *Representative Bryant Clark and Senator John*

Horhn v. Governor Phil Bryant, State Fiscal Officer Laura Jackson, The Mississippi Department of Education, and State Treasurer Lynn Fitch (May 14, 2017).

32. Affidavit of Senator John Horhn. (EXHIBIT 2). In the Chancery Court of Hinds County, First Judicial District. Case: *Representative Bryant Clark and Senator John Horhn v. Governor Phil Bryant, State Fiscal Officer Laura Jackson, The Mississippi Department of Education, and State Treasurer Lynn Fitch* (May 14, 2017).

33. Governor Bryant's statement, released by spokesperson Clay Chandler, regarding what the governor referred to as a "meaningless academic exercise" (May 18, 2017).

34. Jim Hood, Attorney General, State of Mississippi and Krissy C. Nobile and Harold Pizzetta, *Response in Opposition to Motion for Temporary Restraining Order or Preliminary Injunction.* In the Chancery Court of Hinds County, First Judicial District, made by Will Bardwell, Attorney for the Plaintiffs (Filed on May 30, 2017).

35. Affidavit of Brian A. Pugh (EXHIBIT A). In the Chancery Court of Hinds County, First Judicial District. Case: *Representative Bryant Clark and Senator John Horhn v. Governor Phil Bryant, State Fiscal Officer Laura Jackson, The Mississippi Department of Education, and State Treasurer Lynn Fitch* (May 26, 2017).

36. Jim Hood, Attorney General, State of Mississippi, and Krissy C. Nobile and Harold Pizzetta *Response in Opposition to Motion for Temporary Restraining Order or Preliminary Injunction.* In the Chancery Court of Hinds County, First Judicial District, made by Will Bardwell, Attorney for the Plaintiffs (Filed on May 30, 2017).

37. Hood, Nobile, and Pizzetta, *Response in Opposition to Motion for Temporary Restraining Order or Preliminary Injunction.*

38. Hood, Nobile, and Pizzetta, *Response in Opposition to Motion for Temporary Restraining Order or Preliminary Injunction.*

39. Chancellor Patricia D. Wise, *Final Judgement and Order*, the Chancery Court of Hinds County, First Judicial District, referencing *5K Farms, Inc. v. Mississippi Department of Revenue*, 94 So. 3d 221, 226 (Miss. 2012), quoting *Cities of Oxford, Carthage, Louisville, Starkville and Tupelo v. Northeast Mississippi Electric Power Association*, 704 So. 2d 59, 65 (Miss. 1997), June 2, 2017, 3.

40. Chancellor Patricia D. Wise, *Final Judgement and Order*, the Chancery Court of Hinds County, First Judicial District, referencing *Pathfinder Coach Div. of Superior Coach Corp. v. Cottrell*, 216 Miss 358, 62 So. 2d 383,385 (1953), June 2, 2017, 3.

41. Chancellor Patricia D. Wise. *Final Judgement and Order*, the Chancery Court of Hinds County, First Judicial District, June 2, 2017, 4.

42. *Representative Bryant W. Clark and Senator John Horhn v. Governor Phil Bryant, State Fiscal Officer Laura Jackson, Mississippi Department of Education and State Treasurer Lynn Fitch*, No. 2017-CA-00750-SCT (Miss. 2018).

43. *Representative Bryant W. Clark and Senator John Horhn v. Governor Phil Bryant, State Fiscal Officer Laura Jackson, Mississippi Department of Education and State Treasurer Lynn Fitch*, No. 2017-CA-00750-SCT (Miss. 2018).

44. All nine Supreme Court justices affirmed the chancery court's order: Robert Chamberlin, William (Bill) Waller Jr., Michael Randolph, James Kitchens, Leslie King, James Maxwell, Dawn Beam, Josiah Coleman, and David Ishee. The latter two concurred in part.

45. Gov. Phil Bryant, State of Mississippi Executive Budget Recommendation for FY July 1, 2014, to June 30, 2015.

46. Gov. Phil Bryant's FORTIFY Act presentation created for the legislature, May 30, 2017.

47. Standard and Poor's (S&P) analysis for the State of Mississippi.

48. Gov. Phil Bryant's FORTIFY Act presentation created for the legislature. May 30, 2017.

49. Gov. Ronnie Musgrove, veto message for S.B. 2680 on March 30, 2001. General Laws of Mississippi of 2001, Ch. 521.

50. In 2015 the State of Mississippi received a settlement related to damages caused by the BP Deepwater Horizon oil spill in the Gulf of Mexico that occurred in 2010. In the settlement, the State of Mississippi would receive funds over a period of time that, by state law, were to be deposited into the Budget Contingency Fund (BCF). Governor Bryant proposed abolishing the BCF and replacing it with the Gulf Coast Restoration Reserve Fund, in his original Idea for the FORTIFY Act. Bryant's proposal included the legislature deciding how funds deposited into the newly created fund were to be spent. Although the oil spill settlement funds were not addressed in the FORTIFY Act that was passed, the legislature in the First Extraordinary Session of 2018 created the Gulf Coast Restoration Fund and the State BP Settlement Fund for the deposit of the settlement funds, instead of their being deposited into the BCF. General Laws of Mississippi of the First Extraordinary Session of 2018, Ch. 3. However, the legislature still did not abolish the BCF.

51. General Laws of Mississippi of 2008, Ch. 455, Section 2.

52. General Laws of Mississippi of 2008, Ch. 455, Section 2.

53. Gov. Phil Bryant, State of Mississippi Executive Budget Recommendation for FY July 1, 2015, to June 30, 2016.

54. Standard and Poor's (S&P) analysis for the State of Mississippi.

55. Another important reason that the governor was forced to call a special session was because the legislature had failed to pass the annual appropriation bills for the Mississippi Department of Transportation (S.B. 2978) and the Office of the Attorney General (H.B. 1492) during the 2017 legislative session, and those agencies' appropriation bills were passed during the special session.

56. General Laws of Mississippi of 2016, Ch. 459

57. Geoff Pender, "Legislature Sweeps Special Funds to Cover Shortfalls," *Jackson Clarion-Ledger*, April 15, 2016.

58. S.B. 2362, Section 3(1), provided, "From and after July 1, 2016, the expenses of the following enumerated state agencies shall be defrayed by appropriation of the Legislature from the State General Fund: the State Fire Marshal, the State Fire Academy, the Office of Secretary of State, the Mississippi Public Service Commission, the Mississippi Department of Information Technology Services, the State Personnel Board, the Mississippi Department of Insurance, the Mississippi Law Enforcement Officers' Minimum Standards Board; the Mississippi Tort Claims Board; the Mississippi Gaming Commission; the Mississippi Oil and Gas Board; the Mississippi Department of Revenue—License Tag; the Office of the State Public Defender; the Mississippi Workers' Compensation Commission; the Office of Attorney General; and the Mississippi Department of Finance and Administration."

59. Joint Legislative Budget Committee, State of Mississippi Budget Bulletin for FY 2017.

60. Adam Ganucheau, "Hood's Ruling on Special Funds Will Apply for Now," in *Mississippi Today*, August 9, 2016.

61. Geoff Pender, "Hood: Legislature Used 'Cover-Up' to Hide Budget Holes," *Jackson Clarion-Ledger*, June 21, 2016.

62. Attorney General's Opinion, "Opinion regarding the Effect of Senate Bill 2362 on the Mississippi Tort Claims Act," requested by Ms. Lea Ann McElroy, Administrator. 2016 WL 3876460 (Miss. A.G.). Opinion No. 2016–0026. June 13, 2016.

63. Attorney General's Opinion, "Opinion regarding the Effect of Senate Bill 2362 on the Mississippi Tort Claims Act."

64. Attorney General's Opinion, "Opinion regarding the Effect of Senate Bill 2362 on the Mississippi Tort Claims Act."

65. Ganucheau, "Hood's Ruling on Special Funds Will Apply for Now."

66. Interview with State Fiscal Officer Laura Jackson (August 19, 2019).

67. Gov. Phil Bryant, State of Mississippi Executive Budget Recommendation for FY July 1, 2017, to June 30, 2018.

68. General Laws of Mississippi of the First Extraordinary Session of 2017, Ch. 7.

69. Interview with State Fiscal Officer Laura Jackson (August 19, 2019).

70. Gov. Phil Bryant, State of Mississippi Executive Budget Recommendation for FY July 1, 2019, to June 30, 2020.

71. Bryant, State of Mississippi Executive Budget Recommendation for FY July 1, 2019, to June 30, 2020.

72. Bryant, State of Mississippi Executive Budget Recommendation for FY July 1, 2019, to June 30, 2020.

73. Bryant, State of Mississippi Executive Budget Recommendation for FY July 1, 2017, to June 30, 2018.

74. Bobby Harrison, "Lottery Has Momentum, Not Embraced by Legislature's Presiding Officers," *Northeast Mississippi Daily Journal (Jackson Bureau)*, December 29, 2017.

75. Sarah Ulmer, "Speaker Philip Gunn Creates Lottery Study Commission," *NewsMississippi*, May 4, 2017.

76. Adam Ganucheau, "Lawmakers Hesitant to Gamble on Lottery," *Mississippi Today*, August 22, 2016.

77. Harrison, "Lottery Has Momentum, Not Embraced by Legislature's Presiding Officers."

78. General Laws of Mississippi of the First Extraordinary Session of 2018. Ch. 2.

79. Bryant, State of Mississippi Executive Budget Recommendation for FY July 1, 2019, to June 30, 2020.

80. Ganucheau, "Lawmakers Hesitant to Gamble on Lottery."

81. H.B. 1 provided revenue bonds in the amount not to exceed $300 million, which was authorized to be issued and the proceeds allocated as follows: up to $250 million to the Emergency Road and Bridge Repair Fund and up to $50 million to the 2018 Transportation and Infrastructure Improvements Fund. General Laws of Mississippi of the First Extraordinary Session of 2018. Ch. 1.

82. Geoff Pender, "Special Session: Here's What Happened," *Jackson Clarion-Ledger*, August 29, 2018.

Index

About the Author

Credit Dominique Pugh

Brian Pugh currently serves as the executive director of the Stennis Center for Public Service and as an adjunct professor at Mississippi State University. Prior to working at the Stennis Center, Pugh worked in state government for over a decade for the Mississippi Department of Finance and Administration (DFA), the Governor's Office, and the Legislative Budget Office (LBO).

Foreword

Ronny Frith is an attorney and committee counsel in the Legislative Services Office of the Mississippi House of Representatives, with over forty-two years of experience in that office, beginning in September 1977. He has served longer than any attorney in the history of the Legislative Service Offices of both the house and the senate, and longer than any active member or staff of the house or the senate. He is the committee counsel for the House Appropriations Committee, and he has drafted numerous pieces of legislation on a variety of topics and issues throughout his lengthy career. He was significantly involved with nearly all of the budget-related legislation that was enacted by the legislature during that time.

Printed in the United States
By Bookmasters